PRISON JOURNAL

GEORGE CARDINAL PELL

PRISON JOURNAL

Volume 2

The State Court Rejects the Appeal

14 July 2019–30 November 2019

IGNATIUS PRESS   SAN FRANCISCO

Quotations from George Cardinal Pell's breviary are from *The Divine Office*, 3 volumes (Sydney: E J Dwyer, 1974).

Cover photograph courtesy of George Cardinal Pell

Cover design by Roxanne Mei Lum

© 2021 by Ignatius Press, San Francisco
All rights reserved
ISBN 978-1-62164-450-7 (PB)
ISBN 978-1-64229-143-8 (eBook)
Library of Congress Control Number 2020945860
Printed in the United States of America ∞

CONTENTS

CHRONOLOGY

16 July 1996	Pope John Paul II names Auxiliary Bishop George Pell the archbishop of Melbourne, Australia.
26 March 2001	George Pell becomes the archbishop of Sydney, Australia.
21 October 2003	Pope John Paul II makes Archbishop Pell a cardinal.
25 February 2014	Pope Francis appoints Cardinal Pell to the newly created position of prefect of the Secretariat for the Economy, which manages the finances of the Holy See and the Vatican.
29 June 2017	Australian police charge Cardinal Pell with multiple historical sexual assault offences.
5 March 2018	Having denied the charges and voluntarily returned to Australia, Cardinal Pell appears in Melbourne Magistrates' Court for the filing of the charges against him.
1 May 2018	After dismissing several of the charges, a Melbourne magistrate rules that the cardinal will stand trial for the others.
2 May 2018	Cases are divided into two trials: the first will concern charges dating to when Pell was the archbishop of Melbourne in the 1990s; the second will deal with charges dating to when he was a young priest in the 1970s.
20 September 2018	First trial, which began 15 August 2018, ends in a hung jury.
11 December 2018	Retrial, which began 7 November 2018, ends in a guilty verdict.

26 February 2019	Prosecutors drop the second set of charges dating to the 1970s.
27 February 2019	Cardinal Pell is remanded in custody and taken to prison.
13 March 2019	Cardinal Pell is sentenced to six years in prison.
5–6 June 2019	Appeal is made to the Supreme Court of Victoria.
21 August 2019	Appeal is rejected 2–1.
10–11 March 2020	Appeal is made to the High Court of Australia.
7 April 2020	High Court overturns all convictions by 7–0 decision, and Cardinal Pell is released from prison.

WEEK 21

Relapsing into Paganism

14 July–20 July 2019

Sunday, 14 July 2019

Elijah has returned, not as John the Baptist, but in excerpts from the Book of Kings which will run in the breviary as the first reading for the next week.

He is one of my heroes, from the ninth century B.C., Elijah the Tishbite from Tishbe, "the troubler of Israel" who confronted Ahab, King of Israel, who "did evil in the sight of the Lord more than all that were before him", and the even more formidable Queen Jezebel.

I have a beautiful two-hundred-year-old Russian icon of Elijah in my private chapel in Rome, and I revere him because he saved monotheism when it risked being eclipsed by paganism, in this case by Baal. The good Lord chose Elijah with Moses to represent the ancient dispensation at the miracle of the Transfiguration.

It is not enough to be spiritual in a sentimental, episodic fashion, because we are called to acknowledge and love the one true God. Immense consequences follow in daily life from the presence or absence of monotheism, as we are beginning to see in Western societies as God is obscured. George Steiner was one of the most brilliant, if maverick, intellectuals of the twentieth century, and he ascribed the visceral, counterproductive, and insane Nazi hatred of the Jewish people to the fact that Hitler and the Nazi leadership, as heads of arguably the most diabolical movement in all history (only Stalin's or Mao's Communism would be competitors), hated the Jews because they were the chosen people who brought monotheism into history. This wasn't the Nazis' stated aim or explanation, but it has

9

a ring of truth for me. Their hatred was blind, fanatical, driven by a Force even greater than their infamous selves.

The breviary excerpt recounts the start of Elijah's story as he confronts Ahab and prophesies the drought. Forced to flee, not for the last time, he is fed by ravens at the Cherith brook and then by the widow and her son, also starving, at Zarephath from her inexhaustible meal in the jar and oil in her cruse. She gave something from nothing, at Elijah's request, and was rewarded with a constant supply until the drought broke.

My self-awareness alarm almost worked such that I missed only the early part of *Mass for You at Home*, celebrated again by Fr Michael Kalka, who preached a good moralistic sermon.

Prime Minister Scott Morrison attended the Hillsong Conference[1] last weekend and prayed publicly, but he wasn't present today with Pastor Houston,[2] who preached on the rain in your life, once again reverting to pattern, from an Old Testament text in Genesis. The congregation was different from last week, a little more animated, and he prompted the best response when he defended "good old-fashioned lettuce" against this newly arrived kale. He got my vote on that issue.

Joseph Prince's[3] theme was similar, as he talked about "the year of latter rain". Untypically, his text was from the Old Testament Book of Deuteronomy. As always, he was Christocentric when he preached on the harvest of plenty and the damage wrought by plagues of locusts in our personal lives.

Songs of Praise was again from a British church, St John's in Hackney, and featured a mixed black choir singing Negro spirituals. These developed among the tens of thousands of slaves on the plantations in North America from the Protestant hymns of John and Charles Wesley and Isaac Watts. These beautiful hymns move at different levels, religious, sociological, almost political. When Joshua "fought the battle of Jericho, the walls came tumbling down"; they sang that

---

[1] The Hillsong Conference is a televised, annual, week-long event hosted by the Hillsong Church in Sydney, Australia.

[2] Brian Houston (b. 1954) is the senior pastor at Hillsong Church, whose services and programs are televised.

[3] The evangelist Joseph Prince leads a televised worship service called *New Creation Church TV*.

"my trials will soon be over" and that the famous chariot swung low—"coming for to carry me home".

A couple of exercise sessions outside under an overcast sky and drizzle in the afternoon. The inventory of what the property section believes I have in my cell arrived, thanks to the section's cooperative senior officer. It wasn't completely accurate, but I passed two books and two *Quadrant*s to Kartya.[4] After a quiet couple of days, we have a noisy banger and shouter, in short bursts. But he doesn't sound distraught.

The life of Elijah and, indeed, St Thomas More's own life and execution show that More was correct when he wrote to his children twenty-five years before his death, "We cannot go to heaven in feather beds."

Monday, 15 July 2019

As I was about to enter the exercise yard for my afternoon spin, a tremendous and hostile banging came from the cell I was passing. Off and on during the day, we heard these alternate bursts of banging and profanity. The poor man was most unhappy. The warder muttered, "He's doing that with his head. He's sick." Naturally, I don't know the cause of the distress, but the aftereffects of ice [methamphetamine] would be the first possibility. The warder also confirmed, what I had concluded, that they separated those they guessed would be noisy at one end of the unit away from me and the other "quiet" prisoners. Sr Mary[5] had said that I might qualify as a model prisoner.

My nephew Nicholas came in for a pleasant hour. He looked well, although explaining he was tired. His project to build a new home with Julie, his wife, is progressing.

In the breviary today, we have the dramatic story of the contest between Elijah, the only remaining prophet of the one true God, and the 450 prophets who followed Baal, the god of the pagan

---

[4] Kartya Gracer is a senior associate and solicitor assisting Paul Galbally, a partner in the law firm of Galbally and O'Bryan and the principal solicitor for Cardinal Pell.

[5] Sr Mary O'Shannassy, a Good Samaritan Sister, is a chaplain at Melbourne Assessment Prison.

Sidonians (1 Kings 18:20–40). There was a power imbalance like that between David and Goliath. Elijah provoked the contest, challenging the people to stop "limping with two different opinions" and choose between the Lord God and Baal. The terms of the competition are well-known, as each side had to kill a bull, cut it into pieces, lay them out, and call on God or Baal to send down fire to destroy the offering.

The pagan prophets were the first to start, limping for hours around the altar, slashing themselves with swords and lances until the blood ran. Elijah mocked their lack of success, suggesting their god might have gone on a journey or fallen asleep, but "there was no voice, no one answered, no one heeded."

He then moved into action setting up a wooden altar for the pieces of meat and surrounding it with a deep ditch. He doused the meat and altar, then filled the ditch three times with water from four large jars. Elijah called down fire from the Lord God of Abraham, Isaac, and Jacob, so that the people might know that he is God in Israel and that Elijah is his servant. Quickly, the fire of the Lord came down and consumed the burnt offering, the wood, the stones, the dust, and the water in the trench.

At this stage, events took an unexpected turn, when Elijah urged his newfound followers to seize the exhausted prophets and take them to the brook of Kishon, where he killed them. In those days, "the winner takes all."

Eugene has been a friend of mine since the '60s and was a frequent visitor to court for my trials and appeal as well as a regular letter writer. Today, he sent a recent article from *The Australian* by Greg Sheridan on Britons finding something to believe in.[6] I have mentioned how much I miss reading *The Australian*, and I hope that [the owner] Rupert Murdoch has taken effective steps to ensure it continues long after his departure. If it were to close, or even if its standards slipped badly, the damage to the public conversation in Australia would be drastic.

Just as the fortunes of Judaism fluctuated in Old Testament times, as Elijah's story demonstrates, so have the fortunes of Christianity and Catholicism waxed and waned across the ages in different countries

---

[6] Greg Sheridan, "Is Christianity Making a Comeback?", *Australian*, 6 July 2019.

and in Australian history. In many ways, Catholicism has slipped in Australia since the '60s, but early-nineteenth-century Australia was famously irreligious, and the public celebration of the Mass in Australia was banned until 1803.

Sheridan details "the radical loss of belief and meaning" in Britain, a decline since about 1920, but outlines "tentative signs of a counter-trend". Are the vigorous Catholic parish at Brompton Oratory and the Rev Nicky Gumbel's nearby Anglican parish and its Alpha program,[7] which has been followed around the world by about twenty-six million people, "really signs of hope, maybe of a turn at last, or are they more like crowded lifeboats bobbing around in the wake of a sinking ocean liner?" Time will tell, and Sheridan is cautiously optimistic. More than twenty million people are a lot.

Sheridan doesn't hide the grim reality. While he doesn't mention that there are more worshipping Catholics in Britain than Anglicans, he points out that 7 percent of eighteen- to twenty-nine-year-old Brits identify as Anglicans, and 6 percent identify as Muslims. Sheridan sees this as the end of nominal Christianity. I hope not, as I have a lot of sympathy for imperfect Christians.

Fr Gumbel doesn't see Christian decline as inevitable, ongoing, or irreversible, and it was consoling to hear that in 1750, before the revivals of the Wesleys and William Wilberforce,[8] there were ten thousand sex workers walking the streets of London while sixteen people attended Easter services in St Paul's Cathedral there.

Gumbel is the convert son of a German secular Jewish refugee and knows what it is like to be without belief. He doesn't accept that people can find "ultimate purpose and meaning outside of our relationship with God".

Gumbel is one example of a Gospel Christian, encouraging a transcendental experience of God, which offers forgiveness through the death of Jesus and provides hope and meaning in a distinctive

---

[7] The Alpha Course, an introduction to Christianity supported by a wide variety of Christian denominations, was developed by Rev Nicky Gumbel, vicar of Holy Trinity Brompton, London.

[8] John and Charles Wesley were English clerics who led an eighteenth-century revival movement within the Church of England known as Methodism. William Wilberforce (1759–1833) was a deeply religious British politician and social reformer who led the movement to abolish the slave trade.

community of faith and trust. He offers an expanded Alpha program for Catholic parishes.

Many secularists imply that sin is startlingly modern, their invention, or that they are the first generation to define sin out of existence. However, sin goes back beyond Ahab and Jezebel, to Adam actually. It is very old-fashioned. Genuine Christianity is the novelty, and only Gospel Christianity promotes growth.

God our Father, we pray that you may grant us the simplicity of the dove as well as the wisdom of the serpent. May we be wise enough to speak to unbelievers in ways they can understand and simple enough to remember that the answers are always to be found in the teachings and person of Jesus.

Tuesday, 16 July 2019

During my first exercise, which began early at 8:45 am, I phoned Tim O'Leary[9] to ask him to pass on to Fr Alexander Sherbrooke[10] in London my congratulations on England's win in the cricket World Cup and to tell him that the shame I felt at being sent to jail was something like my shame when England slaughtered Australia in the first semifinal. Tim also recounted what a fantastic and close game the final between England and New Zealand was and how well the Kiwis comported themselves after the narrowest of defeats. He said it was all good for sport and good for cricket. The final was not shown on free-to-air television, so I missed it, learning only that England had won a close match.

Sr Mary called for our small prayer service and Communion. Sr Mary McGlone's[11] sermon showed she was still in top form, but a bit hostile to lawyers. I farewelled Mary by saying I would see her next Tuesday, but was not sure about Tuesday week.

---

[9] Tim O'Leary is a senior executive of the Archdiocese of Melbourne and a friend of Cardinal Pell.

[10] Fr Alexander Sherbrooke is the parish priest (pastor) of St Patrick's Church in Soho Square, London.

[11] Sr Mary McGlone is a Sister of St Joseph of Carondelet and a historical theologian in the US. Her reflections on the Sunday Gospel readings appear in the *National Catholic Reporter.*

My reading program goes ahead, but slowly. When Fr Peter Joseph[12] visited, I told him I was reading Hobbes' *Leviathan*. He quickly responded, "It's unreadable, isn't it." It was written about fifty years after Shakespeare, in 1651. I am reading a reprint of the original edition, and it is a hard slog. I have reduced my daily ration to ten pages plus, and I hope to have finished the read by the time I leave prison. I am about eighty pages into the actual *Leviathan* text, and, true to his principles, Hobbes is still spelling out his definitions.

After finishing *War and Peace*, which was my bedtime reading here for months, I have replaced it with Peter Brown's *Through the Eye of a Needle: Wealth, the Fall of Rome, and the Making of Christianity in the West, 350–550 A.D.*, an immense 750-page work, which is also immensely learned. My history lectures on the Early Church were always well received when I could draw on Brown. I adopted his technique of explaining ancient realities by comparing and contrasting them with contemporary ideas and institutions. Brown is regularly illuminating, e.g., claiming that, quoting James Bury,[13] Constantine's conversion "had been the most audacious act ever committed by an autocrat in defiance of the vast majority of his subjects". I have wondered publicly, once during a dinner speech at the North American College in Rome (where US and Australian seminarians are trained for the priesthood), whether history will ever see a Chinese Constantine. I hope so.

This morning I felt a bit lightheaded and wondered to myself whether my blood pressure had dropped. The nurses did the tests, with me sitting and standing, and the readings were low but OK. I slowly improved during the day and went out for my afternoon exercise. The day was overcast.

As I write this around 5 pm, after the prison shutdown thirty minutes ago, a couple of prisoners are conversing loudly from their cells, as sometimes happens. Someone interrupted briefly from my end with a mad yelling. Yesterday, as I was returning from my afternoon exercise, there was another dramatic performance, loud, obscene shouting and some banging, evidence of dismay, but not evidence of

---

[12] Fr Peter Joseph, parish priest (pastor) of St Dominic's, Flemington, is a close friend of Cardinal Pell.

[13] J.B. Bury (1861–1927) was an Anglo-Irish historian and classicist who wrote several books about the Roman Empire.

the deepest suffering. One warder muttered, "Well that won't make the top ten."

Sr Mary confirmed X's story about prison conditions in the past, and S., the boss of [Melbourne Assessment Prison] MAP, also confirmed it by saying that when he started as a prison officer thirty years ago in Castlemaine, six prisoners in one cell had an open bucket for their toilet needs during the night and the cells had no running water.

Some time ago, Sue Buckingham, the driving force and inspiration of David's Place [in Sydney], sent me a copy of their *Emmaus Newsletter*. David's Place is a community of "our most marginalised friends", which meets weekly for Mass and goes on excursions, and the friends generally support one another. They are poor. It is a Catholic group, open to everyone, which I managed to help and visited for Mass once a year. In this letter, Sue devoted her editorial to my defence, wrote a number of kind things, including "I cannot doubt that a most serious injustice has been done—that he is innocent."

I, too, worry, like Fr Alexander in Soho, that the Church is not as close to the poor as we should be. A genuine concern for social justice is essential, but it does not substitute for being with the battlers in the way Sue is. Sue is at the heart of the Church, with her friends. I once publicly disagreed with a St Vincent de Paul speaker when he claimed that the St V de P had a good relationship with the Church. This is not true, I insisted. You might have good relations with the bishops, but you are a vital *part* of the Church. You are one embodiment of the Church. So as Catholic archbishop emeritus and a brother Christian, I am proud of who Sue is and what she does and grateful for the community prayers for me and her courageous defence.

God our Father, we pray that we will always be mindful of chapter 25 in Matthew's Gospel, where your Son Jesus explained what would happen on the Last Day of judgement, when the Son of Man will come for the final separation of the sheep from the goats, of the good from the bad.

May we come to believe that when we help the hungry, the thirsty, the strangers, the naked, the sick, and the imprisoned, we are helping Christ himself, and may we put into practice what we believe.

Wednesday, 17 July 2019

Last night I watched the final two hours in a three-part series on the American program, launched by President Kennedy, to place a man on the moon in the sixties. They succeeded on 15 July 1969, fifty years ago this week. The event occurred during the summer break when I was writing my thesis at Oxford. Working through the holidays, I was too busy to watch much of it on television.

The program was well made, and I thoroughly enjoyed it, watching all three sessions. I doubt whether this would have happened if I were not in jail. The landing remains a stunning technological achievement, spurred on by the ambition to place the Stars and Stripes on the surface of the moon before the Soviets planted their flag.

The Cold War was a serious business for most Australians, and certainly for an anti-Communist like myself, an admirer of Bob Santamaria[14] and Prime Minister Bob Menzies.[15] Ten years earlier, in 1959, during my last year at St Pat's College, Ballarat, I remember going out onto the main oval one night during study time to watch the Russian satellite *Sputnik* orbit overhead. I was disturbed and a bit worried that they had achieved this before the Free World. We overestimated their strength then, before Reagan and Thatcher and Pope John Paul the Great with the Polish Solidarity movement brought down the Western Communist world. This was unexpected.

Soon after I was appointed an auxiliary bishop in Melbourne in 1987, I attended an international seminar on Russia and Communism. Only one speaker, the Melbourne intellectual Frank Knopfelmacher, claimed that the Russians were now very weak and the party was almost over. I remember being at morning tea with some of the overseas speakers following his talk, and they were totally dismissive of him. I hoped he was right, but wasn't at all sure. Pope John Paul II said that he was confident Communism would be brought down, but never dreamt it could be achieved without bloodshed. Some years later I was talking to Knopfelmacher and reminded him

---

[14] B. A. (Bob) Santamaria (1915–1998) was an Australian Roman Catholic, a writer, and a political leader. He was an important figure in Australia for sixty years.

[15] Robert Menzies twice served as prime minister of Australia, 1939–1941 and 1949–1966. Through the course of his political career, he was a member of three political parties: Nationalist, United Australia, and the Liberal Party, which he founded.

that he was the only speaker at the conference who was right. "Of course", he replied.

Another reason for my lack of attention in 1969 was that I didn't approve of the expenditure of such a huge sum, then $24 billion, which would probably be around $75 to $100 billion today.

My day has passed profitably with two exercise periods outside and an hour in the gymnasium. At the gym, I asked for a basketball and was told they were only available at the weekend. With my usual subtle and understated style, I replied that this was nonsense as I had used a basketball on my two previous visits. I don't think I had any chance of obtaining a ball, but my response ensured that was the case.

Tim O'Leary's envelope arrived with a couple of depressing articles on the October Synod on Amazonia and Church life in mainland China, as well as Chris Friel's[16] summing up in eight-thousand-plus words of Milligan's[17] book, all of which I read avidly.

We seem to have only one serious shouter, although there was a commotion around 2 am this morning. Our shouter does not perform regularly, but most of the time he is almost cheerfully obscene, like a child crying when every adult knows he is not seriously distressed.

Not surprisingly, Jezebel was furious at the defeat and death of the prophets of Baal and threatened to do to Elijah the next day what he had done to them. We are told that, on hearing this, Elijah "went for his life", first of all to someplace in the countryside a day's journey from Beersheba, where he was fed miraculously, before travelling for forty days and forty nights to Mt Horeb.

There he stood on the rock for the Lord to pass by. I suspect the good God was showing Elijah and us the nature of godliness. God was not in the great wind that rent the mountains and broke the rocks to pieces, not in the earthquake, not in the fire, but in "a still small voice". And Elijah heard it, telling God that, despite all his efforts, he was the only remaining prophet of the Lord, the God of hosts. That

---

[16] Chris S. Friel is a theologian and philosopher located in Wales, UK, who wrote a series of more than 130 analytical papers on the Pell case, which he made available online at Academia, https://independent.academia.edu/ChrisFriel.

[17] Louise Milligan is an investigative television reporter and the author of *Cardinal: The Rise and Fall of George Pell*, which was published in 2017 and fostered a negative view of Cardinal Pell before his trial.

was enough, because God sent him to anoint Hazael as King of Syria, Jehu as King of Israel, and Elisha as his successor (1 Kings 19:9–18).

Jesus was born unnoticed in the stable in Bethlehem. Unlike Moses and the Buddha, he did not grow up in privileged circumstances. He was killed like a slave, almost unnoticed in Jerusalem. A still small voice.

St John Fisher,[18] like Elijah, spoke truth to power. A martyr, he was the only English bishop to reject Henry VIII's attempt to make himself head of the Church in England. This is part of the sermon he preached in the year before Henry VIII became king.

Lord, according to your promise that the Gospel should be preached throughout the whole world, raise up men [and women] fit for such work. The apostles were but soft and yielding clay till they were baked hard by the Holy Ghost. So, good Lord, do now in like manner again with thy Church militant; change and make the soft and slippery earth into hard stone; set in thy Church strong and mighty pillars. Amen.

Thursday, 18 July 2019

It was a decent Melbourne winter's day: overcast, but not dark, no rain, and about 15°C [59° F] maximum. It wasn't a Ballarat day. The winters in Melbourne were a pleasant anticlimax when I arrived in 1985 from Ballarat.

A deal of shouting during the day, but very little gave evidence of genuine distress. Two cells were flooded into the passage as I passed. The warder explained that the prisoners block up the toilets to create a flood: mischief-making, a sign of protest. He had to clean up about 40 litres [10.5 gallons] of water. Last night during the shouted discussions, I did hear one prisoner claim he was distracting himself by throwing paper balls into the toilet. In solitary, I live a sheltered life, blessed that I can read, write, pray, and receive letters, without the pluses and minuses of dealing with an interesting cross section of

---

[18] St John Fisher (1469–1535) was an English Catholic bishop, cardinal, and theologian, who was executed by Henry VIII for refusing to recognize him as supreme head of the Church in England.

people. I am not inclined to romanticise the situation, as someone would almost certainly attack me if I went around freely.

The highlight of the day was the visit of Robert Richter[19] with Paul.[20] He continues to be busy with the case following up some spectacular leads. It will be fascinating to see where we finish, and it is not contradicting Friel's scenario. Apparently the choirboy's father was a policeman, and J[21] stayed with them for four months in 1998, when, it is alleged, they were dealing in drugs.

The letters continue to arrive, and I have a buildup of letters I might draw on for this journal. I received a promise of prayers from a Carmelite nun in Sweden and a fascinating page from a Mercy Sister in Ireland, who once a year travels three hundred miles to help organize the adoration at the Church of the Assumption in Wexford town. While in the church, she saw an elderly man praying earnestly. He placed a slip of paper near the tabernacle as he left. The note asked for prayers for me and gave my address for letters. So Sr Therese wrote me a note of encouragement (explaining that I "had been in her prayers all along") on July 1, the feast day of St Oliver Plunkett, the last Irish martyr in 1681.

The leaders in the Catholic Women's League of Victoria have been regular with their prayers and letters, and the last one contained fourteen prayer cards for Sr Mary Glowrey, Servant of God. Sr Mary was born in the Western District in the Diocese of Ballarat, was among the first women to graduate in medicine in Victoria, helped found the Catholic Women's League, and then as a nun went to India, where she continued working as a medical doctor, after receiving special permission from Pope Pius XI to do this. Her cause for canonisation has been taken up strongly in India, where she founded the Indian Catholic Health Association, which is now an immense organization. The number of Catholics in India, a small minority, is only a little less than the population of Australia. Sr Mary is worthy of canonisation, and I hope the Ballarat Diocese rallies behind the proposal, because, like us all, it could do with a boost. I am not sure I can do much, if anything,

---

[19] Robert Richter, a Queen's Counsel and a criminal barrister, led the cardinal's defence during the trials in September and December 2018.

[20] Paul Galbally, a partner in the law firm of Galbally and O'Bryan, is the principal solicitor for Cardinal Pell.

[21] J was the complainant.

with the prayer cards, but in God's providence one never knows. Her brother, Fr Glowrey, was a kindly old chaplain at Loreto College in Dawson Street, Ballarat, where I started my education.

The life of Elijah and the immediate aftermath continue in the breviary. Ahab and Jezebel are an appalling couple of individuals, and we read of their encounter with Naboth the Jezreelite, who was unfortunate enough to have a fine vineyard next to Ahab's palace which Ahab wanted to purchase. When Naboth refused to sell, Ahab took himself off to bed and refused to eat. Jezebel arrived and was mightily displeased, rebuking him for his unkingly behaviour and promising to remedy the situation. She organized for Naboth to be accused falsely of cursing God and the King. He was found guilty and stoned to death.

God ordered Elijah out of his mountain retreat to confront Ahab and condemn him, which he promptly did. "Have you found me, O my enemy?" exclaimed Ahab fatuously in Elijah's presence. The prophet answered in the affirmative and promised to bring evil upon him and sweep him away.

Unlike his wife, who remained steadfast in her paganism, Ahab performed the ritual penances and went about dejectedly. The author of Kings acknowledges his humility but does not ascribe repentance to him explicitly, and the word of the Lord inspired Elijah to post-pone the punishment from Ahab to his son's house (which would be little solace for a good parent). Ahab was a tyrant and a coward, but he acknowledged Elijah's authority and seems to have possessed some glimmer of faith.

The prayer with which we conclude does not deal with the Naboths of this world, but talks of the situation of most of us most of the time.

Little headaches, little heartaches
Little griefs of every day,
Little trials and vexations,
How they throng around our way.
Let us not then through impatience
Mar the beauty of the whole,
But for love of Jesus bear all,
In the silence of our soul.

Friday, 19 July 2019

Elijah does not go to heaven in his fiery chariot until tomorrow's breviary reading, although interesting sections from St Ambrose's *De Misteriis* (*On the Mysteries*), about the sacraments, provide solid instruction, which has passed into mainstream Catholic thought. When I was at Oxford, this was one of the university texts taken by Anglican ordinands, and in that vanished age, most of the Oxford humanities students also studied Gibbon's *Decline and Fall of the Roman Empire*, which charted the triumph of Christianity and barbarism. My supervisor, Prof S. L. Greenslade, regius professor of Church history, used to give a few lectures in an attempt to balance up Gibbon's bias. Rodney Stark's *The Rise of Christianity*, the most effective riposte I have read, was thirty years into the future.

The prison was closed down forty-five minutes early this afternoon because two warders had been assaulted and a staff meeting was called for a briefing and discussion. I heard a dog whimper outside in Unit 8, but there was no commotion. My guess is that some prisoner was moved, perhaps one or both of the flooders. So far all is quiet, no lamentings and no conversation.

The day was cold, but clear and fresh, with only light clouds. I put together three pages of thoughts on Friel's summing up of Milligan's book that have to be meshed with the results of the verdict and the investigations. My legal friend Joseph wrote again, enclosing the Dublin text of Richard Rex's (from Cambridge) lecture on Hilary Mantel's treatment of Thomas More and Thomas Cromwell,[22] which my Irish friend Fr Tom McGovern had attended and told me about. It is not surprising, I suppose, that many of my friends have common interests. More on Joseph's missives (three in the last month or so) in a day or so.

A card arrived last week from Fr Eamonn O'Higgins of the Legionaries of Christ seminary in Rome, with a beautiful printed book of photos illustrating the fourth tour of the Vatican's St Peter's Cricket Club to England in July last year [Fr O'Higgins is the team chaplain]. The Queen is photographed with them on the front cover, and Pope

---

[22] Hilary Mantel, *Wolf Hall* (Picador, 2010) and *Bring Up the Bodies* (Picador, 2013). The third volume in the series, *The Mirror and the Light*, was published by Henry Holt in 2020.

Francis is on the back cover wearing a St Peter's cricket hat. While I am the proud patron, the team is the brainchild of John McCarthy, then Australian ambassador to the Vatican, and the result of his extraordinary persistence and powers of persuasion.

They play regularly against the Archbishop of Canterbury's XI and the Windsor Castle team and, in 2018, played a Commonwealth team and one from the Houses of Parliament. The Queen has received them each year, and on the occasion of the first Rome versus Canterbury match in England, more Anglican and Catholic bishops attended together than had been seen for years. They have played Muslim teams, and the whole initiative is a great social, ecumenical, and interfaith success.

My most regular correspondent is a long-term prisoner who has been in jail for decades. He is highly intelligent, well-read, a voluminous correspondent, and knows prison life backward. I believe he helps quite a few prisoners with legal advice.

He consoles me, assures me that God is by my side, and has developed the theme that as the good thief recognized the injustice of what was happening to Jesus, so many offenders acknowledge they have been rightly condemned and deeply believe that punishment of the innocent is wrong. He points out the irony of the situation that "alleged persons of ill repute can see the injustice—but the so-called honourable cannot."

The basic point in his letter is that "what has befallen you is so very dangerous to all in society on so many different levels." He believes, in prayer, that I will be acquitted and that this should be an opportunity to "draw the line in the sand", for the Church authorities to be more clearheaded in acknowledging and rejecting false accusations, in combating "a surge of falsehood that is being allowed to become the truth". Over the years, he writes, he has often been "amazed at how people can come to believe ardently in their lies".

The false accusations against me are not unique, as events in the US and England have demonstrated. Just as it was wrong to reject accusations instinctively and without examination, so it is unjust to issue that accusations do not need to be examined closely and do not need to be established legally. This is a vexed and difficult business as many priests and teachers feel the pendulum has swung too far against the presumption of innocence. Just as wisdom and discernment are needed, so, too, courage is required of those investigating and judging so they can be independent of the tidal waves of public opinion.

My prison correspondent is no longer a Catholic, after having been turned away by a Melbourne parish priest. He had told the priest he was just out of jail, but before he could go farther, the priest rejected him, thinking he was wanting money. In fact, he wanted to go to confession. Such is life.

We now have some noise in the unit (around 6 pm), but the voices are different. A couple of verses in Psalm 68 from today's Office of Readings seem appropriate.

> *How can I restore*
> *what I have never stolen?*
> *O God, you know my sinful folly;*
> *my sins you can see.*
> *Let those who hope in you not be put to shame*
> *through me, Lord of hosts;*
> *let not those who seek you be dismayed*
> *through me, God of Israel.*

Saturday, 20 July 2019

A special interest in Elijah goes back to my days as a young priest preparing the Sunday sermon on the Transfiguration. Initially, I did not find the topic easy, and I remember how impressed I was to meet a German priest theologian who had written a three-hundred-page thesis on the event!

By any criteria, Elijah's life story is interesting, but why had Our Lord chosen him to represent the prophets during the Transfiguration apparition, with Moses representing the law? Elijah had written nothing, and we have masterpieces from Isaiah, Ezekiel, and Jeremiah. My conclusion was and is that his contribution to the preservation of monotheism was unique and outweighed his violence and his literary silence.

Elisha accompanied Elijah as he travelled to Bethel, Jericho, and the Jordan preparatory to his departure. Elijah asked if there was anything he could do for him, his successor, and Elisha requested "a double share of your spirit". He wasn't lacking in self-confidence, because if he was to be half the prophet Elijah had been, this would have sufficed. "You have asked a hard thing", Elijah explained, but it shall be so if you see me ascend to heaven in a fiery chariot with horses. He did so, and Elisha picked up Elijah's mantle, struck the water of the River Jordan, which parted, and then crossed. The sons of the prophets from Jericho came and revered him, because Elijah's spirit was resting on him.

As I never anticipated writing on this incident, I haven't read any exegetes, believers or unbelievers, to deepen my understanding. It is not an option for me simply to dismiss it all as exotic mythology. A couple of things can be said safely. Elijah spent a good deal of his life on the run, fleeing the grasp of hostile powers, when he wasn't anointing or rebuking kings. His departure was a spectacular demonstration of divine approval.

Elijah was persecuted for his faith, for his monotheism, which he defended with such flair. The monotheists had been reduced to a tiny minority, but he did not compromise on the essential issue, and of course many believers, or half believers, who had been cowed stepped up in response to his bravery.

There is a lesson for us here. Those of us who love the Church are grieved by the decline in Mass-going and the formal departures from the community which often follow as the light of life dims or people explicitly reject Christian teaching on forgiveness, sin, life, suffering, family, or sexuality. These are sad developments, which we must resist in every way possible, natural and supernatural. Sometimes our sins have accelerated the exodus.

But one worse alternative exists, that pagan teachings merge into and replace the official doctrines of the Christian churches. Monotheism melts away into spirituality, respect for Mother Earth, and rediscovery of the ancient pagan religions. Forgiveness is rejected as weakness, another teaching of Western Christendom we have surpassed. Christ is not the Son of God, who drove the corrupt money changers from the Temple, but a kindly and tolerant teacher or, worse, a weakling who allowed himself to be crucified. Suffering is without meaning. Moral autonomy, sometimes called the primacy of conscience, replaces the Ten Commandments, and self-affirmation or definition displaces the natural law. And the beautiful package of Christian teachings on life, family, marriage, and children is regarded as hate speech, not to be publicised, especially the essential linking of sexual activity, procreation, and love.

Such a virus will not take over the Catholic Church, but it has not been eliminated or even contained. Tragically, it is often spread by Christians who believe that unless the churches adopt some or more of these teachings, modernise, and go along with the times, then the churches will continue to slip into oblivion.

It is a variation of the heated public debate in the late Roman Empire, which then had Christian leadership. Many pagan intellectuals and leaders felt that Christian doctrines had weakened and betrayed the Western Empire, which was falling into pieces under the attacks and invasions of the barbarian Germanic tribes. So today, especially in Western Europe, the best thinking requires Christians to abandon their antiquated notions, which are incompatible with modernity, for the wellness of society and the churches' survival.

This is a double mistake. Christians are not free to reject or rewrite the apostolic tradition. With it we stand and fight, or we fall. The irony is that contemporary history demonstrates clearly that the more quickly and radically Christian groups adopt the tenets of modernity, the more rapid the collapse. Once-Catholic Holland, Belgium, and Quebec, as well as all the radically liberal Protestant communities, such as the Episcopalian Church in the United States, are examples of this iron law in action.

Elijah would not be pleased by this grim spectacle, these debacles, but he would not be surprised.

Elijah went to heaven in a fiery chariot, while St Thérèse of Lisieux uses a somewhat different image to pray. Both belong to the same tradition.

> *Help me as I fly toward the warmth of the sun,*
> *the Son of God, on eagles' wings of Divine Love.*

WEEK 22

Expecting a Reckoning

21 July–27 July 2019

Sunday, 21 July 2019

I omitted to record that yesterday was a double triumph food-wise. A pie or a pasty is the usual Saturday lunch, but as I returned late after my exercise in the gym, the warder allowed me to heat the pie in the microwave. The result was that I had a pie that was initially too hot to eat, an enormous success with tomato sauce, and the first hot meal since I came to jail.

On Saturday afternoons, different from the usual routine, we regularly have a sweet of jellied fruit and cream. Going out to exercise, I mentioned how much I enjoyed it, and after my return I received, unbidden, an enormous second serving. I don't know if the warder is a Christian, but it was an act of Christian kindness. Thank God for simple pleasures. Good weather on both days, cold and clear with no rain.

I woke at 5:30 am, which was perfect for the 6 am *Mass for You at Home* celebrated by Fr T. Kerin, a canon lawyer and parish priest, who celebrated with dignity and preached an exemplary sermon on Mary and Martha. He mentioned our capacity to be distracted, to take refuge in our work like Martha, and come to the end of our life and find we have missed the boat, have not been following Christ. We don't want to be like the person who works for hours on his computer, then presses the wrong button and loses the lot.

Pastor Houston's session was a rerun. His voice was fresher, and the listeners a little more animated than usual. He told how his congregation had once prayed for rain in a drought and their prayer had been heard. In fact, he said to them that "you have power over rain", like Elijah, whom he mentioned explicitly and who was an ordinary person like us. The congregation was urged to pray for the nice and nasty, and the destruction of Sodom and Gomorrah by fire and brimstone was mentioned.

Joseph Prince's theme was "the confidence that brings great rewards", and as always his New Testament emphasis on Christ, vivacity, and community singing and music contrasted strongly with the Australian Hillsong service. Grace is an unmerited favour, Jesus is the "exceeding great reward", and faith in Jesus brings forgiveness of sins past, present, and to come.

I will conclude with a few words on a recent article by Rita Panahi in the Melbourne *Herald Sun*. Most of her admirers would be social conservatives, many of these Christians. She makes no secret of the fact she is an atheist, judging that this strengthens her claim to objectivity with the middle ground. Being a Christian seems to confer no advantages and could be seen as another difficulty in claiming credibility. When I was a young priest, atheism was not a plus even for a newspaper columnist.

When speaking as a bishop, I strived to give people hope, not at the expense of truth, but by presenting each situation accurately, often by pointing out periods in history that were similar or worse and then by listing at least a few tasks we could accomplish or challenges we could face and surmount.

Some of our black-armband ecologists are still reaching the heights. Panahi quotes an American singer, Miley Cyrus (whom I don't know), who is not going to have children "because we know the earth can't handle it". Prince Charles feels we have eighteen months "to restore nature to the equilibrium we need for our survival".[1] We shall see.

A few hard facts, quoted by Panahi, are needed to put this pessimism into context. Famine has been almost abolished. Two hundred years ago, 90 percent of people lived in extreme poverty; today, it is 10 percent. Last year, the world had twelve ongoing wars, sixty autocracies, and ten thousand nuclear weapons. Thirty years ago, there were twenty-three wars, eighty-five autocracies, 37 percent of people in extreme poverty, with sixty thousand nuclear weapons. Nearly

---

[1] Rita Panahi, "Time to Lift This Misery," *Herald Sun*, 19 July 2019.

everywhere, except perhaps Africa, we have made huge gains in longevity and literacy. Living standards for most Australians have improved a lot in my lifetime. The doomsayers do not have the best lines.

This human progress is good, but when it becomes our first priority, we find it harder to see or know God. We can see the stars more clearly when we are away from the light of the cities, but we can see the stars even more clearly with a telescope.

Some lines from Psalm 57 are a consolation, supposedly written when David was hiding in a cave from King Saul.

> Show your greatness in the sky, O God,
> and your glory over all the earth. . . .
> I have complete confidence, O God;
> I will sing and praise you!

Monday, 22 July 2019

Today the chief justice returns to work. Please God, we are closer to some information. Last night, I watched two television programs, one on the planet Jupiter and the other on volcanoes. My ignorance on both topics was profound: almost total for Jupiter and slightly less for volcanoes, because I had got to the stage of wondering whether they were like dinosaurs in the story of evolution, serving no good purpose. I do remember Fr Brendan Purcell[2] denying that proposition, but I never followed up for further information.

Some scientists speak of a weaker and stronger anthropomorphic principle in the universe, because of the fantastic number (literally) of "coincidences" which have occurred to produce the conditions congenial to human life, without forgetting the supreme mystery of human life itself, an even more improbable development.

NASA now has a satellite with a camera circling this immense planet, Jupiter, 130 times the size of Earth. It had been presumed that the order and nature of the planets circling the sun, with the smaller, solid planets closer and the larger gaseous ones further away, was the

[2] Fr Brendan Purcell, who previously taught philosophy at University College Dublin, is now assistant priest at St Mary's Cathedral, Sydney.

usual pattern for planets around a star. This is not the case, and it seems that Jupiter is the cause. Billions of years ago, Jupiter veered off course, producing the belt of asteroids further out from Earth, so preventing the more predictable development of another planet and so contributing to the specific physical conditions we enjoy on Earth. Moreover, because of its enormous bulk and consequential gravitational pull, it mops up and draws to itself many stray comets which might come our way. As a theist, I see providence at work.

Most of Earth's surface is covered by water, and scientists wonder how this was achieved. One popular theory is that water was produced by the outpourings of myriads of volcanoes over millions of years. We find other beneficial consequences, also. The ashes from the most active volcano in Africa, Mt Nyamuragira, have helped create the Great Rift Valley, an immensely fertile area of land, which is unique for the number and variety of wildlife it sustains. Scientists have discovered how Mt Kilauea, the active volcano near Hawaii, has sparked unique forms of evolution. In fact, some scientists see volcanoes as not only contributing to biodiversity, but playing a crucial role in the birth of life itself.

Science cannot bring us to God, but it does demonstrate the existence of extraordinary patterns, and we can calculate the odds against blind chance throwing up congenial environments for "mechanisms", and more than mechanisms, which know and decide, love and hate. Human life is a singularity, unique in the universe.

I have expressed my conviction that philosophy is essential for the academic preparation of priests. So, too, universities and theological colleges should be offering courses on theism and atheism, on evolution, on the interface of science and religion.

It was beautifully clear and brisk for my morning exercise, a little less so in the afternoon. Two bonuses were that a Qantas airliner crossed my brief patch of sky in the morning and a melodious splash of birdsong punctuated the afternoon session, although I could not see the birds.

Bernadette and Terry Tobin[3] were my visitors between 1:00 and 2:00 pm, and I brought them up-to-date on recent developments

[3] Bernadette Tobin is the director of the Plunkett Centre for Ethics; her husband, Terry, is a Queen's Counsel.

and the Friel papers. They are long-term friends and strong supporters. I owe them a lot.

Managed to return to Hobbes' *Leviathan* and made some good progress, and I again conquered the very easy Sudoku in the *Herald Sun*.

We conclude with a psalm excerpt (89:1–4).

> *O Lord, you have been our refuge*
> *from one generation to the next.*
> *Before the mountains were born*
> *or the earth or the world brought forth,*
> *you are God without beginning or end.*
>
> *You turn men back into dust*
> *and say: "Go back, sons of men."*
> *To your eyes a thousand years*
> *are like yesterday, come and gone,*
> *no more than a watch in the night.*

Tuesday, 23 July 2019

No news again today from the appeals court. I am coping with this, although I wobbled briefly toward exasperation when I was outside for my afternoon exercise. No point in that. The appeal was brought on earlier than usual, and extra waiting can be offered for the strengthening of the Kingdom as well as more serious problems.

I had forty-five minutes in the gymnasium this morning and am a bit tired now. Sr Mary brought Holy Communion and another thought-provoking sermon from Sr Mary McGlone, pointing out that Jesus led a busy life, like Martha. But he spent long hours in prayer, also.

A big puddle in the first exercise pen showed it had rained heavily overnight, but a beautiful morning and an overcast afternoon.

My legal friend Joseph has recently sent about fifty pages of material for pondering on topics like Shakespeare and Catholics, Boris Johnson and crashing out of the EU, and the Battle of Stalingrad through the dispatches of Vasily Grossman,[4] who was an important source for Antony Beevor.[5] [As previously mentioned, he also sent a lecture on Hilary Mantel's treatment of Thomas More and Thomas Cromwell.] And by a strange coincidence, my Dublin priest friend Fr Tom McGovern, who is an enthusiast for St Thomas More, wrote that he was going to attend a lecture at University Church, Dublin, Newman's old church, given by the Cambridge Don Richard Rex on "Two Thomases: Thomas More and Thomas Cromwell". He had been slightly apprehensive, but he need not have worried. It was one of the finest lectures I have read for years—concise, elegant, and balanced in its judgements on the two characters and the reasons why their fortunes have recently been reversed.

Thomas More has always been a popular figure across the centuries, with four biographies even in the Tudor era. Rex pointed out that there were more editions of William Roper's life of More than there were biographies of Cromwell, who scored three before 1950. It was G. R. Elton in the 1950s who returned Cromwell to respectability, presenting him as a pioneer of cabinet government, a statesman and architect of modern Britain. More had gained enormous popularity from Robert Bolt's *A Man for All Seasons*, a play turned into a popular 1960s film, and Elton correctly objected to More being portrayed as a champion of individual conscience. He wasn't, as he died for the Catholic faith.

Hilary Mantel's *Wolf Hall* is a novel which she originally presented also as history and which moved Elton's thesis forward spectacularly. More is now the villain, and Cromwell the hero. The duel between these two figures dominates her narrative.

Mantel has next to nothing good to say about More, who is presented as an unpleasant hypocrite, psychotic, a persecutor and torturer. Although there is no evidence he aspired to the priesthood, he did spend some years, without vows, living in the London Charterhouse. So Mantel depicts him as a failed priest and frustrated preacher, someone who condones lying to heretics and tricking

---

[4] Vasily Grossman (1905–1964), a Russian Jewish author and journalist, served as a war correspondent for the Red Army during the Second World War and wrote two epic novels that were subsequently censored by the Soviet government.

[5] Antony Beevor (b. 1946), a British historian who has written much about the Second World War.

them into confessions, is obsessed with sex and excrement, and is hypocritical in his personal penances. It was Cromwell who used the Act of Attainder in the 1530s to bypass judicial process and declare individuals guilty of treason, and Mantel has Cromwell ascribing this expedient to More. Absurdly, without any evidence, she has More in the Tower of London masterminding and financing a plot to capture the Protestant Bible translator William Tyndale on the other side of the Channel. The Renaissance man, the author, and the humourist, who, almost uniquely, insisted on a good education for his daughters, has disappeared.

Mantel presents Cromwell as a nice man who had once been violent but was converted by the frescoes in Florence. As a child, he felt pity for the heretic burnt to death. He is kind to prisoners and visits the Holy Maid of Kent in prison, even though she is the most dangerous figurehead of opposition to Henry VIII. Cromwell is "impeccably modern", scorning superstition and the priesthood, sceptical but Protestant, and opposed to hunting because some larger mammals, their entire species, have been driven to extinction.

By any standards, Cromwell was formidable, a poor boy who made good, a ruthless agent for his ruthless King, Henry VIII. Until his own execution, he was the ultimate fixer, who made himself and his family very rich and set out to destroy the Catholic Church. This is why he is so appealing to Mantel and to her enthusiastic readers today.

For Rex, "Cromwell and More symbolise the spiritual struggle of our times, both in their historical reality and in the distorting mirror of Mantel's fiction." Rex feels compelled to intervene on the side of truth "because when a book presents an essential historical novel bolstered with a remarkably well-researched body of circumstantial trivia but characterised by wild misrepresentations and grotesque anachronisms, [it] will misinform and it will mislead." Rex goes on: "To destroy More, the symbol of Catholicism, More must be diminished to the scale of an ant, that Cromwell may trample upon him."

I have seen Holbein's portraits of More and Cromwell in the Frick Collection, New York, and believe he captured both of them perfectly. For years I claimed Holbein to be the greatest portrait painter, but I then realised he had an advantage with me, because I know his subjects so well, better than I know Pope Innocent, whose portrait by Velasquez is often claimed to be the finest, better than I know the Renaissance popes painted by Raphael. Whatever of that, Holbein got these two portraits right. More stands for something beautiful, imperfect but a saint. Cromwell was a brutal adventurer, empty and evil.

Let me conclude with some lines from another prayer of St Thomas More, written in the Tower of London the year before his execution.

Bear no malice or evil will to any man living. For either the man is good or wicked.... Let me remember that if he be saved, he will not fail (if I am saved too, as I trust to be) to love me very heartily....

And on the other side, if he will continue to be wicked and be damned, then is there such outrageous eternal sorrow before him that I may well think myself a deadly cruel wretch if I would not now rather pity his pain than malign his person.

Wednesday, 24 July 2019

A couple of local developments, before dealing with the breaking news of yesterday evening.

In the mid-afternoon, one of the warders on duty in the unit, a woman, came with the news that Dr Shane Mackinlay had been appointed bishop of Sandhurst, i.e., the Bendigo Diocese. Shane had been in year twelve at St Pat's, Ballarat, when I came to live with Bishop [James] O'Collins in the early 1980s. He was a brilliant maths and science student, whose father lectured with me in mathematics at the Aquinas campus of the Institute of Catholic Education. He was a seminarian when I was rector of Corpus Christi seminary in the mid-1980s, still an outstanding student who earned a doctorate at Louvain University in Belgium after priestly ordination. A Ballarat priest, he became master at the Catholic Theological College in Melbourne, while living and serving in the Bungaree parish, where I had been in 1984.

Catholicism is in steady decline in country Victoria,[6] possibly more than in Melbourne, so he faces a strategic challenge. Thirty-five years

---

[6] Country Victoria, also known as regional Victoria, consists of all the areas of the state of Victoria outside of Melbourne.

ago, seminarian opinion in Corpus Christi College, Clayton, was facing resolutely in the wrong direction, so I wish the new bishop every blessing and success. He was well regarded in his parish.

The second development touched on my case. Ruth[7] and Kartya called in this morning, explaining that the court had informed them of a New South Wales court decision which had some similarity with the third ground of my appeal, that I was improperly arraigned. Both sides have been asked to submit views before 31 July. We do not believe the interstate decision has any relevance, but this means that the first week of August is the earliest possible date for a verdict. I am pleased about the clarification and knowing the reason for the delay.

Ruth also mentioned that the complainant (J) not only asked the prosecution that there be no second trial, but told them that getting at least one person to believe his story at the first trial with the hung jury was probably as good a result as he was likely to obtain! I asked Ruth to examine all the Friel material, and she is lunching with Robert Richter tomorrow. Kartya brought three *Spectators*, and I received two of them. Swept out my cell and took both my exercise sessions. Unfortunately, my sister was not answering her phone.

The big news last night was the anticipated victory of Boris Johnson, who received two-thirds of the votes of the Conservative party members in the UK. This is good news, but as prime minister he faces giant problems. As a supporter of Brexit (a personal view from the other end of the world), I welcome the appointment, despite the paranoid hostility he provokes.

The left-wing press will always be hostile to him, which makes evaluation difficult. He received a mixed verdict as foreign secretary, was twice a successful lord mayor of London, winning the popular vote in a left-of-centre city, a successful editor of the *Spectator*, and is a fine writer. I enjoyed his biography of Churchill more than any book I had read for some years.

He came to my notice when I read his work, perhaps twenty years ago, defending the teaching of Greek and Latin classics, explaining their importance today, although I was surprised at his open admiration for the pagans rather than the Christians.

---

[7] Ruth Shann, a junior barrister to Bret Walker, senior counsel and leading barrister in both appeals.

When I had a pleasant twenty-minute chat with him thirty months ago, I recounted this fact, and he cheerfully confessed. I mentioned Rodney Stark's book *The Rise of Christianity* as an antidote to Gibbon's pagan enthusiasms. While he did not know of Stark, one of his staff intervened to say he had read him and that it was a quality work. Johnson muttered something about also having to read it.

He told me he was baptised a Catholic but confirmed as an Anglican. Someone, I think it was a grandmother, was a daily Mass-goer, and he has a Catholic nun somewhere among his relatives. He is a great political campaigner and a charming companion. While his personal life is alleged to be colourful, this is not unique in political life.

I was in Rome when the Brits voted to leave the European Union. I had not expected Leave to win, although I had expressed my conviction that their vote would be 2 to 3 percent better than in the polls, when people would not confess their unpopular position.

On a couple of occasions, I did my bit to defend Brexit. One senior Italian politician had been urging me to accept Communion for the divorced and [civilly] remarried, which I cannot accept because of Christ's teaching on divorce and Paul's teaching on the conditions necessary for the reception of Communion. I was a bit irritated because I had anticipated this friend would share my views. When he went on to condemn Brexit emphatically, I was constrained to point out that the English nation had enjoyed self-government for a thousand years, while Italy had a national history not much older than Australia's. This helped explain the vote and his reaction. We left the discussion at that point.

The Japanese ambassador to the Vatican did not have strong views but muttered the conventional line that the vote to leave was unfortunate. I countered by wondering whether Japan would fancy being governed from China. He, too, did not pursue that line of discussion.

Early in July, my friend Joseph sent me a detailed account of the controversy John Finnis, formerly of Oxford University, provoked by his proposal that the executive, the prime minister through the lord chancellor, might prorogue Parliament by not presenting for royal assent any bill to prevent Brexit, so that membership would lapse on the set date. Johnson has refused to rule this out, and it remains a possibility, unless deemed to be illegal by the courts before October 31.

Whatever of the legalities on this crucial, but abstruse, point, I believe Johnson and his team must plan publicly and efficiently for a departure with no deal and be prepared to implement it, but also to use this as a bargaining tool. This should have been done by Prime Minister May at the start as a consequence of her proclamation that "no deal is better than a bad deal." One major factor explaining the obduracy of the European authorities is fear, their awareness of the financial weakness of Greece, Spain, and Italy and of the growing populist hostility to the Union in many countries, even in France.

I don't believe Prime Minister Cameron should have put the motion on Brexit to a referendum, but since he did so, the decision of the majority should be accepted.

Catholics of course are free to take any position they choose on the European Union and Brexit. My opinion has the same status as that of any non-British observer. But it is such a fascinating mess, another example of tension between the deplorables and the elite, that it is an irresistible topic for examination and comment (at least for myself).

There could be no sterner test than this (short of war) for a new prime minister. It will make Boris or break him. Leaving will renew England, even if the Scots were unwise enough to depart from Britain.

It is difficult to know what prayer to use after considering such a topic. What would Thomas More think? These words of his are certainly a good start.

O Lord, give us a mind that is humble, quiet, peaceable, patient, and charitable, and a taste of your Holy Spirit in all our thoughts, words, and deeds.

Thursday, 25 July 2019

I have been watching the Tour de France on most days, enjoying the skill, grit, and endurance of the riders and particularly enjoying the changing panoramas of the French countryside from the northeast to today's racing in the Alps.

I know marginally more about the racing itself and am delighted that the Australian Caleb Ewan, a fine sprinter, has won two stages. I am also developing an empathy for the French rider Julian Alaphilippe, who has led the Tour in the yellow jersey for eleven or twelve days. He has a pleasant personality, and the commentators keep predicting his demise.

The ride today commenced the first of three very difficult and long daily climbs in the Alps before heading for the finish in Paris next week.

I don't know whether I shall finish my stay here in early August, but it has been a decent stint of five months in solitary confinement, when the usual maximum is three months. Gargasoulas[8] might be here for years.

I don't anticipate any great trials, like the three [Tour de France] mountain climbs, during the next week, but I do have to keep focused on my daily routine of prayer, exercise, sleep, reading, Sudoku, and writing. The letters I receive and the visits of family and friends are a marvellous solace. Like all the riders in the Tour, I have to keep myself together, focused and not self-absorbed, as I head toward what (I hope) is the final stretch. It is beyond doubt that prayer and Christian perspectives help you retain balance and a sense of purpose.

Today's first reading in the breviary is from Paul's Second Letter to the Corinthians. Because of his faith in the risen Lord, Paul tells them "we never become discouraged, even though our physical being is slowly decaying, yet our spiritual being is renewed day after day. And this small and temporary trouble we suffer will bring us a tremendous and eternal glory, much greater than the trouble. For we fix our attention, not on things that are seen, but on things that are unseen. What can be seen lasts only for a time; but what cannot be seen lasts for ever" (4:16–18).

This is the aim, this is the program, and these convictions bring life and peace. But my part is a work in progress, incomplete.

Writing this diary helps, also. Only today, a prisoner wrote to me explaining that he writes letters to keep his sanity. In Sydney and Melbourne, we have priests struggling to complete their doctoral theses. Six months in jail, with outside distractions removed, would be ideal for that total immersion needed to finish!

---

[8] James Gargasoulas was convicted in 2018 of murdering six people and injuring twenty-seven others when he drove a car through the Bourke Street pedestrian mall in central Melbourne in January 2017.

Anne McFarlane paid a visit, but Tim could not escape from his mediation.[9] My time in the gymnasium passed quickly and pleasantly. Young Tom Langrell sent me a great letter and an invitation to his October wedding to Billy. Good news. Wrote to John Howard[10] to congratulate him on his eightieth birthday and thank him for his public support, which has not been cost free.

Apparently Andrew Bolt had an article in today's *Herald Sun* about the man in England who has been found guilty and jailed for falsely accusing a number of senior British figures of paedophilia.[11]

A woman from Eldorado in Victoria wrote to tell me she was going to the Irish shrine of Knock, where she would pray for me, and sent the first and last two lines of a favourite poem of hers by Gerard Manley Hopkins, which I do not know.

> *Myself unholy, from myself unholy*
> *To the sweet living of my friends I look . . .*
> *No better serves me now, save best; no other*
> *Save Christ: to Christ I look, on Christ I call.*

Friday, 26 July 2019

In Unit 8 of the Melbourne Assessment Prison, where there are twelve cells for those of us condemned to solitary confinement, each person is allowed to have six books and six magazines. You are also allowed, inter alia, six pairs of socks and jocks [underwear], one pair of shoes or runners, and no hooded jackets. No tissues are issued or sold, so I have been using toilet paper as a handkerchief, which is effective, but the paper quickly breaks up in your pocket.

The system, nearly every aspect of the system, is designed to be slow and cumbersome, to remind us of our prisoner status; and the

---

[9] Tim and Anne McFarlane are close personal friends of Cardinal Pell. Tim is a solicitor and mediator.

[10] John Howard was the prime minister of Australia from 1996 to 2007. He was a member of the Liberal Party.

[11] Andrew Bolt runs Australia's most-read political blog and writes for the *Herald Sun* and other newspapers.

fact that staff are regularly shifted to different sections of the jail, with consequently different interpretations of the rules, compounds the challenges. You need patience and sometimes perseverance to negotiate the mazes. All this explains how I received my copy of the 29 June *Spectator* a couple of days ago. The system is not malicious, but usually punctilious.

I quickly noticed Christopher Akehurst's article, "All Aboard the Anti-Catholic Bandwagon", on the Victorian government's plan to allow sex-abuse victims to have a second dip at compensation. My possibly imprecise recollection is that the sums were set by the Melbourne Archdiocese bearing in mind the rates of crimes' compensation. I wonder if those, too, are up for review.

Akehurst correctly identifies the contest, which is the campaign of the ideological Left against the Catholic Church. He continues, "The Left has been very successful at exploiting child abuse. The sins of a small minority of flawed individuals have been seized upon to paint the Church as rotten to the core, so that its moral opposition to the Left's social agenda, especially in such matters as abortion, will be dismissed by public opinion as hypocritical."

He then continues a line of argument which is plausible but might not prove to be totally correct. "Catholic moral authority doesn't count for much in the Western world anymore", he opines. "Leftist propaganda has done its bit, but the general collapse of belief has done more." This is correct, but elderly parishioners in upper-middle-class parishes, like reporters who have never been in a parish church on a Sunday, are regularly unaware of the strength of working-class Catholicism in the suburbs, not all of it foreign-born.

Catholic political influence on the ground has fallen dramatically since Bob Santamaria's movement threw out the Communist leadership in the unions after the Second World War.

Even in the 1970s, we were much stronger. In the mid-seventies, as director of the Aquinas campus in Ballarat of the Institute of Catholic Education, then preparing Catholic schoolteachers, I was involved in a campaign to encourage the federal Labor government to extend its new funding for Catholic tertiary institutions to the Ballarat campus. In those days, throughout country Victoria, we could call on the Knights of the Southern Cross and the members of the National

Civic Council as well as the Catholic Women's League; all were present in many places, an active and interested network. Where such groups still exist, they are but shadows of the past.

When we were received in Canberra by Kim Beazley Snr, then minister for education under Whitlam[12] (who did a lot for Catholic schools), he complimented us on the quality of our campaign, saying he was sure Aquinas would continue long after he was gone, although he declined to help us. Federal funding for Aquinas came when John Carrick was minister for education in the Fraser government,[13] which also did a lot for Catholic schools.

During our campaign, Joh Bjelke-Petersen, the Queensland premier, was speaking in Daylesford when a delegation met him to seek support. His greeting to me was a classic: "Your job is like my job: I tell people the truth, and they will not listen. You tell them the truth, and they will not listen." He promised his enthusiastic support, well aware that the Queensland government would not be called on for funds. Those days are all gone.

I think the recent federal election result is a pointer to the future, because unease on religious issues such as religious freedom and the wider social agenda was one factor at work. Turnbull could never have provided reassurance to Gospel Christians in all the churches, but Morrison did.[14]

Most of Catholic history has not been lived in democratic societies, and this is also true of most Protestant history since the Reformation. In a democracy, everyone has a vote, including every Christian adult. Every citizen still has a right to free speech and to associate for social and political purposes. Ecumenical and interfaith cooperation, when possible, is the way forward to win majority support, to protect Christian virtue and institutions, and preserve the Judaeo-Christian underpinnings of our type of civilisation. Without this, it is impossible to find any way forward.

We turn again to James McAuley, who was active in the culture wars around the middle of the twentieth century, a founder of

---

[12] Gough Whitlam was prime minister of Australia from 1972 to 1975.

[13] Malcolm Fraser was the prime minister of Australia from 1975 to 1983.

[14] Malcolm Turnbull was the prime minister of Australia from 2015 to 2018, and Scott Morrison was elected as his successor.

Quadrant.[15] He told us, "It is not said we shall succeed"; we know this. Then he continues:

> *Nor is failure our disgrace:*
> *By ways we cannot know*
> *He [Christ] keeps the merit in his hand,*
> *And suddenly, as no-one planned,*
> *Behold the kingdom grow!*[16]

Saturday, 27 July 2019

Today I begin with a sports report. Last night, Richmond thrashed Collingwood in the AFL [Australian Football League] by thirty-two points, taking their place in the top four. I confidently predicted in the second round of the season that Richmond would not be premiers this year. Now, after five consecutive wins, expert opinion varies from describing them as a serious contender for the top prize to naming them the clear favourite. I think they should be favourites.

To my mind, they are a better team than when they won in 2017, due to Tom Lynch at full forward, signed this year (he kicked five goals last night), and the young aboriginal Sidney Stark, while the two ruckmen [Ivan] Saldo and the tall Sudanese [Mabior] Choi are together better than [Toby] Nankervis, the premiership ruckman.[17] Dusty [Dustin] Martin is back to form, but the team is not as dependent on him as it was. Here's hoping.

Yesterday's stage of the Tour de France was called off before completion because of a snowstorm in the Alps, more evidence of global warming. Unfortunately, Julian Alaphilippe lost the yellow jersey, losing his leadership position as the experts had been predicting for thirteen days. As a bit of a contrarian, I regretted this.

After pondering my situation, I yesterday phoned and left a message for my solicitors, urging them to send in their response for comments

---

[15] James McAuley (1917–1976) was an Australian poet, journalist, and literary critic. He was the first editor of the literary magazine *Quadrant*, which was started in 1956 by the Australian Committee for Cultural Freedom.

[16] James McAuley, "Retreat" (1956).

[17] In Australian Rules football, ruckmen are midfielders who follow the ball throughout the game and are some of the most important players.

on the New South Wales decision as soon as possible and requesting them to inform the court that their client does not require five days' notice of the verdict, as five minutes would suffice. I don't anticipate that this will make much difference, but it helped me feel better. My friends outside are more irritated and frustrated than I can afford to be. In the larger scheme of things, a few days more don't make much difference, provided the judges have recognized the truth. And in the Christian scheme of things, extra time in confinement will help balance out all the extra penances I have not performed during a long and comfortable life.

Yesterday, I focused on Christopher Akehurst's estimate of the position of the Catholic Church in Australian life today. My story is a cause and one consequence in this changing scenario.

Mark is now a middle-aged man, a committed Catholic, who worked in my youth team in Melbourne in the mid-1990s. He recounted a discussion he held recently on my case with two work-mates. He explained to them objectively why he believed I was not guilty. At the end, they conceded that I could be, or most probably was, innocent, but that this doesn't matter, because I "still deserve to be in jail because of the behaviour of some priests and inaction of some bishops". They admitted there was no logic in their argument, but didn't care.

A second case involves one of the lesser lights in the culture wars, a journalist who is as active and committed to the new paganism as the best of the Christians are to our cause. After the guilty verdict, he said on a couple of occasions at least that he did not believe I was guilty, while insisting to another lawyer that I was. Probably his real opinion was best expressed on yet another occasion, when, surrounded by people, he casually remarked that I probably wasn't guilty, but he was not concerned by the sentencing because "Pell had made his career on bashing the homosexuals and the divorced."

Each incident has significance but for different reasons. The second expression is entirely predictable as one example of the battle of ideas and the regular ad hominem attacks on defenders of social conservatism, of Judaeo-Christian ethics. It shows scant respect for law or truth.

The first incident is an example of scapegoating. Keith Wind-schuttle of the *Quadrant* wrote that the different verdicts of the two juries, moving from irreconcilable differences in the first trial to a guilty verdict against me in the second, are explained by the fulsome apologies of the prime minister [Scott Morrison] and the leader of the opposition [Bill Shorten] to the victims loudly proclaiming that complainants are to be believed.[18] These two men are on different points of the spectrum on social values and attitudes to Catholicism, but both felt their extravagant language was justified by Catholic crimes over generations and a perceived Catholic political weakness. Facing up to the facts, to the intrinsic evil in our communities, has, we hope, rid the Church of long-term cancers, but the weakness has been exploited by the advocates of the New Order, by the powerful forces of political correctness nourished in the universities and imposed by much of the media.

The result is that good people with a rudimentary sense of justice want someone to be punished, some type of balancing up, however indiscriminate the retribution. Elements in the police force are prone to this infection, and so are juries. Victoria is the only state in Australia where trial by a judge is not an option in criminal cases. This should be changed, because public opinion can be exploited and corrupted. It is foundational to our society that the judiciary especially, and the police also, are committed to the search for truth, to striving for justice, and to defending the presumption of innocence.

The Second Epistle of Peter places these legal considerations in an ultimate and godly context. What we are waiting for is what he promised:

The new heavens and the new earth, the place where righteousness will be at home.

So then, my friends, while you are waiting, do your best to live lives without spot or stain so that he will find you at peace. Think of our Lord's patience as your opportunity to be saved (3:13–15).

---

[18] Keith Windschuttle, "Why the Second Jury Found George Pell Guilty", *Quadrant*, 30 May 2019.

WEEK 23

Copycat Testimony

28 July–3 August 2019

Sunday, 28 July 2019

My self-waking mechanism went awry this morning as I woke two hours early and then only slept lightly before rising at 5:45 am for *Mass for You at Home*, again celebrated by Fr Tony Kerin.

Like some others from around his time and earlier, he has the habit of looking at the congregation while praying to God in the Mass, not simply when he is greeting the people. I don't think it was a conscious levelling, but enlightened liturgical opinion at one stage favoured church buildings in the round so people could see God in each other's eyes.

Whatever of that, Fr Kerin's celebration was faithful and reverent, and he again preached an excellent sermon which didn't simply repeat tired old patterns. He recounted a story of the seventeenth-century rabbi Ben Esra, who reproached one of his congregation for praying too emphatically. His congregant explained that he was telling God he was a sinner who sometimes mistreated his wife and children (but God knew what they were like), occasionally cheated a bit in his business, and told the odd lie. However, he went on and told God that his sins were worse, as God allowed earthquakes, droughts, storms, and wars. Finally, he explained to God that they should strike a deal. He would forgive God's sins if God forgave his. What did the rabbi think of this? There was a pause, and the rabbi finally said that he was surprised his friend had let God off so lightly. He should have insisted that God had to send a Messiah and effect redemption for all he had done. Fr Kerin summed up by saying God expected our prayers to be persistent, and I couldn't help thinking that the prayers for my release and exoneration certainly met that criterion.

Pastor Houston at Hillsong had a new backdrop of the façades of tenement houses, still no Christian symbols, and a differently arranged congregation, and he was sporting a recent haircut. He took his theme from Psalm 34 and used next to nothing from the New Testament as he recounted why he had built their church building. He emphasised that it all started with leadership, lauded creativity in worship, and explained that a worshipping church is a high-capacity church. A band was lined up on the stage when he was finishing, but we never have music or singing in his televised half hour. The reasons for his success elude me, as there seems to be no Gospel strategy (on the TV), but he draws large congregations in godly worship.

Pastor Joseph Prince of the New Creation Church preached on the "latter rain", which falls in springtime, as compared to the earlier autumn rain for planting, and he preached graphically on the scourging and the crowning with thorns Jesus endured for our sins. He always starts with a swinging hymn, sung enthusiastically by all his immense congregation. It is a reverent, slick, and expensive production.

I was told as a young person that it is "the Mass that matters", and more than ever that is my position. In the Catholic liturgy, as distinct from Protestant worship and some Catholic devotions, the emphasis is on the beauty of tradition rather than novelty of expression, and this is as it should be. But the format and the locale of the *Mass for You at Home* haven't changed in more than thirty years, with the same small and often aged congregations and the pleasant, pious music of that earlier time, too, e.g., "Come as You Are". Apparently the financial constraints on the Melbourne Archdiocese are considerable, and the archdiocese is to be commended for continuing to sponsor this service, but a more broadly financed television Mass, with an hour of available time screened at a better time of day, would be a more effective witness. It remains strange that Hillsong can afford to film a large congregation and we cannot, while a significant percentage of the Catholic population is housebound. I am sorry I am no longer in a position to push for a feasibility study because the present format is tired.

Took my customary double exercise period. In the afternoon, a few birds sang enthusiastically for a while, while still unseen, and the prisoners outside and below sounded like a happy school at recreation time. Failed to make contact with both my brother and sister when I phoned.

It is strange to be unable to celebrate Mass, and this is another reason why I look forward to a not guilty verdict and freedom. So I pray with Psalm 118:

> *Lord God, let my lips proclaim your praise*
> *because you teach me your commands.*
> *Let my tongue sing your promise*
> *for your commands are just.*

Monday, 29 July 2019

Today is the feast of St Martha, and this occasioned one of St Augustine's finest sermons; and there is no better homilist. Recent competitors for the top position in this genre would include Pope Benedict XVI and Cardinal Newman, but for the range of human emotions and earthiness as well as theological truth, I would retain Augustine at the head of the list.

Augustine tells us we are all heading toward the contemplation of God in heaven "still as pilgrims, not yet at rest; still on the road, not yet home; still aiming at it, not yet attaining it".

We should not lament that we do not see the Lord in the flesh, because we see him in the least of those around us. Martha did well because she "received him (Christ) just as pilgrims are received. But it was the servant receiving her Lord, the sick woman receiving her Saviour, the creature receiving her Creator."

In heaven, we shall find no pilgrims, no hungry, no thirsty, no sick. We shall find "what Mary has chosen: there we shall be fed, we shall not feed others. And so what Mary chose here will be full and perfect there." Augustine even seems to suggest that in heaven the Lord will serve us, but I wouldn't want that. Perhaps I am repeating Peter's failure to understand at the washing of the feet, but Our Lord's redemptive service was completed when he ascended into heaven, where he is the Alpha and the Omega of all creation and time. Once again, nearly 1,600 years after his death, Augustine is still able to provoke a lively theological argument (sermon 103).

In the early hours of this morning (Australian time), the riders finished the Tour de France in Paris. The Australian Caleb Ewan won this final stage, his third stage victory, demonstrating that he is the finest sprinter among the road racers. The Colombian Egan Bernal, at twenty-two the youngest winner in over a hundred years, won the overall Tour. He came through as a modest, pleasant man, who blessed himself after his victory and was absolutely delighted. Julian Alaphilippe, who won fifteen of the daily stages, came in fifth, enhancing his stature and popularity especially at home, so that he now is, as one Australian commentator explained, "world famous in France".

I am not sure I am a convert to the sport, but I enjoyed watching and am wondering whether I am eligible to join the cycling fraternity, "the best family in the world", according to the advertisements, because I peddle fifteen to twenty minutes a day on a fixed exercise bike when I am at home. When I was at school in Ballarat, together with my siblings, we often rode to and from school. This was healthy, and my sister as a young teenager was able to cycle up the Dana Street Hill in Ballarat without rising from the bicycle seat, no mean feat!

More than fifty years ago, in 1965, I attended the final stage of the Tour in Paris. I was there on a six-week French-government scholarship to study language and culture, and I must have looked foreign and a bit lost as a French policeman asked me if I would like a ticket into the stadium where the cyclists were finishing. I gratefully accepted, entered the stadium, and watched the Italian [Felice] Gimondi win the Tour.

One small encouraging development today, as a warder asked me to write an authorisation to Kartya to collect my property and to write another letter to the prison property section to inform them of this authorisation—in the event that I win the appeal. I don't know whether surmise prompted this request or some court information.

Took my two exercise sessions and noticed that there seemed to be more birdsong. It is still a bit early for spring to be in the air.

Prompted by St Augustine's thoughts on the nature of life in heaven, I conclude with another heavenly prayer from a different age, from someone (not a priest or bishop) who died in very different circumstances: St Thomas More's prayer "For Heaven" from his *A Treatise on the Passion*.

Almighty Jesus Christ: Give us your grace so to keep your holy law and so to reckon ourselves for no dwellers but for pilgrims upon earth that we may long and make haste, walking with faith in the way of virtuous works, to come to the glorious country wherein you have bought us inheritance forever with your own precious blood.

Tuesday, 30 July 2019

I was fifteen years of age when I first saw television, as it was introduced into Australia only in black-and-white, for the Melbourne Olympics in 1956. My family was not among the first to have a set, which my father only purchased after some months or a year or so. In the very early days, sets were placed in shop windows, and people would gather on the footpath to watch. Television has changed the world. Decades ago, I remember, some religious commentator pointed out that half the people whom we would have in our lounge room on the television would never be allowed past the front door by good parents. Around 1990, I was in a Cambodian village, where Caritas Australia was working on agricultural development, when the peasants gathered around in the open for their first vision of television. They were entering a new world, which, with all its faults, was a giant step forward from Pol Pot, who was not long gone.

Over the decades, I did not watch much television, never in the morning, often only later in the evening after appointments or meetings, but I regularly watched the AFL "match of the day" and the Test cricket.

Therefore, I have watched more television during my five months in jail than I have in any other period of my life. I watch Channel 7 *Sunrise* while I have my breakfast after my morning prayers and have become a fan of Sam Mac.[1] At night, the SBS[2] hour of news follows my shower as I eat my meal, often a salad in a plastic container, which I prefer to hold over rather than eat when it is distributed around 3:15 pm. So most of the time, I have watched SBS, except for the AFL football on Channel 7 (and *Sunrise*).

[1] Sam "Sam Mac" McMillan is the colourful weatherman on the *Sunrise* morning show.
[2] The Special Broadcasting Service (SBS) is an Australian public radio, online, and television network.

A couple of things struck me. SBS is so politically correct: exaltation for homosexuals, understanding for gender fluidity, and a remorseless endorsement of global warming, like the Soviet propaganda of old in its simplicity and certainty. And both Channel 7 and SBS have plenty about the royals; Channel 7 has regular updates on royal gossip, and SBS often reruns BBC features on the history of the British monarchy, especially in the twentieth century. I was surprised by this.

Among my earliest book purchases as a young teenager, apart from the Biggles and the Just William books (many of which I received from my older cousin Kevin, who had returned from England with his family), were a few books about Queen Elizabeth and Prince Philip. And on Monday night, SBS showed the last in an excellent series on the Windsors and the castle, respectful but with a lot of honesty. The stations can only be doing this because of popular demand.

Windsor Castle claims to be the oldest royal fortress anywhere, continuously inhabited by a royal family since it was constructed by the Normans, to keep an eye on the locals, one or two days' march from London, not long after 1066. The popes only moved into the Vatican in the late-fourteenth century when they returned from Avignon, and they were assured they could garrison troops in nearby Castel Sant'Angelo.

Queen Elizabeth has done a fine job, despite the marriage failures of three of her four children and the Diana debacle. Constitutional monarchy, with a wise sovereign, is a bulwark of democratic stability. It is equally true that the system works well in Australia, also, and any replacement system must be able to demonstrate advantages for us. I am clearer in my own mind than I was twenty years ago about the importance of maintaining a Westminster system of government in any new arrangement, rather than moving to an executive president or a directly elected president.

I was pleased to dine with the Queen when she visited Melbourne in 2000 and prayed the grace, as the senior of the two archbishops, for the luncheon in the ballroom at Government House.[3] This was built in the Gold Rush days, when Melbourne was one of the richest cities in the world. When London heard about the size of

---

[3] Government House is the Melbourne residence of the governor of the state of Victoria. Built between 1872 and 1876, it is considered one of the largest and most beautiful mansions in the country.

the ballroom, larger than the ballroom at Buckingham Palace, they wrote, instructing that the dimensions be reduced, but somehow the letter arrived too late.

At the meal, the Queen was a little subdued until Cathy Freeman, the Olympic champion, asked about her corgis and Damien Oliver, the jockey, followed up with racehorses.[4] Conversation then took off, the atmosphere became relaxed and pleasant, and, please God, less of a penance for Her Majesty.

To my surprise, she was slightly nervous when she rose to speak. Later, I was telling my niece about this and added that the Queen has done very well, as she has never, or rarely, "put her foot in it", said the wrong thing, when she was speaking. My niece quickly responded that this was not something people would ever say about me! Genes will out.

Afterward, I was struck by the fact that more people asked me about my lunch with the Queen than asked about any other event or encounter in my life as a priest or a bishop.

I won't be seeing an Australian republic in my lifetime, and if the monarchy can survive Charles, and if William and Kate continue up to the mark, the monarchy is likely to be secure here in Australia for fifty to seventy years at least.

When I was growing up, the Australian flag was flown regularly, the Union Jack much less so (unlike the situation until at least World War I); but we still celebrated Empire Day, and "God Save the Queen" was the national anthem. It is a song I still love to sing.

So my concluding prayer is, to the dismay of at least some of my Irish Catholic ancestors:

May God save the Queen.

Wednesday, 31 July 2019

After the rest and recreation day yesterday, writing about the Windsors and constitutional monarchy, we are back to serious business

---

[4] Cathy Freeman is an Australian sprinter who won a gold medal at the 2000 Summer Olympics. The jockey Damien Oliver has won more than a hundred Group 1 races and has been inducted three times into the Australian Racing Hall of Fame.

today with the feast of St Ignatius of Loyola. Unusually for me, I did not sleep well last night, waking up early—and I believe one reason was that I was anxious about what I might write on the Jesuits. Naturally, I wanted to be just and accurate, which is made more difficult in prison when access to information is almost nonexistent.

Ignatius is one of the greatest saints and reformers. The Jesuits spearheaded the Counter-Reformation. Ignatius was a Spaniard, and Spain is remarkable for the number of Church reformers it has produced. First of all, St Dominic. Then Teresa of Avila and John of the Cross from about Ignatius' time, and more recently two of the most influential twentieth-century founders and reformers, St Josemaría Escrivá of Opus Dei and Kiko Arguello and Carmen Hernandez Barrera of the Neocatechumenal Way. Secularism is powerful in modern Spain, where the Civil War continues under the surface and 40 percent of the churchgoers are from Opus Dei and the "Neo-Cats" (as they prefer not to be called).

Ignatius' warm heart is well concealed as he was tough and demanding. I remember a story about St Francis Xavier, who was labouring with spectacular missionary success in India. Letters came rarely on the sailing ships, and on one occasion Ignatius did not write to Francis in order to help strengthen his detachment from worldly things!

I have only gratitude for the four years I spent under the Jesuits at Corpus Christi seminary in Werribee. They were good priests, prayerful men, and generally humane, implementing a seminary model that would be changed by the Second Vatican Council. The academic formation, which is important, but less important, varied between adequate and occasionally woeful, for Latin-language textbooks are not ideal for classes of mixed ability. However, we were following a system which had worked for four hundred years.

All around the world, the availability of good-quality priests to direct seminary formation is a pressure point, exacerbated in our time by large numbers of seminarians.

Campion Hall does not have collegiate status at Oxford University, but is a constituent private hall. In the late '60s, it had about sixty students, mostly postgraduates like myself, Jesuits and other clergy, with some laymen, a strongly international group. Campion is a Jesuit institution.

It took me a while to settle in, but I came to love the life and my good friends during my four years there (1967–1971). Fr Ted Yarnold, the master, was quiet and shy, a learned man, if a bit boring as a lecturer, and a prayerful, serious priest. Fr Michael Kyne was the spiritual director, and I learnt from him never to count your eggs before they are hatched as he once received a letter appointing him provincial of the English Province which was countermanded before the due date. Br Jim Higgins, an older man, became a dear friend. The English Jesuits led self-contained lives with a level of community life among themselves lower than Australians and Americans were used to.

I have been known to say that there is no man better than the best Jesuits, and that these are few. This claim is at least initially defensible, especially in those days, when they had a rigorous spiritual formation as well as a first-rate intellectual preparation in philosophy, theology, and some areas of secular learning. Here, too, standards have slipped. The Jesuit provincials with whom I worked were serious, prayerful priest leaders. Fr Peter Steele, the poet and English professor at Melbourne University, was a friend who prepared the text for the Stations of the Cross at World Youth Day, 2008. I am very grateful that Fr Frank Brennan[5] has used his formidable talents in my defence during my recent troubles. This list could be continued.

Unfortunately, the Jesuits today have fewer than one-third of the 36,000 members they numbered in the 1960s. This represents an incalculable loss to the Church and society across the world. India is almost alone as a province with a good number of vocations.

For decades, a struggle has taken place among the Jesuits, since the time of Fr [Pedro] Arrupe as superior general (1965–1983) at least, as to whether revelation, as developed from the Scripture by the Magisterium, has the last word or whether this belongs to modernity, contemporary learning, and insights. Is the priority evangelisation or working for social justice; personal conversion, prayer, and repentance or caring for Mother Earth; building faith communities or striving for structural reform? Most poignant of all, is homosexual activity still sinful, or does respect for persons amount to an endorsement of such behaviour as a legitimate expression of human love?

---

[5] Fr Frank Brennan, SJ, is a Jesuit priest, author, and lawyer as well as rector of Newman College, University of Melbourne.

One fears the worst when one hears the superior general wondering whether anyone can say what Christ taught as they didn't have a tape recorder! His predecessor as "the black pope" hardly mentioned Jesus in his first sermon in office. These are not proofs sufficient to convict, but they are disturbing.

The Jesuits need reform. On the feast of St Aloysius Gonzaga, I expressed my belief that reform is possible. I stand by this, as I acknowledge it would require a miracle, not quite like the Resurrection, but a huge miracle nonetheless. But, Gospel Christians believe in miracles.

Sr Mary called yesterday for our prayer service and to bring Holy Communion. I welcome her coming at every level, and the warders usually give us a good hour. She spoke about Eugenio Pacelli [future Pope Pius XII] and said a couple of Ballarat priests, who had been jailed for paedophilia already, were in court once again. This is sad news.

The challenges which confront the Jesuits are those facing all Christians in the Western world and, indeed, in every country where the elite are Western educated. A couple of verses from Psalm 94, which always begins the day's prayer, reminds us of our priorities.

> Come in; let us bow and bend low;
> let us kneel before the God who made us,
> for he is our God and we
> the people who belong to his pasture,
> the flock that is led by his hand.
> O that today you would listen to his voice!
> Harden not your hearts as at Meribah,
> as on that day at Massah in the desert
> when your fathers put me to the test;
> when they tried me, though they saw my work.

Thursday, 1 August 2019

It has been a frustrating day. I couldn't say it was deeply frustrating or that I had an overwhelming reason to be frustrated. However, I still have not heard from the court when the verdict will be delivered.

My agitation was provoked by the fact that Paul [Galbally], my solicitor, had promised to visit today, saying when we were on the phone on Tuesday that he had some news to deliver personally. But he didn't arrive.

Until nearly 4 pm (and we closed down for the night at 4:30 pm), I was fearful that I would not get my afternoon exercise spot, preventing me from phoning my sister—and the lawyers. After a couple of polite requests, I was successful and phoned to find my sister, Margaret, in good form. *Deo gratias*. Paul was not in the office, so I spoke to Kartya by phone. Margaret had received a garbled message from cousin Elizabeth in Perth that the ABC[6] had announced over there that I would be released, but with some conditions attached. Kartya knew nothing of this, but informed me that Neil Mitchell had told his radio audience, today presumably, that I would be released.[7] On my return inside, I mentioned this to the warders, commenting that Mitchell must be better informed than I am. One warder, who gave me extra food last night and a box of tissues (for a brief series of sneezes), laughingly claimed that Mitchell was always right.

Had nearly an hour in the gymnasium, walking and doing strengthening exercises for my arms and thighs. The thighs are strengthening, as I am able to rise from a chair more easily and with a little more grace.

Fr Victor Martinez, my confessor from Sydney, came down from Castlemaine, where he was giving a retreat. I went to confession, we had a good chat, and he brought greetings from friends in Australia and overseas. Still quite a number of vacancies for new bishops across the Australian dioceses.

We prisoners in Unit 8 at the moment seem to be a dull lot as we have no serious shouters or bangers. We had one banger yesterday, but he did not sound too serious. A warder shouted, "Louder, louder", a couple of times. I wondered whether this was a good tactic as the banger responded more loudly for a while and then fell silent, completely silent. I heard nothing today. The warder had correctly recognized the genre. Some shouters are exultant, especially if they have an audience. Some are petulant performers with no deep emotion. Some are bitter and hostile, shouting and banging simultaneously, probably dangerous to confront, while some are frantic,

---

[6] The Australian Broadcasting Company (ABC) is the national, government-funded television and radio network.

[7] Neil Mitchell hosts the popular *3AW Mornings* radio show broadcast by a Melbourne news and talk station.

anguished, and angry. Most of us don't put on public performances, while the last four or five days have been quieter than any other during my five months. Late night or early morning performances are the most annoying, but not always the most distressing. Occasionally cell doors are open as you pass on the way to exercise or the medical centre or visitors. Few if any have books in their cells.

The first cricket Test at Edgbaston, UK, started against England, the old enemy. The Aussies began badly, being 3 for 82 at lunch, with the local crowd (no vacant seats) vigorously booing the Australian cheaters as they came out to bat, singing lustily Blake's beautiful hymn or poem about this [England's] "green and pleasant land",[8] confident, relishing the Australian discomfort and hoping much more would follow.

Today is also the feast of St Alphonsus Liguori (1696–1787) the founder of the Redemptorist Fathers, whose main work is to run missions, renewal weeks of Mass, devotions, and sermons in the parishes. Their house of studies was in my home city of Ballarat, an immense, cold bluestone building with a beautiful chapel, which had to be sold as their numbers collapsed and the religious orders consolidated their theological centres in Melbourne.

The building has now been turned into apartments, but was vacant for some years, squalid, a haunt for dossers [vagrants] even the chapel. A beautiful image of Our Lady of Perpetual Help remained among the desolation, high up in the chapel. A friend managed to extract it, and it is now in a Melbourne worship centre. A small work of redemption.

As a seven- or eight-year-old, I walked with my mother through the darkness and chill of Ballarat winter mornings along Rowe Street to the 7 am Mass for the mission at St Alipius, Ballarat East. We had missions when I lived in the parish as a priest in the seventies, which were well attended by a sizeable number across all age groups.

I still remember a fourteen-year-old boy, with his mates, asking on what nights the missioner would be talking on hell and on sex, because he was coming on those nights. St Alphonsus himself was a humane and moderate moralist, but some of the priests were colourful

---

[8] The words are from the last line of William Blake's poem "And Did Those Feet in Ancient Time" (1804), which was made into the hymn "Jerusalem" with music Hubert Parry in 1916.

and tough preachers. In a Gippsland church, one of the most colourful performers was orating and berating as he walked back and forth behind the altar rail. One young boy was a bit discomforted, telling his mother, "I hope he doesn't get out." The "Reds" did a lot of good.

The Redemptorists converted many and probably reconverted more, urging them back onto the narrow path to salvation, bringing peace and calm, leading them closer to the Lord. Psalm 34 talks of the tens, indeed, hundreds of thousands who flocked to their missions over the decades.

> *I sought the Lord, and he answered me;*
> *and delivered me from all my fears.*
>
> *Look to him and be radiant;*
> *so your face shall never be ashamed.*
> *This poor man cried, and the Lord heard him,*
> *and saved him out of all his troubles.*
> *The angel of the Lord encamps*
> *around those who fear him.*

Friday, 2 August 2019

August 1 has come and gone, the day when the dream had predicted I would be freed. Neil Mitchell's announcement that I would be freed is not equivalent to the verdict of the judges! As someone who is innately sceptical, but believes strongly in the reality of the supernatural, I would have been surprised if the situation panned out as predicted. I know, too, from my reading, of the significant number of inexplicable events and coincidences, whether they be paranormal or supernatural, but that even in miraculous apparitions, e.g., Fatima, the specifics, the detailed predictions can be wrong. Prophecy is inexact, does not bring the predictability of scientific laws.

When I went to bed around midnight, the Australian cricket situation had deteriorated, England exultant, as we were eight wickets for about 120 runs, Steve Smith having just reached his 50. I was resigned to hearing of a dismal total, when I woke this morning, of much less than 200 runs. As a very small Friday penance, I did not turn on the TV until I had made my bed, said the morning Office, and sat down for breakfast. To my amazement, Australia had scored 284 runs, with Smith making 144 in what the TV commentator breathlessly described as one of the greatest innings ever! And unbelievers will persist in claiming there are no miracles.

I had been expecting Ruth and Kartya in the afternoon, so I was surprised to be told late morning that I had a professional visit. It was Paul Galbally, the senior solicitor. He had decided not to send on to Tim O'Leary my comments on the Friel synopsis as he did not want any signed document of mine on the loose. While I believe this is excessively cautious, I went along with the advice. He also reported that Kartya had accepted an invitation yesterday from the registrar of the Appeal Court to go to the court and walk through the procedures required in the event of my being exonerated. It was agreed that, as I would then be a free man, I would be entitled to leave by the main entrance, as I preferred.

Kartya and Ruth came as anticipated in the afternoon, clutching the Friel documents. Ruth was more impressed than when she first read them, believing his forensic skills developed as he went on, as he received more information. She made the very good suggestion that he be invited out to continue his investigative work and be given access to all the court transcripts. When I reported this to Tim O'Leary, he thought it an excellent suggestion. I don't know what would be the minimum time that would be useful, much less whether Friel would be available to travel from Wales. Robert Richter's opinion would be important.

Ruth mentioned in passing that the local publicity about the conviction and jailing of the fraudster who made false accusations against establishment figures in the UK was good and useful, not just for me, but more generally in the interests of justice.

By a coincidence, today I received from Sheryl, a regular correspondent from Texas, a copy of the 15 May 2019 post on the blog *These Stone Walls* written by Fr Gordon MacRae. The article was entitled "Was Cardinal George Pell Convicted on Copycat Testimony?" Fr MacRae was convicted on 23 September 1994 of paedophilia and sentenced to sixty-seven years in a New Hampshire prison for crimes allegedly committed around fifteen to twenty years previously. The allegations had no supporting evidence and no corroboration.

It is one thing to be jailed for five months. It would be another step up, which I would not relish, to spend another three years if my appeal were unsuccessful. But we enter another world with a life sentence.

Australia is not New Hampshire, and I don't believe all the Australian media would blackball the discussion of a case such as MacRae's.

The late Cardinal Avery Dulles, SJ, whom I admired personally and as a theologian, encouraged Fr MacRae to continue writing from jail, stating, "Someday your story and that of your fellow sufferers will come to light and will be instrumental in a reform." Fr MacRae recounts the extraordinary similarities between the accusations I faced and the accusations of Billy Doe in Philadelphia, which were published in Australia in 2011 in the magazine *Rolling Stone*. Earlier this year, Keith Windschuttle, editor of the quality journal *Quadrant*, publicised the seven plus points of similarity, pointing out that "there are far too many similarities in the stories for them to be explained by coincidence."[9]

The author of the 2011 *Rolling Stone* article was Sabrina Rubin Erdely, no longer a journalist, disgraced and discredited. In 2014 she had written, and provoked a storm which reached Obama's White House, about "Jackie" at the University of Virginia, who claimed she was gang-raped at a fraternity party in 2012 by seven men.[10] As MacRae points out, "The story was accepted as gospel truth once it appeared in print."

Jackie's account turned out to be a massive lie. A civil trial for defamation followed; the seven students were awarded $7.5 million in damages by the jury; and *Rolling Stone* was found guilty of negligence and defamation.

The allegations behind the 2011 *Rolling Stone* article, published in Australia, have also been demolished as false by, among others, Ralph Cipriano's "The Legacy of Billy Doe" published in the *Catalyst* of the Catholic League in January–February 2019. No one realised in 2015,

---

[9] Keith Windschuttle, "The Borrowed Testimony That Convicted George Pell", *Quadrant*, 8 April 2019, https://quadrant.org.au/opinion/qed/2019/04/the-fanciful-testimony-that-convicted-george-pell/.
[10] Sabrina Rubin Erdely wrote "The Catholic Church's Secret Sex-Crime", *Rolling Stone*, 15 September 2011, and "A Rape on Campus", *Rolling Stone*, 19 November 2014. The magazine retracted the latter article on 15 April 2015.

when the allegations against me were first made to police, that the model for copycat allegations, or the innocent basis for the remarkable similarities, was also a fantasy or a fiction.

I am grateful to Fr MacRae for taking up my cause, as I am to many others. These include in North America George Weigel and Fr Raymond de Souza and here in Australia Andrew Bolt, Miranda Devine, Gerard Henderson, Fr Frank Brennan, and others behind the scenes.

I will conclude, not with a prayer, but with Fr MacRae's opening quotation from Baron de Montesquieu (1742).

There is no crueler tyranny than that which is perpetrated under the shield of law and in the name of justice.

Saturday, Feast of St Dominic, 3 August 2019

In Australia we celebrate the feast of St Dominic, a Spaniard (1170–1221), whose customary feast day, still celebrated in the rest of the world on 8 August, has been taken over locally by the feast of our only canonised saint, St Mary of the Cross MacKillop.

Our archbishop in Sydney, Anthony Fisher, is a Dominican, an invaluable support for me, and earlier today, this morning, he ordained seven new priests. Three of them had been among the seniors when I came to live at the Homebush seminary two years ago and were kind and welcoming. I had anticipated being present, and my absence is personally disappointing. Naturally, I offered my prayers today for all of them, also remembering in particular the three Neocatechumenal ordinands from Redemptoris Mater seminary.

My daily routine continues without disturbance. The fact that I am not woken an hour earlier each morning to receive my medication is a bonus, as it now comes around breakfast. Yesterday, unexpectedly, I had a blood test for my liver. I objected, asked whether they had chosen the correct patient (the African nurse, very efficient, replied emphatically, asking, "How many George Pells are in jail?"), but I went along. I think the doctor should have informed me. A warder mentioned that the young nurse who regularly needed multiple attempts to extract the requisite amount of blood from my ancient veins had been moved on.

Had forty-five minutes in the gymnasium, doing the usual round of exercise. As it is a Saturday, basketballs are allowed. My bouncing-the-ball skills are now respectable, and I managed to throw, under-arm, three goals. At the age of seventy-eight, practice does not make perfect, but practice does bring improvement. My knees gave no trouble on the stairs, and I am now able to ascend and descend without clutching the bannister, so my sense of balance is also improving.

We once again have a shouter, but he is a pale exemplar of the tumultuous best. He must be at the other end of the unit, as I cannot hear him clearly. The noise is muted, rather brief, but tinged with anguish.

The gent in the exercise pen next to mine put on quite a show this morning when I wouldn't reply to his repeated requests for my name. He was rough spoken, incoherent for a good deal of his diatribe, but it was quite clear he disapproved of the silent "dog" next door. It was no big deal, but a little something to be offered up for the new priests. I pray for them now.

Lord God, Creator, Light of the faithful and Shepherd of souls, whose servant Anthony ordained seven young men to the priesthood, to feed your flock by their teaching and form them by their example, grant that they may always keep the faith taught by your Son and follow the way he walked.

WEEK 24

Transfiguration

4 August—10 August 2019

Sunday, 4 August 2019

Today, I begin with the less important pieces of information. Richmond had another solid AFL win against lowly Melbourne, which has slipped badly from last year. Chris Meney,[1] who has accompanied me on my trips south, is a Melbourne supporter, as his great uncle, my distant cousin Dick Hingston, was a top player there just before the Second World War. Chris' daughter suggested to her father that he arrange for six Melbourne players to carry the coffin at his funeral. "Why?" Chris asked innocently. "So they can let you down for the last time", his loving daughter responded. I believe Richmond is a better team than when they won in 2017, but the reigning premiers West Coast are formidable, too.

Barring another miracle inning from Steve Smith and the lower-order batsmen, Australia will be comprehensively beaten by England in the cricket.

The story of St Ignatius of Loyola convalescing after being wounded at Pamplona and having only *The Life of Christ* and *The Flower of the Saints* to read, rather than his usual diet of "aimless and exaggerated" historical tales, is well-known. He eventually realised that after reading of worldly heroics he left dejected and empty, while he remained content and peaceful after reading of the austerities of the saints. From this his teaching on the discernment of spirits developed.

A good friend sent me a copy of Chris Pavone's *The Paris Diversion*, a thriller set in the world of finance and terrorism. It has been

---

[1] Chris Meney, chancellor of the Archdiocese of Sydney, is Cardinal Pell's cousin and friend.

well received and is well written, with about four different strands of the story running in parallel and therefore alternating. When you are desperately wondering what will come next, the author returns to another narrative stream. It wasn't that I didn't like this "escapist" yarn, because I could have simply stopped reading. I continued. My distaste came from the fact that all the characters were thoroughly unpleasant. I couldn't find a hero or heroine; the husbands and wives were regularly lying to one another, and the only altruist was the Muslim who was duped into martyrdom by non-Islamic crooks.

It was the only book of this genre I have read in jail, and it just didn't fit with my state of mind. But on top of that, I well understand what Ignatius felt, although I don't doubt that Pavone is a better writer than Ignatius' Basque authors. I also suspect that the unrelieved emptiness and wickedness was worse in the *Diversion*. No food for the soul of a jailed man, but the gift was still a kind thought.

I woke up after 5:00 am and comfortably made it to the 6:00 am *Mass for You at Home*, where Fr Kerin preached another excellent and unusual sermon against avarice, urging that we build up a store of good works and think of leaving something in our wills for the Church or, more precisely, for Catholic Missions, which is the sponsor. They also sang a (newer?) hymn I didn't know.

Pastor Houston at Hillsong kept ploughing on, giving a good talk on the importance of God and worship. Once again, there was no mention of Jesus, apart from a passing reference to the prodigal son, but the Spirit was invoked.

It is not as though Houston were an Arian who denied the divinity of Christ because the Lord is not mentioned. On release, I must find out whether they bill themselves as Christian and only talk about him later to the initiates.

Joseph Prince was not at his best, but he warned us against avarice, very effectively pointing out that tithing is an excellent antidote to greed.

Hymns of Praise came from the ancient headquarters in London of the Order of St John, now known as St John Ambulance. The order was refounded in the nineteenth century, after being suppressed by Henry VIII in 1540, and traces its origins to Gerardo Sasso, born in Scala, Italy, in the eleventh century, who set up the first Christian hospital in Jerusalem after that city was taken by the First Crusade in 1099. The Knights of Malta, of Lazarus, and of St John are all knights "hospitaller", i.e., they cared for the sick as well as being soldiers. The Knights Templar did not run hospices or hospitals.

Scala is a beautiful small town in the hills behind Amalfi, on the Italian coast south of Naples. It was my titular see while I was an auxiliary bishop in Melbourne. St Alphonsus preached his first Redemptorist mission in the crypt of the cathedral there, under a splendid Gothic crucifix.

The most precious possession of the cathedral is a magnificent jewelled mitre donated by the Norman ruler Charles I of Anjou (1226–1285), after a narrow escape from disaster off the coast of North Africa. He eventually went on to become King of Jerusalem.

When I made an official visit there in 1988, they asked whether I would like to use the mitre when I celebrated the Sunday Mass during their official welcome. Just before this, I had been invited to wear a mitre that had belonged to Pope Paul VI, but it was much too small. Remembering this, I replied that I would be honoured to do so, but anticipated it wouldn't fit me. To my immense surprise, it did fit, and I wore it for the Mass. I suspect the mitre had been reconstituted at some stage over the past eight hundred years, when some bishop might have had a large head like mine, which I probably inherited from the Norman Burkes and Fitzgeralds, or during a period when they used wigs. I later saw the mitre again at an exhibition of Norman treasures from Italy held in the Palazzo Venezia in Rome. It was from a balcony at this palace that Mussolini addressed his Fascist rallies.

God our Father, I thank you for the many blessings I have received during my life, human as well as spiritual. Continue to stay with me in my present circumstances, and help me when I am freed, now or later, to continue to work for the spread of your Kingdom.

Monday, 5 August 2019

I was wrong. We had a second miracle in the cricket, with Smith scoring another century with [Matthew] Wade's century, too, so that near the end of the fourth day, Australia declared at 7 for 487, a magnificent second inning's total after a poor start. The last day will be a classic Ashes struggle,[2] even if, as lately, the English have to bat for a draw. For many noninitiates, especially my Italian friends, this is the ultimate absurdity; to play for five days and have a drawn result. The wheel has turned as Australia hasn't won a series victory in England since 2001.

We have two shouters and bangers in the unit, and as I write this, the worst of them is performing; or was, as he has just paused. He is seriously aggrieved and disturbed.

Once again during my morning exercise, I had a show next door, possibly the same man who abused me yesterday. He talked to himself loudly and laughed at his own jokes. He is quite mad, probably alcohol damaged, with or without drugs. He wasn't abusive toward me, despite his abuse of the guards and ferocious banging on the door to the exercise area. As one warder commented, "He has a kangaroo loose in the top paddock." The warder must have grown up in the country. While this was continuing, a more subdued banging was occurring in one of the cells. I can hear the main culprit singing, almost happily, in his cell at this moment. Both his mood changes and pauses are unusual, but he is in a sad way.

The morning weather was crisp and clear, with a few more light clouds in the afternoon. The birdsong is increasing even here in the CBD.[3]

A few days ago, another encouraging letter arrived from Peter Jensen, emeritus archbishop of the Anglican Diocese of Sydney, with whom I worked. He wrote about Psalms 22 and 23, which begin with Our Lord's lament on the Cross, "My God, my God, why have you forsaken me?"

He pointed out that his preacher had explained that the psalter has "couplets", i.e., neighbouring psalms which dialogue with each other. So the grim beginning to Psalm 22 deals with what is painful in our lives, then carries us through the latter part of the psalm to

---

[2] The Ashes is a series of Test cricket games between Australia and England. Test matches are of the longest duration in the sport of cricket.

[3] CBD stands for central business district. The Melbourne Assessment Prison is located just west of Melbourne's city centre.

better things and on to the quietness, abundance, and joy of perhaps the best known of all, Psalm 23: "The Lord is my shepherd, I shall not want", as I lie down in green pastures, am led beside quiet waters, and guided along right paths. The archbishop concluded, "Certainly, I have found Psalm 23 to be more and more precious to me as I journey through the exile which is this world."

During the last couple of mornings, I have used the two psalms for meditation. Thanks be to God, so far at least in my life, I have never been tempted to think that God might have abandoned me. Our Lord was not a stoic, philosophically speaking, and one of the charms of the psalms is that they enable you to express the worst, knowing a correction will follow in the same psalm or the next one.

Two stories of imprisoned bishops remind me not to lament my situation; it could have been much worse. A regular correspondent from Singapore sent me a couple of pages from Cardinal Robert Sarah's book *The Power of Silence*, which tell of his predecessor in the Archdiocese of Conakry, Guinea, Archbishop Raymond-Marie Tchidimbo, who was in solitary confinement, forbidden to speak to anyone, in a sordid prison for nine years. He was in fear of torture and in fear of his life, and in this silence he encountered God.

Another loyal and frequent Australian writer sent me the story of Blessed Bishop Vasil' Hopko, who was ordained in 1929 and began work with his Greek-Catholic flock in Prague. The Communists were busy, and Fr Hopko worked especially with the youth.

After the war, when the Communists took over Czechoslovakia, they suppressed the Greek Catholic eparchy and then arrested the newly created bishop. Imprisoned near Prague, he was kept solitary in a dark cell, where he lost count of time. He was tortured, interrogated for a year, charged with subversion, and condemned to fifteen years in prison. There he was slowly poisoned with small doses of arsenic, suffered from acute depression, was unable to sleep and hardly able to walk. He was released in 1966, and in 1968 the Greek Catholic Church was reestablished. He died in peace with the nuns on 23 July 1976.

One conclusion which we should draw from the two short accounts is to thank God that our Australian society is so different from the countries described. We enjoy freedom of speech and freedom of religion. Our judicial system might be imperfect, but it is not corrupt; and despite the Lawyer X scandal in Victoria,[4] our police force is increasingly held to account.

Closer to home, my situation in jail could not be more different from that of the two bishops. I am well fed, warm, with my own shower, able to pray, write, read, and watch television, including the religious programs. Perhaps most importantly because I am in solitary, the guards are decent human beings, humane. The power plays are rare enough and usually petty. And I have been able to receive between 1,500 and 2,000 letters as well as visitors twice a week.

I am sure that Archbishop Tchidimbo and the Blessed Hopko followed Paul's teaching in Romans (12:14–16):

Bless those who persecute you; bless and do not curse them. Rejoice with those who rejoice, weep with those who weep. Live in harmony with one another; do not be haughty, but associate with the lowly.

Tuesday, 6 August 2019

Today is the feast of the Transfiguration, that glimpse of Christ in his transcendent glory with Moses and Elijah which was his gift to Peter, James, and John. It is like what awaits all of us after death, provided we make the grade: the unknown journey we all will take to encounter God's love. It was an experience which strengthened the leadership group within the twelve apostles as they continued toward the darkness of Good Friday, a foretaste and promise of the reward to come.

The Transfiguration is now the fourth in the Mysteries of Light, which St John Paul II added to the three sets of rosary mysteries. For some reason, it took me a while before I could easily meditate on them as I recited the rosary; it was a change in the routine. On some days, in jail, while praying and taking my exercise in the tiny yard, I didn't feel much like meditating on such a joyful topic. My situation seemed far away from Mt Tabor.

---

[4] The Lawyer X scandal was the discovery that a criminal defence barrister, Nicola Gobbo, was also a registered police informant through the 1990s and during a gang war in the early 2000s, when two criminal organizations waged a bloody fight for control of Melbourne's illegal drug trade. Gobbo was both defending and betraying her mobster clients.

Sr Mary called as usual today, and we both wondered whether we would meet again next Tuesday, if I haven't been liberated. Still no news on a verdict date. As the Italians say, "Pazienza". Mary again brought me Sr Mary McGlone's sermon from last Sunday, when she recounted a marvellous tale from the Russian novelist Dostoyevsky, which merits repeating regularly.

A guardian angel went weeping to God because her charge, a woman, had been sent to hell for her wickedness. God asked whether she had ever done anything good, and the angel replied she had once given an onion to a beggar. God told the angel to find the onion and use it to pull her charge out of hell. All went well when she held out the onion to the woman, who grasped it as they started to ascend. Seeing what was happening, the other sinners also wanted to escape by grabbing and hanging onto the woman's legs. She kicked them away, shouting, "It's my onion!" The onion broke and they all fell back into the abyss. That's a useful little tale for any sermon on avarice and the nature of the afterlife.

It was drizzling this morning but had cleared up in the afternoon. At different stages this morning, our shouter was loud and disturbed, but all is quiet now. He has either settled down or been moved on; I don't know. Just as I don't know why the whimpering dog, with its manager or with the squad, was outside but in the unit last night.

A minor kerfuffle midafternoon when I was called to the medical centre and told I had to take my afternoon tablets when I received them and as observed by the warden and the nurse. I said I could not see any reason to change the procedure followed for five months, that I would tell them if I wasn't going to take the tablets, and that I wanted a written direction from the doctor, with reasons, before I would do as they were directing. None of my other tablets are taken immediately, much less under supervision. The tablet involved is warfarin [a blood thinner], and my blood levels are excellent. I said that the reason they offered for the change, "to be sure I was taking the medicine", was ridiculous and unnecessary. It was a petty power play, which I felt should not be indulged.

The senior officer present said a warder would come in the afternoon when the tablet is distributed. He and the nurse arrived while I was taking exercise, and she gave me the tablets in the plastic envelope. I thanked her and put them in my pocket, and the warden said

OK, and they left. I had said that I was happy to talk with the senior doctor, and I am to meet him tomorrow morning. We shall see.

I mentioned the encounter to Sr Mary, and she repeated that it is a feature of prison life, often in small matters, and that she, as chaplain, also encounters it occasionally. It would be wrong to make a mountain out of a molehill, but capricious authoritarianism should be resisted. It says a good deal about the jail that I was allowed to take the stand I did.

God our Father, give me patience and discernment, continue to help me act and speak courteously, to realise that the judgement will soon be given and that a further delay of some days, in the real scheme of things, doesn't matter much. After surviving the major challenges, help me not to trip over the smaller last hurdles. I make this prayer in the name of Jesus, your Son.

Wednesday, 7 August 2019

Yesterday's feast of the Transfiguration distracted me from the cricket, which is better than the situation being the other way around! Australia won the First Test by 251 runs, with [Nathan] Lyon the spinner taking six wickets for 49 runs. A stupendous win, not anticipated by me or anyone else I know. I think England has a better team than this result suggests. In the last Ashes series in England, which Australia lost, there were huge contrasts in the results. If the two teams had been racehorses, they would have been swabbed.

Today the New South Wales Parliament is debating the decriminalisation of abortion, though abortion on demand has been the practice for decades. In Western Australia, a bill has been introduced to legalise euthanasia on the Victorian model. In both cases, the pro-life forces are expected to lose ground.

I have only one suggestion among our arguments: there should be an explicit appeal to the Christian teaching against taking innocent life. For as long as I have been a priest, we, too, kept God out of the debate. We have not had many wins, and the momentum now is against us. For God's sake, we should bring him back into the discussion, as more than 50 percent of Australians are Christians as well as other monotheists. "God wills it" was the battle cry of the Crusaders. Being silent about God helps those who want to exclude religious discussion from the public square. The homosexuality advocates, much more than all the other excluded sinners, don't like being threatened with hell, in which many or most of them don't believe. Those who kill, take innocent life, should be reminded that this is against God's teaching. This won't convince too many of our embittered opponents, although truth can be disconcerting. But many people are confused, under pressure, doing the wrong thing reluctantly. Godly truth would help. There is too much silence about God in the Catholic Church in Australia and not just in the areas of life and marriage. Do we have enough faith to be embarrassed by our silence? I remain intrigued by the claim that Australian Catholic tourists overseas fall silent when visiting a mosque but continue to chatter in churches.

During my afternoon exercise, I phoned my lawyers for an update and received the good news that the High Court had refused an application for leave by the Victorian prosecutors' appeal against the exoneration of Br Tyrrell. He had been accused of sexual offences at a time when he was no longer at the school. Justice Weinberg, who is on my panel of judges, had also been central in the Tyrrell verdict.[5]

My fear and frustration oozed from the hypothesis that the delay in delivering my verdict came from inertia or caprice. Logic told me this was unlikely, but ...

My conjecture, only a conjecture, is that my three judges knew a High Court ruling on Tyrrell was in the offing and prudently waited to see whether there was material there relevant to what they were proposing to write in my case.

This news from the High Court brought me relief and consolation, so that when I returned to my cell, I prayed the Te Deum, the traditional hymn of praise and thanksgiving, which is sung on grand occasions and was sung lustily, in Latin, at the end of every seminary year in my time at Werribee:

[5] On 15 March 2019, the Victorian Court of Appeal overturned the conviction of Christian Brother John Francis Tyrrell, who had been accused of raping a young boy and other offences more than fifty years ago. Tyrrell had been found guilty by a jury following a trial in which no forensic evidence or witnesses were presented. On 7 August 2019, the High Court, without a hearing, dismissed the prosecution's request to challenge the appellate court's decision.

Te Deum laudamus: te Dominum confitemur.
Te aeternum Patrem omnis terra veneratur.

Unfortunately, I did not have a Latin version.

A digression on the Te Deum. After the Allied victory in the Second World War, the French leadership under General de Gaulle gathered in Notre Dame Cathedral in Paris, war damaged but upstanding, for a solemn singing of the Te Deum. During the ceremony, shots rang out in the cathedral, and, quite predictably, confusion and some panic followed. De Gaulle remained standing in his place, unmoved through all the commotion. He is another of my heroes, leader and patriot, brave and also a fine writer. He always opposed Britain's entry into the European Union and would now probably feel justified by Brexit.

With the news this afternoon, I feel we have turned the corner. Bad news, a guilty verdict, is possible, but reputable jurists believe it highly unlikely. There is light at what I hope is the end of the tunnel.

A few verses from the conclusion of the Te Deum follow.

> *Lord, save your people*
> *and bless your inheritance.*
> *Rule them and uphold them*
> *for ever and ever.*
> *Day by day we praise you:*
> *we acclaim you now and for all eternity.*
> *In your goodness, Lord, keep us free from sin.*
> *Have mercy on us, Lord, have mercy.*

Thursday, 8 August 2019

We celebrate today the feast of Mary of the Cross MacKillop, the first Australian canonised saint. I have always felt that she understands me. I prayed at her tomb before my installation as archbishop of Sydney, seeking her help and intercession; was present at her canonisation in Rome in 2010; and was honoured to be principal concelebrant and homilist at the Thanksgiving Mass next day at the Basilica of St Paul Outside-the-Walls, the traditional burial place of St Paul and long associated with English speakers. Before the Reformation, the King of England was regularly an honourary canon at the basilica.

St Mary of the Cross was cofounder with Fr Julian Tenison Woods of the Josephite Sisters, who contributed massively to Catholic education, especially for the poor kids in country areas. They were a blessed force for the faith and human development.

I benefited from their work. Sr Dominic Foley was principal of St Mary's Primary School in Swan Hill, my first appointment, and she was a wise and energetic mentor. Sr Giovanni Farquer, who had been superior general, became the ecumenical and interfaith leader in the Sydney Archdiocese, another wise woman much loved across all the faith communities. Like most, but not all the religious orders, they are now struggling.

I omitted to mention that my cell was checked for contraband yesterday, part of the usual routine. This was preceded by the usual strip search. The warden was pleasant and chatty, but I find the strip searches and handcuffing when I travel to be the most demeaning experiences. It once again says a lot for the jail that this is the worst of it.

You have to leave the cell while it is searched, and as I passed on my way to the exercise pen, I saw the large Alsatian dog that no doubt sniffed around my cell for drugs. I received a clean sheet.

Not surprisingly, no doctor called me today to discuss my medicine taking.

I have long admired St Thomas More, but felt a deeper sympathy for the somewhat more direct approach of St John Fisher, who, unknown to Henry VIII, had urged the King of Spain to do his duty,[6] and more sympathy again for the formidable Archbishop of Canterbury St Thomas Becket with his dramatic resistance to Henry II, whose demands on the Church were similar to those of Henry VIII nearly four hundred years later.[7]

---

[6] In 1533 Cardinal Fisher encouraged Holy Roman Emperor and King of Spain Charles V to invade England and depose King Henry VIII.

[7] The dispute between Thomas Becket and Henry II was about royal authority over the Church. The King had appointed Becket, his chancellor, as the archbishop of Canterbury in order to defend his interests in Church-state conflicts. Instead, Archbishop Becket defended the rights of the Church. In 1170 four knights of the King's court murdered Archbishop Becket in Canterbury Cathedral.

More was a lawyer's lawyer, certainly more devout than Becket. Now with almost two years' experience of the courts, I have a better understanding of the quality of More's legal defences, which, of course, proved inadequate against perjury and the implacable determination of his autocratic King.

More was a politician and once speaker of the House of Commons as well as a lawyer; and "the King's great matter", his determination to discard Catherine and have a son, was well advanced when Henry offered More the post of chancellor. Each of them must have thought, mistakenly, he could influence the other, and Henry probably liked as well as admired More.

Eamon Duffy, the distinguished Reformation historian, once said to me that he thought one reason for Henry's increasing antagonism to Anne Boleyn was that she, in particular, urged him to have More eliminated. She certainly tried to rip Holbein's portrait of More, but my inexpert eye could detect no evidence of this when I was in the Frick Gallery in New York. My admiration of More has grown with my jail reading, and I have already praised the quality and variety of his prayers.

One particular aspect of the suffering of More and Fisher still strikes me. They were so alone. Not one bishop supported Fisher, and no one in More's family, even his favourite daughter, Margaret, agreed with his theological position (although they were personally supportive).

Fr Tom McGovern, the Dublin theologian, has been one of my most regular jail correspondents, and he sent me an excellent book by two US attorneys, L. W. Karlin and D. R. Oakley, entitled *Inside the Mind of Thomas More: The Witness of His Writings*. Their legal clarity and insight were invaluable to me. I propose to write a few lines on one topic only: More's execution of heretics. During More's term as chancellor, how many heretics were executed? What was More's rationale for this? Was he embarrassed, puzzled, or torn on the issue?

While More was chancellor, six heretics were burnt, a painful way of dying, and More was involved in the proceedings of three of these. It was not a personal decision or enthusiasm, but followed what had been the law in all European states for hundreds of years. Only obstinate heretics were prosecuted, and the death penalty for heresy had been introduced into England in 1401 by Henry IV as a response to the public disorder of the Lollards and from John Wycliffe's teaching.[8]

More was opposed to heresy for both civic and spiritual reasons: because it endangered social peace and order, and because it endangered the salvation of the souls of its adherents.

Heresy was sedition, a crime against the state. More well knew of the evil and suffering caused by civil war as the War of the Roses had only concluded in England in 1487. He saw clearly that Protestantism would split Europe, as it did through the terrible wars of religion, and provoke unforeseen upheavals like the Peasants' Revolt, which caused seventy thousand deaths in Germany in 1525. He also realised that Luther and Henry VIII would strengthen the power of rulers, a return to Caesaropapism, with rulers seeing themselves responsible for both state and church.

In the sixteenth century, before the first nonliteral explanation of Pope Pius IX in 1863 and the teaching of the Second Vatican Council on religious liberty, Catholics believed in a strict definition of "extra ecclesiam nulla salus", i.e., no salvation outside the Church. Heretics, therefore, were leading their followers to hell, and it was the sacral duty of a king's ministers to oppose this.

More was not embarrassed by his position on the fate of heretics. After his resignation, he drafted his epitaph, listing his offices and honours, affirming that the King, the nobles, and the populace did not find fault with him, but, he boasted, "he was a source of trouble to thieves, murderers and heretics."

As the son of an Anglican father with many Protestant and secular relatives, I would wish he had been softer, even if it only touched on the nature of the punishment. More was not a shallow sentimentalist, but a man with clear contemporary principles, who was far-seeing. He was also a former judge, and judges must implement the law, even when the consequences are distasteful.

More died for what he saw as the truth, not a truth, not a relativist's "his truth", and he punished heretics because they threatened and damaged the truth.

---

[8] The Lollards were those who followed and spread the teachings of John Wycliffe (c. 1330–1384), an Oxford professor who called for the reform of corrupt clergy and nobility, rejected transubstantiation and absolution, and taught that the Bible is the supreme authority in matters of Church doctrine.

We have three vacancies in Unit 8, and I hope there will soon be one more vacancy. It would have been good to have learnt the date of the verdict on the feast of St Mary MacKillop.

The doctor came down tonight with the nurse and a couple of wardens to clarify the situation of my medicine. She ruled that we should continue to do as we have for the last five months, and I replied that this was an excellent idea as my blood levels were also excellent.

In 1529, when More was away with the King, his barns with their corn and several of his neighbours' barns were burnt down. His son-in-law came to inform More, who then wrote to his wife:

God sent us all that we have lost, and since he has by such a chance taken it away again, his pleasure be fulfilled; let us never grudge at it, but take it in good worth, and heartily thank him as well for adversity as for prosperity.

Friday, 9 August 2019

Today is the feast of Edith Stein, St Teresa Benedicta of the Cross, and I nearly missed it. My breviary predates her canonisation, so it was only when Tess Livingston's[9] letter mentioned her among the August feasts that I remembered and checked my *Scripture Diary*.

As I have mentioned, she is one of my favourite saints, a convert from Judaism, a professional philosopher, a contemplative nun, and a martyr under the Nazis because the Dutch bishops protested against their anti-Jewish policies.

We should seek her intercession for the Church in Germany, which is rich, performs many great works of mercy at home and around the world, has a well-educated clergy and laity, but where, in [Gerhard] Cardinal Müller's recent words, "the Catholic Church is going down." The Church leaders there "are not aware of the real problems", self-centred and concerned primarily with sexual morality, celibacy, and women priests. "They don't speak about God, Jesus Christ, grace, the sacraments, and faith, hope, and love." The

---

[9] Tess Livingston is a writer at *The Australian* and a friend of the cardinal.

cardinal concluded his verdict by lamenting the deep legalism and desperation now flourishing in German society, designated in Pope Francis' terminology as a New Gnosticism and a New Pelagianism. The verdict might be a tad generous as there is also a mighty stream of self-indulgent paganism. The Gnostics were godly-minded, and the Pelagians Christian. For the German cardinal, his nation, like Belgium and the Netherlands, with their inability to promote the Gospel, is now seeing "the consequences of this progressive wave".

Naturally, some German bishops, led by [Rainer] Cardinal Woelki of Cologne, well understand the challenges, which are those of the Western world writ large; but among the laity and the clergy, the orthodox party, the voices of the Gospel Christians, seem to be weaker than in any other great European country. The dominant liberal faction has learnt nothing from salvation history since the Second Vatican Council, and [Reinhard] Cardinal Marx in Munich is central in this rout, this collapse.

St Teresa Benedicta of the Cross, intercede for your Church.

A lively altercation has just taken place (around 5:28 pm) between a warder and the unhappy, poorly spoken prisoner a few cells away, who yesterday denounced and turned away the doctor. He refused to talk to the warder, who was requiring him to remove the paper he had attached across the small window they use to check on inmates. The warden is threatening to leave the light on all night unless he obeys, and my neighbour is shouting, "I don't care." It could be an interesting night. He has been quiet for most of the day, singing occasionally. He is still shouting defiance, but the warden has gone.

Once again, it was disappointing to receive no news today about the date of the verdict. The senior prison official who checks weekly on our welfare told me they had been told "it" would happen yesterday. I am not sure whether "it" was the verdict itself or information on the date. Paul Galbally chose not to phone the court registrar and enquire and had suggested to Robert Richter that the judges might be still "polishing" the document. The date doesn't depend on the presence of prosecution or defence lawyers.

The cold snap has arrived with rain and heavy winds and a metre of snow on some of the snow fields. I took both my exercise periods and finally made contact with my sister, who had been to the specialist doctor yesterday and received a good report.

I was cheered up in the afternoon by the arrival of a second batch of letters, one each from [friends] the Turchis and the Paganis. Another from a Sister of Life recounted her conversion experience at Sydney World Youth Day [2008]. A Mt Waverly woman who had followed me for decades and spoke kindly of the "Cardinal Pell phenomenon" particularly commended me, not for my learning or eloquence or sanctity, but for the fact that when asked about animal suffering ("They haven't committed any sin"), I eventually replied, "It's not really something I've thought about. Maybe I need to think about it now." You never know, you know.

Another category of letter came from an adult secure unit at a mental health centre in a provincial Victorian city, requesting that I persuade the pope to confirm that the writer is the Son of Man, the Lord of Righteousness. All in all, a quiet day, but not without interest.

Perhaps it was John Milton who wrote:

They also serve who only stand and wait.[10]

Saturday, 10 August 2019

Last night in Canberra during the AFL game between Hawthorn and Great Western Sydney, it snowed for the first time during an AFL game. I took a foolish and perverse delight in this widespread snow as SBS television had been proclaiming for days that this was the warmest year in history (although it's not yet December), and I am pleased South East Australia is doing its bit to ward off disaster. I know that climate is constituted by thirty years of weather, but the propagandists for the 1.5 trillion dollar climate change juggernaut recognize this only when it suits their argument. The latest Intergovernmental Panel for Climate Change report is strongly opposed to land clearing and modern farming because they fear that bovine flatulence might pose a bigger threat than the increasing human population.

It drizzled with rain during both my exercise sessions; the gymnasium was open again, and the basketballs were available. I only managed a couple of goals but fastened up the treadmill, happily.

[10] Sonnet 19.

My pasty and tomato sauce were waiting for me when I returned from the gymnasium, but no one suggested I heat it up in the microwave.

At midafternoon, I had an official visit from a couple of senior officers, who handed me a page outlining a regulation prohibiting the distribution of letters or information from a prisoner on the Internet. They accepted that I had no knowledge of any such regulation. One of the Support Cardinal Pell groups had posted my handwritten letter to them on some form of Internet. I had not forbidden them to do so or authorised it, but I am not inclined to blame them. What I wrote had passed through the jail censor. The group members are very loyal, but a bit fierce, and I wrote to them urging, among other things, family unity in the Church. The couple of pages are solid religious advice with almost nothing about prison life, but this momentous development made it to the evening SBS news. They reported me as claiming that my faith has helped me in jail and that I was like Jesus Christ! Would that I was.

As I have noted, during the past few weeks I have been watching the ABC series on the planets of our solar system, and this has prompted me to ponder the role of the Creator God.

We use different images for God's activity such as a small still voice, the dew, the Lamb of God; not the earthquake or the lion or the eagle. But the one true God is the Creator of the universe, and his Son is the Alpha and the Omega, the beginning and the end of all creation, who will set up a new heaven and a new earth when he comes again at the end of time.

Once Western thought had moved beyond the layered image of creation in Genesis, it conceived of the sun as moving around the earth, until Copernicus in the sixteenth century introduced his "revolution", where the earth circles the sun. It was this issue early in the seventeenth century which got Galileo into trouble with the papal authorities, although Copernicus and his earlier writings were not condemned or disturbed.

So we now know the earth is not the centre of the solar system and the sun is not even the centre of the Milky Way, much less of the universe, which has been expanding in every direction at the speed of light for over fourteen billion years.

We might now have the first evidence from space of a black hole, rather than just a theoretical concept, and we do have evidence of stars colliding, dying red dwarf stars, and the occasional marauding comet. Think of the craters on the moon, some of them named after early Jesuit astronomers.[11]

The universe is vast beyond our imagining, much of it dark and cold, but nearly all of it hostile to life and mysterious, with stars immensely larger than our own, sometimes much, much smaller with unbelievably greater weight and pull.

With the naked eye, we can see very little of all this, but it is there, slowly giving up some of its secrets to us, the only intelligent beings in the universe, living in a beautiful world congenial to life, as the end result of billions of coincidences.

What is God up to with his universe? Why such prodigality and extravagance, which is awe-inspiring when not terrifying; and all of it ruled by the elegant and often simple laws of physics? Does God need all this space and time for the systems he devised to throw up planet earth with its loving, thinking, deciding human agents?

I probably should be more awestruck by human sanctity and heroism, by human genius, by music and poetry and the capacity for self-sacrifice, but the beauties of the earth and of the heavens, both seen and especially the unseen, are awe-inspiring calls to worship.

If I am puzzled by the role of Islam in salvation history (and I am), how much more mysterious is God's cosmos, the unfathomable universe as the backdrop to the salvation history of the God-among-us, who will come again. King David expressed this beautifully and much more in Psalm 19:

> *The heavens declare the glory of God;*
> *the skies proclaim the work of his hands.*
> *Day after day they pour forth speech;*
> *night after night they reveal knowledge.*
> *They have no speech, they use no words;*
> *no sound is heard from them.*
> *Yet their voice goes out into all the earth,*
> *their words to the end of the world.*

[11] Bettini, Clavius, Cabei, Kircher, Kugler, Bartoli.

WEEK 25

Love of Money

11 August—17 August 2019

Sunday, 11 August 2019

My sick and sometimes noisy neighbour has been quiet during the day apart from an outburst of song in the morning. We have a couple of shouters at the other end of the unit, one with a young, light voice, and together they put on a great show for twenty minutes after the jail was locked down around 4:30 pm. His mate was very angry, denouncing someone or something in colourful but repetitive language. I was too far away even to catch the drift.

The morning was cold but a little warmer for my afternoon exercise, with light drizzle only then. The MCG had a couple of heavy rain showers, while Richmond enjoyed a solid thirty-point win over Carlton.[1]

My brother, David, told me when I phoned that my letter-writing escapade had made the papers. A storm in a teacup.

I was up past midnight last night finishing yesterday's journal article, but I slept well and was awake for the *Mass for You at Home* celebrated by Fr Michael Kong, who had an Indian seminarian as a server. It was good to see some young people in the congregation of five.

He urged us to be ready for death, reminding us of the importance of faith, of Abraham's example. As a support for his faith argument, he quoted Luther, who remarked that if he learnt he was to die tomorrow he would still be tending his apple tree. Mother Teresa was quoted reminding us that we are not called to be successful,

---

[1] Richmond and Carlton, teams in the Australian Football League, were playing at the Melbourne Cricket Ground [MCG].

but to be faithful. A dignified, prayerful Mass and a well-prepared, slightly Protestant homily.

Pastor Houston had a new backdrop of a huge blue wave about to break and was sporting a stubbly, short-cropped beard and a new set of clothes: faded jeans, a t-shirt, and a grey jacket with silver buttons. He gave an animated performance, building up a head of steam (perspiration) and provoking the large congregation to subdued applause on a few occasions.

His text was taken from Acts, chapters 13 and 14. In Jesus' name, we were to confront difficulties, look them in the eye, and he gave us seven pieces of advice, e.g., do more than you are paid to do, give more, try harder, waste less time, etc. None of them were Gospel teachings, except perhaps the last, give more time to God. Nothing on Jesus' parables or his life or death and Resurrection. The mystery remains.

He correctly told us that we sometimes cannot see a miracle in front of our eyes and that we have to be prepared to be uncomfortable.

As always, Joseph Prince had a new clothes ensemble, dark, and on this occasion sported only a couple of rings, one on each hand. He began as always with a melodious and rousing hymn and told us about our harvest of blessings, which we reap from Jesus' saving activity on the Cross. When Jesus exclaimed "it is finished" and breathed his last, he was rejecting the Jewish notion of generational curses. The congregation applauded. Not his best, but still very good and emphatically Christian.

Untypically, the ABC *Compass* program told us of the marvellous work about thirty Polish Divine Word priests and some nuns are doing in the highlands of Papua New Guinea. My much-loved *Songs of Praise* was set in Wales, where the host, who had starred for years in *The Sound of Music*, interviewed three Welsh Christians, and the hymn singing was performed beautifully by the congregation and choir at Llandaff Cathedral.

I am still moving through Hobbes' *Leviathan*, where the subject matter on the commonwealth is more interesting but still hard going, and I am now making some progress on Katrina Lee's[2] gift, *From*

---

[2] Katrina Lee had been in charge of archdiocesan communications when Cardinal Pell was in Sydney.

Dawn to Decadence, 1500 to the Present: 500 Years of Western Cultural Life, by Jacques Barzun. Immensely learned and elegantly written.

A few lines from St Augustine's *Confessions* (book 10) will serve as a conclusion:

See, Lord, I cast my care upon you, that I may live: and I will consider the wondrous things of your law. You know my unskillfulness and my infirmity: teach me and heal me. He your only One, in whom are hidden all the treasures of wisdom and knowledge, has redeemed me with his blood.

Lord Jesus, bless all those who preach and teach Your Word today. Give us again an Augustine.

Monday, 12 August 2019

An action-packed day, but no action and no information on the main issue of the verdict. Julien O'Connell[3] visited for a pleasant hour in the box, bringing the sad news from Peter Tellefson that Brian Blood had died (RIP) and that both Barry O'Callaghan and Andrew Quinn were unwell in hospital. Julien said it was not a good time for him, with me in jail and two friends very sick. I said no one could blame him for that.

The bad cold weather has moved past us, the warders had pumped out the pen, which was half covered with water from the heavy rain; and while the weather was not balmy for my afternoon exercise, it wasn't too bad.

This morning I managed to speak with Tim O'Leary, who told me that the operation on his son Joe had been delayed for one week and that the publicity on my letter wasn't too bad, although an article in *The Australian* this morning had touched on theology and the Synod on Amazonia in October.

Kartya Gracer called in the afternoon and took down my view of the letter incident, including my judgement that nothing more was likely to be done in the prison.

---

[3] Julien O'Connell is the pro-chancellor of the Australian Catholic University.

My fears that I appeared to big-note myself [brag] by comparison with Jesus were not justified by the text, which Kartya read to me. In fact, it is not a bad letter, urging Church unity and the importance of proper criteria for doctrine and practice. As Tim O'Leary commented this morning, my claims represented basic Christian teachings and had to be invoked.

At the top of the letters page, in the Vox Pop section, today's Melbourne *Herald Sun* ran a small photo of me looking rather startled and the following quotation from "a letter attributed to George Pell": "The knowledge that my small suffering can be used for good purposes through being joined to Jesus' suffering gives me purpose."

It is a key message, highlighting a fundamental difference between Christian and secular interpretations of suffering. I think the issue will die, as nothing was said in the letter on my case or the prison. But one never knows as the Amazonia material might excite a little coverage overseas.

I spent a good deal of the day finishing the short (sixteen-page) autobiography, *By the Grace of God*, by Fr Tom Uzhunnalil, a Salesian priest from Kerala, India, who had been working in war-torn Yemen as a parish priest and a chaplain to the Missionaries of Charity in Aden, who were looking after eighty people during the violence, which brought disease and drastic food shortages. (The Abraham family from Cranbourne had sent the book to me.)

Without any warning, masked Islamic terrorists attacked this home for the elderly on 4 March 2016, killing sixteen persons, including four of Mother Teresa's nuns, and they captured and abducted Fr Tom.

He then spent 557 days as a prisoner in a variety of locations unknown to him and a hostage of these same murderers. He was bound and blindfolded most of the time, lost track of the number of days and nights, was prevented from exercising, unable to communicate in any way with the outside world or receive any news, and in fact he could hardly communicate with his captors as they had no common language, apart from their smattering of English.

He was a good priest, strong in faith, generous enough to volunteer for missionary work in a Yemen torn by Sunni versus Shiite violence and brave enough to return to work there after sick leave in India, only a short time before his capture.

As a good Catholic and a good priest, he prayed when he was in trouble, with not even his breviary. He prayed constantly for his abductors, for his release, remembering the thousands outside who were praying and sacrificing for him. He also prayed to God for a sign that the martyred nuns were already in heaven, and it rained heavily. While I don't believe the prayer was necessary, neither do I think it put God to the test, because the answer was so easy. Fr Tom was also sustained by the hymns of his childhood.

God normally has no hands but human hands, and it is remarkable that his murderous abductors not only did not kill him, but treated him well enough and with kindness. He was always fed regularly, and they found him enough medicine to survive in decent health, despite his high blood pressure and diabetes. They never tortured him and cared for him when he was ill. In fact, Fr Tom was criticised afterward in India for speaking well of his captors.

Naturally, the Catholic bishops, the Vatican, and the Indian government were working for his release, and the Sultan of Oman was influential in the final decision. There was no mention of a ransom.

Perhaps we should let Fr Tom himself have the last word: "Now I have realized that my calling is to tell the world that there is a God, who listens to our prayers and grants our requests."

I am grateful for these words as I await my verdict.

Tuesday, 13 August 2019

The highlight of the day, which was uneventful until around 4:00 pm, was the visit of Sr Mary to bring me Communion. We followed the customary service outline of confiteor, readings, creed, prayer of the faithful, Our Father, and distribution of Holy Communion. Life goes on around us. I nearly always have to return at least once to the cell (while another prisoner is moved), so the setting is not prayerful. We both pray, however, with faith and reverence to the extent we can.

Mary was quite pleased with what she read in the press of the letter incident, because it brought into public view a basic religious teaching. Later in the afternoon, I was speaking with Mr H, one of the jail bosses, and he agreed that the incident's importance had been inflated. He confirmed no further action would be taken in the jail.

Unfortunately, there was confusion with the senior officer over whether my gym session was today or yesterday. It did not take place, but he admitted it was his "stuff up" and promised to make it up this week.

After all this, I had to ask a couple of times to receive only about fifteen minutes' exercise time in the afternoon, which I used for a couple of phone calls.

Earlier, just at the start of the Communion service, a couple of envelopes arrived from the lawyers, which I signed for and accepted. After praying, I opened them, in case there was good news to share with Sr Mary on the verdict. As we used to say in my childhood, "No such luck."

Following my usual practice, I phoned the solicitors to enquire of any developments. Paul was very reluctant to speak, until I reminded him that we are told before each legal call that it is not monitored. He said he didn't have any news, but ... as the head of the court, presumably Maxwell,[4] is going away on Monday, Paul thought we could obtain a verdict this week. I was not to mention this to anyone as the hypothesis might be wrong. I explained that I was sometimes capable of discretion and would say nothing. It is just possible Paul knows a little more, agreeing with me that it has been too long a wait. Another false dawn?

Immediately afterward, I phoned the Tobins, speaking to Bernadette as Terry was out. She told me John Ferguson had a piece in today's *Australian* on why there was a delay and giving the opinion that the judges have to respond to the third ground of appeal in light of the New South Wales court decision. This is plausible.

While I am tempted to frustration at this period, probably more than at any other time in jail, I realise full well that it is much more important for the Church, and for me, that I am found not guilty, rather than my fussing about extra weeks in prison. The two issues are inextricably connected, but the logical priority is clear. May God's will be done—with my preference for action sooner than later and a strong preference for a just decision.

I took time this afternoon to reply to two significant letters from prisoners, both of whom have written previously. The first writer

[4] Justice Chris Maxwell is president of the Victoria Court of Appeal.

mentioned he was reading Hilaire Belloc's *The Great Heresies* and again asked a couple of new questions on behalf of a group of prisoners. Could a long-term prisoner deputise another prisoner to fulfil the requirement to obtain for the prisoner a plenary indulgence in a jubilee year or at some shrine? What did St Augustine mean when he wrote, "Qui cantat, bis orat" (He who sings prays twice)? He mentioned he was a bad singer. I replied as best I could and counselled that he sing quietly, if he regularly cannot find the note.

I thanked him for his reference to Joseph from the Old Testament, who was wrongly imprisoned, and for this prayer: "We praise God, as he knows what is truly good for us while we may not. I pray, therefore, that we have the patience of Joseph and that we may be able to receive the steadfast love of the Lord as he did."

The second correspondent writes beautifully in both Italian and English, and I am envious of his expertise. Two intercessions from morning prayer are helpful:

Christ, our king and redeemer: help us to know your power and your love.
Christ, our refuge and strength: fight with us against our weakness.

Wednesday, 14 August 2019

At about 9:30 am, the wardens, who accompany you when you move through the jail, said that I had a professional visit. While we waited before moving off, one asked me to pray for the repose of the soul of his uncle, who had died in an accident (which made the press). I replied that I could certainly pray for him and the family. They were a bit curious about a visit so early in the morning, and I agreed the timing was unusual.

Kartya was alone when I entered the box, which put me off the scent as I thought Paul would come if there were significant news. Kartya got straight down to business, informing me that the verdict session had been set down for next Wednesday [August 21], a week from today, at 9:30 am in the same court where the appeal had been heard. I was delighted, as I don't like uncertainty and this substantially reduced the uncertainty. Kartya wondered whether I would be concerned about another week of waiting, and I was able to reassure her completely on that score. Knowing the day changed my perspective. If Justice Maxwell, the head of the Court of Appeal, is away next week, he obviously will not be present.

Kartya read me the message she had received, which mentioned there would be time for "submissions" after the verdict. Kartya explained that this would allow us to request bail if a retrial were ordered and would also enable us to apply for an indemnity, i.e., financial recompense for part of our expenses if an appeal were successful.

The court does not want us to tell anyone today, so tomorrow Kartya will inform my brother, David, Michael Casey,[5] and perhaps Danny Casey,[6] who is on holiday in Canada, and I think she also said that the news would be made public tomorrow. She wondered whether any information would leak today. I will have to make sure Chris Meney and Terry Tobin are informed. I know David will immediately tell my sister, Margaret. Kartya had been told today to deal with any press.

Today did not bring a false dawn. On my return to my cell, I prayed the Te Deum twice (I felt I was somewhat distracted on the first run-through) and then said the five Glorious Mysteries of the rosary, which is an easy, repetitive, and calming prayer. I try to be grateful, as I remember the parable of the ten cured lepers, where only one returned to Jesus to say thanks. I am sure the others were also grateful, but were busy and distracted. Failing to say thanks is a mark of immaturity; saying thanks is something young children have to be taught. Not giving thanks is a mark of serious adult selfishness.

Older people can still pray, and sometimes we might pray better than when we were younger. As we age, our energy diminishes; we move more slowly, make more errors (generally small), and of course there is the constant possibility or presence of sickness. But we can still pray, and jail is a good place for prayer, even though I cannot celebrate Mass. Time in jail in my situation is somewhat like an uncomfortable silent retreat, without the sacraments, but with a solid dose of worldliness through the presence of the television.

[5] Michael Casey is the former secretary to Cardinal Pell, 1997–2014,

[6] Danny Casey is a close friend of Cardinal Pell, former business manager for the Catholic Archdiocese of Sydney, and former director of the Secretariat of the Economy.

God works for good in strange ways because he has to adapt to the sins and foibles of everyone. If I had been released earlier, as I had hoped, that probably would have prevented the publishing of my few lines on the Christian view of suffering. Someone might have read it and benefited. One of the consolations from the letters I received was, e.g., to hear the gratitude of some former university students I used to address at the Thomas More Summer Schools. I remember them as happy occasions, where the talks seemed to go down well, but I wondered what was the fruit of these labours. You never know, you know.

It would have been nice to receive a favourable verdict tomorrow on the feast of the Assumption, which was also my mother's birthday. It was she, more than anyone else, who passed on the faith to me.

Today is the feast of St Maximilian Kolbe, the Polish priest executed by the Nazis at Auschwitz when he volunteered to replace the father of a young child who had been selected for a reprisal execution by starvation.

August 21 is the feast of St Pius X, who was a bit of a handful. We might need someone like him next time.

We give you thanks, Almighty God, for all the good things you have given us. We make this prayer through Christ Our Lord.

Thursday, 15 August 2019

When I got out of bed this morning, I could see through my opaque narrow window that the sky was clear and bright. Good weather for the feast of the Assumption.

The morning headlines on *Sunrise* assumed that my verdict would be handed down next Wednesday, 21 August. Apparently the news was also in the newspaper. When I phoned my brother, David, in the afternoon, he reminded me that today was our mother's birthday and that he had been to Mass, a "last opportunity to kick a goal for you". Everyone I spoke to was pleased, and Chris Meney remarked that the feast was an excellent day for such an announcement. Another bonus from the 21 August date is that Anne McFarlane returns from San Francisco on the previous day, 20 August, and so will be home while

I spend a few days with them. The warders, too, are pleased I have a date and have wished me well.

The unit is basically quiet, so I don't know whether my next-door neighbour is still with us. At the other end, we have one noisy malcontent, who has flooded his cell and was engaged in some violent altercation as I took my afternoon exercise nearby. The warder threatened to cut off the water to his cell, but did not do so. This brought a reality dimension into the discussion, but the poor bloke was lamenting that he was locked up for twenty-four hours a day. He has been silent since the dialogue.

I missed my period in the gymnasium as the lawyers called who were representing me in a case where a Melbourne man, who had been abused as a child by a Christian Brother and had been paid compensation by the Order, had now initiated a civil action against a number of agencies and persons for additional damages. As episcopal vicar for education in Ballarat, I had no authority over a Christian Brother in another diocese or any diocese.

Peter Tellefson also made a visit telling me that Brian Blood had received a wonderful send-off, with a Requiem Mass in a packed St Patrick's Cathedral in Ballarat yesterday. I thought he was a little older than his seventy-nine years. As I requested, Peter had been able to express my sympathy individually to each of his five children. Brian and his first wife, Joan, who died about twenty years ago, had been very good to me for more than thirty-five years, and I knew his second wife, Denise, quite well, also. May he rest in peace.

The Assumption is the most popular Marian feast among Australian Catholics, and it used to be a holy day of obligation, when attending Mass was obligatory. The feast celebrates the fact that Mary's body did not remain to decay when she died, but that she was taken immediately, body and soul, into heaven. We, too, shall eventually be in heaven, body and soul, when we take up our bodies again on the Last Day.

Pope Pius XII infallibly declared the Assumption dogma in 1950 after consulting all the bishops. While we find no direct evidence for the Assumption in the New Testament, and Eastern Christianity celebrates the feast of Our Lady's Dormition (going to sleep), Pope Pius' apostolic constitution produces a remarkable number of saints and teachers who uphold this tradition. The eighth- century St John

Damascene, perhaps the feast's greatest champion, was from Eastern Christianity. It is a clear example of the development of doctrine, from within the tradition, which involves no "backflip" away from previous teaching and is consecrated as truth by the successor of St Peter and the successors of the apostles.

A couple of verses from the hymn for morning prayer describe the mother given to us, through John, on the Cross:

> *More glorious than the seraphim,*
> *This ark of love divine;*
> *Corruption could not blemish her*
> *Whom death could not confine.*
>
> *God-bearing Mother, Virgin chaste,*
> *Who shines in heaven's sight,*
> *She bears a royal crown of stars*
> *Who is the door of light.*

Friday, 16 August 2019

Friday is the day when we meditate on the Sorrowful Mysteries of the rosary, so I thought I might say a few words, only a few, on the Vatican finances. It is not all gloom, but remains a sad tale at least since the 1970s, with Calvi found dead under Blackfriars Bridge on the Thames in London, Sindona, and the Banco Ambrosiano.[7]

My day was a good day, as I had two visits from my lawyers and also received about twenty letters, more than double the daily ration for the last week. One was from a priest exorcist in the UK, who at 3:00 pm every Friday performs a general exorcism directed at all the anti-Christ forces, which include "the evil attacks on you".

---

[7] In 1981 Roberto Calvi was found guilty of illegally transferring millions of dollars to foreign countries while he was manager and then chairman of Banco Ambrosiano. Much of the money had been transferred through the Vatican Bank, Ambrosiano's largest shareholder. Ambrosiano collapsed in 1982, and soon afterward Calvi was murdered. An earlier case of fiscal misconduct involving the Vatican occurred in 1974, when the Holy See lost millions of dollars after the collapse of Franklin National Bank owned by Michele Sindona, who died in prison after drinking poisoned coffee.

I believe the spirit of evil is at work in our society, thriving in the Western decline of most forms of Christian life. Certainly the devil is at the heart of the paedophilia crisis, and I also sense a whiff of evil in the forces opposing me.

It is not surprising that the Evil One is active in the Roman Curia, because the papacy and its officials are critical for the life of the universal Church. Most of those who work in the Curia, priests, religious, and the majority of laymen and women, are persons of genuine faith and goodness. A disproportionately high percentage are outstanding in their faith and piety. There are also elements of doctrinal muddle, personal moral confusion, and financial irregularity. Once in a while, in a few individuals, these three weaknesses are present together.

My daily thoughts make up a journal rather than a diary, because of my musings on a disparate array of topics, prompted by the prayer of the Church, the liturgical year, books which I brought with me, the many letters, some of my long-term intellectual interests, the multiplicity of articles and books friends have sent to keep me occupied. And, of course, I reflect on daily life in solitary confinement.

I have decided not to draw heavily on my four years working on the Vatican finances, while acknowledging what is public knowledge from the 1970s through to the writings of Sandro Magister and Edward Pentin in the last few weeks.[8]

The Financial Secretariat, the Council of the Economy, and the IOR Bank[9] have made substantial progress, but the work is incomplete. My information is that the new systems continue to function and that major corruption is no longer occurring, despite the axing of the external audit and the firing of the auditor, who was later exonerated.[10]

---

[8] Sandro Magister is the editor of the Catholic blog Settimo Cielo on the website of *L'Espresso*, an Italian weekly news magazine. Edward Pentin is a regular correspondent for the *National Catholic Register*.

[9] The Secretariat for the Economy, the Council for the Economy and the Institute for the Works of Religion (IOR), commonly known as the Vatican Bank.

[10] In 2015 Pope Francis hired Libero Milone, a former partner of the multinational accountancy firm Deloitte, to lead an audit of the Vatican's finances. Two years later, Church officials accused Milone of espionage and embezzlement, threatened legal action against him if he did not resign, and stopped the audit. Milone has said that these actions were taken to prevent him from uncovering financial misconduct. In 2018 Vatican prosecutors said they were closing their investigation of Milone and would not be filing charges against him.

Therefore, for a prudential mix of theological, ethical, and socio-logical reasons, I will confine myself now to restating two of the major financial challenges facing the Apostolic See and Vatican City, both of which are public knowledge.

The combined two entities, together dubbed as the Vatican, have an overall structural deficit of 20–25 million euros, which in an unusual year can blow out to three or four times this amount. There are no substantial debts, and there are assets which could be devel-oped in the long term (which would require significant attitudinal change and would run the risk of an equally significant corruption), so we have no immediate danger. But a Francis IV or a Francis V will face huge financial challenges unless the annual financial deficits can be curtailed if not eliminated. Pope Francis concurred with the Finance Secretariat's view that the entirety of Peter's Pence cannot be used on Roman Curia expenses. People contribute believing it to be used mainly for charitable purposes, and of course deficits should not be concealed through imaginative bookkeeping.

The second well-known challenge facing the Vatican is the loom-ing deficit in the Vatican Pension Fund. Four years were wasted and extra losses were incurred as officials would concede privately the existence of a large problem, while publicly announcing all was well.

My belief is that we now have a competent pensions board, which is not inclined to overstate the problem but is working to be in a stronger position when the pressures emerge, perhaps in ten years' time. We are talking of a shortfall of hundreds of millions of euros—unless effective measures continue to be implemented. It was never a consolation to realize that most, if not all, European countries could be in a worse situation.

Incidentally, I believe Australia is well placed for the future on pensions, due to the efforts of men like my mentor Sir Bernard Calli-nan,[11] who spoke to me a lot about this problem in the 1970s.

---

[11] Bernard Callinan (1913–1995) was a decorated Australian military officer and a civil engineer. In 1971 he became the chairman and managing director of the GHD, an employee-owned, multinational technical services company, and six years later he was knighted for his services to engineering. He was the only chairman of the Institute of Catholic Education from 1974 to 1991 (now part of Australian Catholic University) and chairman of the National Catholic Education Commission from 1985–1989.

When I left Rome two years ago, contemporary financial best practices had been introduced (and were being implemented with difficulty), and corruption had been stopped. But our investment procedures were still a shambles, and the revenue return on our properties less than it should be. Once in a while, it was spectacular, e.g., 300 properties together producing an annual revenue of €60,000. In the bad old days, one agency was working to reconcile with the Italian civil authorities a common list of what the Vatican did own! I don't know where that finished.

Some senior financial leaders, including Christine Lagarde[12] of the International Monetary Fund, consoled me by explaining that the abuses we were confronting were by no means unique to the Vatican. A small consolation. Our ambition was to be an example of best practice, and our most publicised feat was to discover €1.3 billion worth of unlisted assets. This is better than discovering a debt of comparable size, but the result demonstrated that no one knew accurately where the Vatican finances were, even the one or two officials who claimed they did. If you know where you are, you are so much better placed to confront challenges. And the Vatican now has that capacity.

Money is fascinating and dangerous, and I enjoyed my financial work. Money is a good servant but a tyrannical master, and the Lord Jesus had a lot to say on it, especially on greed. And we have Jesus' dramatic warning recounted in chapter 19 of Matthew's Gospel, where Jesus said to his disciples:

Truly, I say to you, it will be hard for a rich man to enter the kingdom of heaven. Again I tell you, it is easier for a camel to go through the eye of a needle than for a rich man to enter the kingdom of God (23–24).

Saturday, 17 August 2019

The weather was beautiful today, crisp and clear both in the morning and in the afternoon. I was only in the gymnasium for a half hour

---

[12] Christine Lagarde, a French politician and lawyer, was chair and managing director of the International Monetary Fund from July 2011 until September 2019. She is now President of the European Central Bank.

when a "black alert" in Unit 9 sounded over the loudspeaker, some
sort of incident, and all prisoners had to return to their cells. I had
used the weights, practised bouncing the basketball with each hand,
and done some circuits. While I had not been on the treadmill, I did
not mind leaving early too much.

For the last couple of weeks, the breviary readings have been from
the minor prophets, from the fierce denunciations of Amos, through
the more mixed and milder messages of Hosea, to today's famous
passage from Micah, chapter 6, where the good God points out that
he has freed his people from Egypt and deserves their loyalty. He
does not need holocausts of calves or thousands of rams. The Lord
asks only this of us: "to act justly, to love tenderly, and to walk hum-
bly with your God".

But if these activities are not forthcoming, and men are violent,
robbing, and defrauding the people with fraudulent measures and
false scales, then God will (in fact, he has already started to) "strike
you down, to bring you to ruin for your sins.... And what is preserved I shall give to the sword."

To some extent, and in different ways, every age is selective,
gives different weight to different sections of the Scripture teaching. In our comfortable, sentimental age, which I find so congenial
most of the time, we readily accept talk of justice and tenderness
and believe humility must be balanced out with an appropriate self-
assertion, reinforced by the regular affirmation of others. This is
fair enough, up to a point. But we all struggle with Micah's vivid
description of our punitive God's activities. And the farther we are
from understanding Jesus' central teaching, which takes us beyond
Micah, the more difficult it is to understand God's retribution for
sins. Unless we happen to be on the receiving end of human evil.
At our worst, we find it hard to forgive, and we lust for vengeance.
And secularists, even more than Christians, also find it hard to bring
together the obligation to forgive and the inevitability of punishment, restorative retribution.

Our Lord is the last and greatest of the prophets, the Final Divine
Revelation, which enriches and perfects our understanding of the
basic truths about God and man. Let us pray that we will see more
clearly and follow more nearly.

God of my fathers and Lord of mercy,
who have made all things by your word,
and by your wisdom have formed man,
to have dominion over the creatures you have made . . .
give me the wisdom that sits by your throne,
and do not reject me from among your servants.

(Wisdom 9:1–4)

WEEK 26

Appeal Rejected

18 August—24 August 2019

Sunday, 18 August 2019

I am hoping this Twentieth Sunday in Ordinary Time is my last Sunday in jail. Certainly I will finish this journal on next Wednesday evening even if my appeal is unsuccessful and turn to some other writing. But, inside or outside jail, I will be writing, though not necessarily 700–800 words a day as I have for nearly six months.

For these reasons, it was disappointing to wake about 6:15 am and find I had missed the first half, and more, of *Mass for You at Home*. Fr Michael Kong was again the celebrant, but I unfortunately missed his sermon.

Naturally, the survival of the TV Mass is a motive for gratitude, but the time slot of 6:00 am is not ideal for older people, or for any reason. Frequently on Channel 7 in the morning program, we find a section on fortune-telling from the stars. (If it is not a daily segment, it is a regular each week.) I only watched one part of one session, and I don't even know under which star I was born. Superstition, not pseudo-scientific unbelief, usually comes in to occupy what was God's space.

As a Catholic, because of decades of practice, but more for doctrinal and theological reasons, I need the sacraments, the formal rituals of worship, and I have come to love the solemn Sunday cathedral liturgies over more than twenty years. The Mass is the Mass, but the trappings of *Mass for You at Home* are not cathedral style.

And as a Catholic, I find I am not sufficiently nourished by an exclusively Protestant emphasis on the ministry of the word, as we find in Pastor Houston and Joseph Prince. But I am very grateful for their regular witness, which I have followed each Sunday. As has been demonstrated many times, I preferred the contribution of Joseph Prince, because it is explicitly Christocentric as well as being more dynamic and slickly produced. I appreciate his World Youth Day type music, although I am not suggesting WYD is the musical prototype.

Songs of Praise is regularly beautiful and often performed in ancient and splendid settings, as it was this morning with the hymn singing from the small old Cathedral of St Asaph in Wales. Many of the Anglican community hymns are excellent, and if I were a parish priest, I would try to introduce more of them into our Masses. A lot would depend on the composition of the local congregation, but such music must not be lost. Congregations also sing it, love the melodies, and learn from the words. Cross-fertilization in this area makes good sense. I suppose the hymns I am thinking of are the Anglican or Protestant equivalents of our much-loved Latin Benediction hymns or upmarket equivalents of Hail Holy Queen.

Another strength of Catholic worship is the act of sorrow for sin at the start of every Mass. I prefer the "confiteor", but all the official alternatives seek God's forgiveness. This discussion is also entirely missing in the teaching of my two evangelists. However, they both jogged my conscience over the small amount of Old Testament material I have used over the years in my sermons. I should have done more ...

I received a good batch of letters today, which gave me a lift and a good deal to think about. From Archbishop Fisher,[1] whose sermons are always exemplary, Fr Brendan Purcell, a couple of prisoners, and Mary, an eleven-year-old from Jindera in New South Wales.

A university student thanked me for the "pastoral letter" (his words) which I wrote to Mrs Kathy Clubb and which he found "quite encouraging".

I was also encouraged by a marvellous letter of support from Noel Henry, a classmate at St Pat's, Ballarat: acute, humorous, but grateful for what we received while acknowledging, lightly, the martinets and the waspish tongue of our best teacher.

---

[1] Anthony Fisher, O.P., archbishop of Sydney.

He wrote, "I thought I should, as an old Inter A habitué, drop you a line of support and wish you, by God's grace, the very best. Only trivial anecdotes and small beer on offer, I'm afraid. No philosophical frolics." Noel has a gift for understatement.

The St John Paul Pilgrimage group on a twenty-mile-a-day pilgrimage through Norfolk to Our Lady of Walsingham (in the UK) wrote, promising their prayers for me, and one kind woman (St Paul also boasted) wrote to thank me for my catechesis talk in 2002 during World Youth Day in Toronto, which "strengthened my faith these years past".

I also received Fr Paul Stenhouse's[2] July issue of *Annals*, which included the prayer of Bishop Synesius, who died in A.D. 414 in North Africa (Libya), nearly twenty years before St Augustine's death.

> *Lord Jesus think on me*
> *and purge away my sins;*
> *From earth-born passions set me free,*
> *and make me pure within.*
>
> *Lord Jesus, think on me,*
> *nor let me go astray;*
> *through darkness and perplexity*
> *Point thou the heavenly way.*

Monday, 19 August 2019

More birds were about this morning when I went outside despite the cold. The sky was clear apart from a few light clouds, although when I returned outside this afternoon, the first exercise pen had an immense puddle of water, the benches were wet, and the sky overcast. I think snow was forecast across Victoria above 500 metres. Spring is announcing its arrival despite the cold.

About a month ago, my friend Eugene was wishing I could see his daffodils, although I don't know at what stage they are now.

---

[2] Fr Paul Stenhouse, MSC (1935–2019), was a distinguished scholar and writer. From 1964 to 2019, he edited *Annals*, the longest-surviving Catholic journal in Australia.

Neither have I enquired about the wattle or the tulips in the Dande-nongs.[3] I love the traditional European-type gardens you can grow in Melbourne and Ballarat, and you appreciate spring more after a cold winter. A less exuberant spring is the price we pay for the mild and pleasant (usually) winters we have in New South Wales.

A couple of warders asked whether I am going to publish a book when I am released. I said that depends... They also enquired whether I would write well or badly about them, and I replied honestly that it would not be bad.

Since I am in solitary confinement, my knowledge is limited, although I can hear a good deal of what happens in the unit, especially when there is trouble. This unit is well run, the exercise of authority is not capricious, although protocol requires that requests are met slowly. The staff here like to suggest that they are "better" quality because the work is difficult, especially with the damaged ice [meth] addicts. The dialogue is sometimes vigorous and colourful, but I have been surprised for the better. We have enjoyed a few days of quiet, with no bangers or shouters. Some other sections are now blessed with their presence. I received a letter from a prisoner who had been a couple of cells away from me for some days before moving on. Apparently, he is a frequent guest. I have benefited from many small acts of kindness from warders. Some have asked me to pray for them or family members, others wished me well with my appeal, and one or two said they would pray for me.

My brother, David, and his wife, Judy, called for an hour-long contact visit. As I phone each week, no one had much family news. My sister, Margaret, has settled well in Bendigo, and my old school friend Fr Michael Mason will be with her in Bendigo while the ver-dict is delivered. For some reason, a warder sat in the large visits room about ten metres [eleven yards] away. I objected mildly and asked why this was happening, as it had never occurred previously. Initially the warder said he was there to protect me, claiming that this is the new regulation for all contact visits. Who knows?

Prof Tracey Rowland of the University of Notre Dame, Australia, sent me her contribution to the festschrift for Msgr Livio Melina,

[3] The Dandenong Ranges are low mountains (the highest peak is just shy of 2,100 feet) about twenty miles east of Melbourne.

formerly president of the John Paul Institute for the Family in Rome, who, together with some kindred spirits, has been removed from his position. This is a sad development. It weakens the pope, the successor of Peter.

The essay has the rather grand title of "The Salvific Relevance of Moral Action and the Totality of Intellectual Formation", but it is a learned and accessible piece defending the moral union of scriptural teaching and natural law, of faith and reason as they impinge on judging the morality of actions.

Msgr Livio is named after the Latin writer and historian Livy, or Titus Livius, and Tracey feels barbarians are now on the prowl and Rome's defences have been breached, once again.

In this journal, I have defended what I see as Gospel Christianity in the Catholic tradition, and Prof Rowland gives a learned and sophisticated account of what this means for Catholic moral teaching.

What is the basis for Christian living in successive generations, now spanning almost two millennia? Is our activity important for salvation? Why is there such moral confusion even in the Catholic Church?

The basic moral truths have been given to us by Christ and the apostolic tradition, which builds on the Old Testament. There is development but from within the moral tradition, so that Christ's teaching in the Sermon on the Mount does not discard the Ten Commandments, just as we are not entitled to discard Christ's explicit moral teaching, not entitled to start "from the position that it is not what Christ said or did that matters, but how he related to his context."

If we get the basics wrong, then it is inevitable that specific errors follow, often worsening or, as we proceed, arriving at the autonomy of secular human values, spelled out in cultural theory or intellectual Marxism.

Prof Rowland explained her thesis this way. As Luther's errors "began the long and tragic process of the secularization of German culture and along with it the cultures of formerly Catholic countries influenced by German scholarship", there has been an almost total collapse of the faith.

Our task is to present the Catholic moral tradition as a life-force, sometimes hard and challenging, but especially enriching and liberating as our social capital declines and identity politics strives to limit free speech.

Tracey prefaces her tribute with a caption from Livy's *Ab Urbe Condita*, about the terrible Roman defeat by Hannibal's ambush at Lake Trasimene in 217 B.C.: "Pugna magna victi sumus." (We were defeated in a great fight.) But in the end, Hannibal did not win. After fifteen years in Italy, he returned to Carthage, unable to capture the city of Rome. And then Carthage was destroyed.

Tuesday, 20 August 2019

Sr Mary McGlone is one of the best sermon writers, beyond any doubt, despite the fact that she writes for the *National Catholic Reporter*. Good things can come out of Nazareth. Her sermon on Jesus bringing fire and causing division is one of her best.[4]

Sr Mary proposes that, in his passion and directness, Jesus is his mother's son and, citing her Magnificat prayer, points out that she, like Joseph and her Son, was nourished by the writing of the Hebrew prophets, who preached their share of fire and brimstone and suffered the consequences of persecution and division.

She quotes St Ignatius of Loyola's discernment of spirits to explain that "when a good spirit touches a soul inclined to evil, the result is discord.... When a prophet speaks for God to a sinful people, conflicts ensue."

She then moves on to the Swiss theologian Hans Urs von Balthasar, who cheerfully warns us about the danger of getting involved with God. We might want a quiet, peaceful life, but, says Balthasar, "God draws us beyond our limits into the divine adventure, which is always fatal."

The readings last Sunday will not let us off the hook, but we are consoled by the cloud of witnesses, the communion of saints, which "offers us the universe's largest extended family for encouragement".

If our churches only offer us comfort and peace, we have to ask, according to Sr Mary, whether "they are centres of Christianity or just spas with uncomfortable chairs."

This is Gospel Christianity, elegantly expressed.

[4] "Twentieth Sunday in Ordinary Time", Sunday Resources, *National Catholic Reporter*, 17 June 2019.

The day passed busily with a couple of outside exercise sessions under an overcast sky and a session in the gymnasium, where a friendly warder set up a table-tennis table so you could play by yourself. Once again, I discovered that I can't do now what I once could, but once again I improved with practice (a bit).

At the final roll call tonight, as we stood with one hand in the trap to be counted and identified, James Gargasoulas called out my name from next door, banged on the wall, and wished me the best of luck for tomorrow. He is unlikely to live to see a day such as mine for himself. Mr Harris, the senior officer, and the two warders also wished me well, and I thanked him for his leadership and his kindness.

Ruth, my barrister, and Kartya, my solicitor, called, and we had a pleasant chat. As always, they were cautious about tomorrow, but cautiously optimistic. Apparently the ABC is running a live stream.

I awoke this morning around 5:00 am and spent the next couple of hours dozing and pondering what I might write in this penultimate offering.

Naturally, I would never have chosen to spend six months, less one week, in jail. I hope it does not continue, and I would never want it to be repeated. But it is something God permitted, and I have survived in good health, through the grace of God, and the prayers and encouragement of thousands of well-wishers, friends, and family. I have done a fair bit of reading and more regular writing than I have for years. So, too, my prayer life has been regular, sometimes dozy, often distracted, but daily. After Matthew's Gospel, I moved on to meditating on the psalms, moving through from the first one. For half the time, however, especially when I was outside, I used the simple John Main[5] method of repeating one or two phrases time and time again: "Jesus, Son of the Living God, my Creator, Redeemer, Brother, and Friend." During each of my two walking sessions, I recited the rosary.

I was not surprised to discover that the advice I gave to priests when they were under stress worked also for me: keep up a routine of daily prayer, not too much food or alcohol, daily exercise, and regular sleep at night, not during the day. I always recommended daily Mass, but that was impossible in jail, and no alcohol was available.

[5] Fr John Main, OSB (1926–1982), was a British Benedictine monk who taught the use of a prayer phrase or mantra for meditation.

In the early weeks, until reminded, I did not perform any exercise for my upper body, but I then remedied this deficiency.

Many of the letters I received were deeply spiritual and nourishing. Too many writers were too generous toward me, but many kind words of thanks were expressed, which I would never have received in any other circumstance.

Writing was therapeutic for me, as it is for many prisoners, and I had no writer's block. I even wondered whether the Spirit was giving me a hand as I put pen to paper. I don't type, much less use a computer, and neither machine was available to me. I can now understand why Solzhenitsyn's[6] novels are so long.

Each of my days followed a fixed pattern, which varied somewhat to allow for AFL football, Test cricket, the Tour de France, and a surprising number of good documentaries, many of them on the British royal family.

At 9:00 pm, a woman's voice came over the intercom telling me I would be called at 6:00 am to go to court tomorrow morning and that there was no need to pack anything.

However, I have been packing, especially the reams of paper I have collected. If I am unsuccessful in the appeal, I will simply unpack on my return. I have ordered a Wednesday newspaper, but, please God, I won't be reading it here.

I will conclude with three intercessions from morning prayer.

God our Father,
Help us to realize that our troubles are slight and short-lived;
they are as nothing compared with the joy we shall have
*   when we reach our home with you.*
— Stay with us, Lord, on our journey.

Take away our pride, temper, and anger;
may we follow you in gentleness; may you make us humble
*   of heart.*
— Stay with us, Lord, on our journey.

---

[6] Aleksandr Solzhenitsyn (1918–2008) was a Russian novelist, philosopher, and historian who spent eight years in Soviet prison camps and was then exiled for three years because of what were considered disrespectful remarks made about Stalin.

Give us the fullness of your Spirt, the Spirit of sonship;
make our love for each other generous and sincere.
— Stay with us, Lord, on our journey.

Wednesday, 21 August 2019

Deus, in adiutorium meum intende.
Domine, ad adiuvandum me festina.

This is the old Latin introduction to the daily prayer of the Church.
In English:

O God, come to my assistance.
O Lord, make haste to help me.

Today, the appeal judges found against me, rejecting my appeal
2 to 1. The chief justice of the Supreme Court and the chief judge
of the Court of Appeal, both civil lawyers, found against me, and
in a minority dissenting opinion, Justice [Mark] Weinberg upheld
my appeal.

I was astonished and badly upset. I could not believe judges could
come to a decision upholding the jury after studying the evidence. I
said to my lawyers it was "an interesting" decision, and to my slight
surprise they agreed.

Their instinct is to appeal to the High Court, and I will wait to
see what Bret Walker [senior counsel] recommends after reading the
judgements: 201 pages from Weinberg and 120 pages combined from
the majority judges.

This has close to destroyed my faith in justice in Victoria, so I am
not confident of success in the High Court (even though it is not
in Victoria). This court decision brings a number of consequences,
first of which is three more years in jail, unless the next appeal is
successful, and then a life in disgrace. The prime minister has already
announced that my Order of Australia should be removed (this is not
in the government's power), but the governor general said that he
would await the finalisation of the appeal process.

The Australian Catholic Bishops' Conference put out a bland
statement accepting the decision, but the Roman statement was more

helpful, recognizing my right to appeal, while Frank Rocca in Rome from the *Wall Street Journal* explained there was a lot of scepticism in Rome about the charges, and most thought I was not guilty.

We have twenty-eight days in which to lodge an appeal with the High Court, three or four months for a decision to grant leave to appeal, and the same period (or more) before the appeal is heard.

Terry Tobin supports an appeal and will consult family and friends, and I asked him to contact Fr Frank Brennan and his circle. It will, of course, once again be an expensive business if the appeal goes ahead.

The boss of the jail, Nick Selisky, came for a chat this afternoon and spoke about getting me out of solitary confinement. The lawyers thought I might be going to Ararat,[7] but his view was that I should stay in MAP in a freer environment, mixing with other prisoners. Something will happen on this occasion, unlike in the past, given my appeal has failed. Selisky was genuinely sympathetic about my appeal failure. The decision also means that any thought I had of publishing extracts from this journal before Christmas have vanished completely. Perhaps it will never see the light of day.

I had been thinking that I would conclude today, but I shall continue for the moment, if only for personal therapy.

This afternoon Paul Galbally and Kartya Gracer called for a useful chat, bringing the Weinberg judgement, which they had read. They were most enthusiastic and said I would be also, believing his judgement could be just what we need for the High Court. Apparently Walker, who sent me his sympathy, had devised his Appeal Court methodology mindful of the High Court requirements.

I might be excessively pessimistic at this moment, but after two successive failures, when I was confident of success, more reticence is warranted.

I will now have to devise some reading or intellectual program for the months or years ahead. As with every suffering, even unwelcome and unexpected, all can be offered to the Lord for the good of the Church. This is a great consolation. After three more years in jail, I am not sure what time or health I might have to cut a dash, almost as a nonperson. Facing up to such a prospect, by writing about it, is already a help.

[7] Hopkins Correctional Centre in Ararat, Australia, a medium security prison for men.

One basic point was made by the prison director. A 2 to 1 judgement is certainly better than appealing against a unanimous decision.

That a majority of judges found against me, as well as a jury, will increase the scandal and damage to the Church.

Yesterday I prayed for the realization that our troubles are slight and short-lived, when compared to the joys of heaven. Today I pray simply:

Jesus mercy. Mary help.

Thursday, 22 August 2019

My jail life is returning to its useful patterns, and I am regaining my equilibrium after yesterday's upheavals. I have an intermittent banger next door, who has ceased for the moment, and at the other end of the unit, two or three shouters swear at one another intermittently. (It is 10:15 pm.)

Paul and Kartya called for twenty minutes this morning to cheer me up and bring the 120 pages (combined) of the two civil law judges who rejected my appeal. Paul said to me that almost certainly they will appeal, and I let this go unchallenged.

I spent the day reading the 201-page verdict of Judge Weinberg, which encouraged me enormously. A Supreme Court judge told Paul Galbally that it is a masterpiece and that he has deep respect from the High Court judges.

I have been known to say that if there were one Church history book I would like to have written, it would be Peter Brown's *Augustine*. To that list of material I would like to have written, I would now like to add Weinberg's judgement.

It is explicit, clear, methodical, and wise. Some details in particular I loved. He wrote that "the complainant's account of the second incident seems to me to take brazenness to new heights, the like of which I have not seen. The use of the term 'madness' may have been a rhetorical flourish" (1095).

In the next paragraph, he began, "Nevertheless, I would have thought that any prosecutor would be wary of bringing a charge of this gravity against anyone" (1096).

He acknowledged that the charges against me were implausible: an archbishop, still in his vestments, in a sacristy after Mass in his cathedral, grossly violating two young servers whom he did not know, at a time when the sacristy was full of other servers (adults) and he was with his master of ceremonies on the front steps of the cathedral. Justice Weinberg was particularly struck by the bizarre nature of the second incident, but it would also be an interesting exercise to find other cases as bizarre as the first set of accusations. Even the Billy Doe charges are not quite as spectacular.

A couple of quibbles. I thought the judge was a bit too severe on the moving visual representation. I am not sure it was as tendentious as he judged. Similarly, I am not sure the judge grappled with the strangeness of two "victims" in one terrible incident never mentioning it to each other at any later stage. Even among the wildly different patterns of reporting abuse, that claim is a stand-out.

It is as though the Weinberg judgement had been written for the High Court, to guide them through the deliberations. Therefore, I am more settled, less committed to the worst outcome as the most likely.

Terry Tobin said yesterday that only judges could be as silly as the majority judges. More than fifty years ago, I remember Bertrand Russell, the atheist British philosopher, saying something like: you had to be very clever sometimes to be very silly. The prevailing wisdom is that no one can tell what the High Court judges are thinking, and they are such formidably clever persons they could find "good" reasons for many absurdities.

Friday and Saturday, 23–24 August 2019

Spent Friday studying Weinberg's text, listing points of interest, and making points for discussion with Ruth and Kartya. I had not finished when they arrived, but we had enough to talk about.

I am returning to equilibrium. Was much heartened by the Aussies dismissing the English in their first innings for 67 runs. We then made around 250, giving us a lead of 359. However, on Saturday night Australian time, the Poms rallied to be at 3 for 150 plus with Root and Stokes still batting. (Three days later, we were beaten when the Poms hit a record second innings.)[8]

[8] The cardinal is describing the Australia-England Ashes 2019 cricket match. Joe Root and Ben Stokes play for England. Poms is an Australian slang word for people of English origin.

As I had stayed up to watch the English collapse, I was tired on Saturday, even more so after my workout in the gymnasium, where I increased the weight exercises for my thighs and walked for seven and a half minutes on the treadmill. It sounds very little, when you write it, but it still left me tired. However, my physical strength is slowly increasing, and my weight continues to fall slightly—on Saturday, it was 115 kg [253.5 lbs]. However, I am not feeling hungry, not least because of my nightly Cadbury's chocolate and the chocolate bullets!

Put in an application to receive a larger size of gym boots [shoes], as my size 15 are slightly tight, exacerbating my two left-foot corns and inhibiting the curing of my left big toe's ingrown nail. Spoke with the doctor about this and about a spot on my right lower leg. Also received some ointment for my cold sores on lower lip. Otherwise—all is well.

Terry Tobin and Bernadette are both keen that I appeal and believe this should be announced on Monday. It can be filed when the legal work is completed.

I spent some hours this afternoon reading the combined hostile judgement of [Judges] Maxwell and Ferguson. It is a clumsy rerun of the prosecution case. The complainant is judged to be "credible", and everything he says is evaluated in this light. When he is making some bizarre claim, this is judged as evidence of his truthfulness, because no liar would be so silly.

Portelli's and Potter's evidence[9] is to be set aside as unreliable, and they claim there is no "direct" evidence that the rehearsals took place. Potter's five- or six-minute pause is identified as the time when attacks occurred. This is a physical impossibility for a number of reasons. I will make a substantive critique for Ruth and Walker. I find it hard to believe two senior judges could be so mistaken and so biased. Tim O'Leary labelled it pathetic.

Archbishop Comensoli [of the Archdiocese of Melbourne] announced in a Neil Mitchell interview[10] that J might have some credibility because he had been attacked, but not by me. I wonder what

---

[9] Msgr Charles Portelli, former master of ceremonies to Archbishop Pell, and Maxwell Potter, former sacristan at St Patrick's Cathedral, Melbourne, testified on behalf of Cardinal Pell.

[10] "Full Interview: Melbourne Archbishop Peter Comensoli Reacts to George Pell's Failed Appeal", *Mornings with Neil Mitchell*, 3AW, 21 August 2019, https://omny.fm/shows /mornings-with-neil-mitchell/full-interview-melbourne-archbishop-peter-comensol.

prompted him to make this statement. I mentioned this to Bernadette and Terry and then told them in Italian about Robert's two pieces of information. Bernadette replied that she understood what I was saying. Terry said the theory of another assailant could be widespread among the clergy, as Gerry Gleeson[11] had already mentioned it to Bernadette.

On Thursday, Tim and Anne McFarlane had called, urging me strongly to keep going and to appeal. I acknowledge that my reluctance to appeal was partly irrational, but not completely, as there must be some realistic prospect of success. I owe the appeal to my supporters, especially as I am innocent, and it would be foolish to acquiesce to more than three years' jail time without fighting.

I haven't stopped my usual routine of prayers or my eating or exercise, and my sleep is improving after Wednesday and Thursday. However, even these impaired nights of sleep seem to compare well with the patterns of minor insomniacs. *Deo gratias.*

The "psych nurse" interviewed me, and I managed to reassure him. He explained that warfarin in a very large dose can be used for suicide, so that was the ostensible reason why they wanted me to ingest it before them. As always, I explained that I could come for help if I felt I needed it.

I know that misfortune is not a sign of divine disapproval and, indeed, can be a sign of God's special love, as long as God realizes how weak and imperfect I am, as well as being someone who is keen on a comfortable life and even a quiet one. However, I will take what comes, perhaps becoming more like Job and complaining a bit, and try to use it for God's good purposes—for the Church, victims, family, and friends. My family and friends have been marvellous in their support and encouragement.

Psalm 54 is helpful:

> *He (God) will deliver my soul in peace*
> *in the attack against me:*
> *for those who fight me are many,*
> *but he hears my voice.*

[11] Very Rev Gerald Gleeson is the vicar general for the Archdiocese of Sydney.

WEEK 27

Forging Ahead

25 August—31 August 2019

Sunday, 25 August 2019

I slept through to 6:18 am and so missed *Mass for You at Home*—probably a result of my exercise in the gymnasium.

I decided to bypass Hillsong, but watched Joseph Prince and the following Gospel session from Houston, Texas, led, as it turned out, by the son of Joel Osteen. [He spoke of how] Jabin, who had nine hundred chariots, and Joshua prevailed over the Canaanites. Grace is beyond strength. He wore dark jeans and a zipped-up top, with three rings on his hand.

Apparently, both Joel Osteen and his wife, Victoria, are evangelists, and his son has inherited their genes. About twenty-five years plus or so, he speaks well with a pleasant personality. His theme was "The Love of the Father", or God's love for us. God is the biggest fan of each one of us, especially when one is tempted to give up. Not surprisingly, the message brought me comfort.

He urged us to go straight to God, as we don't need pastors or priests or saints to contact God. Go direct, because "you are God's biggest deal."

God takes our side, our burdens. God forgets our mistakes (not forgives our sins). Jesus took on our penalties. No one can earn being a son, and when the father ran to greet "the prodigal son", his younger boy, this is the only image we have of God running!

Only a one-word reference to sin, nothing about repentance, much less anything on the four last things: heaven and hell, death and judgement. He obviously has a significant defence in his topic "the love of the Father" for not mentioning these unmentionables. I have plenty of weeks in jail ahead of me to discover whether my suspicions are justified.

A beautiful, clear late-winter day, and I was given two longer periods outside. Richmond had a solid five-goal win over Brisbane, so this was about as welcome as the English cricket team's low score in their first innings.

While watching the news on the TV after the football, I saw that I had decided to appeal to the High Court. I had tried to phone Katrina [Lee] to ask her to inform the Tobins of my decision to go ahead, but I was unable to make contact. I am not sure how it progressed after this, but I was pleased with the announcement.

Received a substantial number of letters, only one or two written after my appeal's failure. One such was from the dreamer, who is very intelligent, reads the play well, and is probably adept at seeing the best results in his prognostications. While his understanding of his role is bizarre, he still claims all will be well, that he was reluctant to discourage me by being too pessimistic about my appeal, and that the answer to my problems lies in the past of the complainant. This clarification will be extra-judicial and urge a high level of activity from, e.g., the Church and others. Not surprisingly, he claimed, before the event, that I would be dejected after the failure. He could be wrong on both counts, i.e., I will not be exonerated and freed legally and not helped by developments establishing my innocence. He says, quite rightly, that some extra-judicial development or revelation demonstrating my innocence would be better than even a High Court acquittal.

We have a very mad fellow at the other end, who breaks out loudly, sometimes in acrimonious dialogue with one or two neighbours. He is sick. I think he was in the next exercise pen, talking and swearing to himself, when I was out this afternoon. I heard my first brief jail blasphemy from him.

Two days ago, we celebrated the feast of St Rose of Lima. When we were in Peru en route to the World Youth Day in Rio de Janeiro, Brazil, in 2013, we visited the large mansion in Lima where Rose had lived in a tiny hut in the house garden, infested with mosquitoes. She was heavily into penance, and I did not find her image particularly attractive as a way to sanctity.

However, the breviary extract from her writings on grace and suffering were powerful and accurate. She is very clear about the importance of suffering. "Let them be on their guard against error or deception: this is the only ladder by which paradise is reached; without the cross, there is no road to heaven."

So marvellous is grace, we should be searching for trouble to obtain it. "Would that mortal man might know how wonderful is divine grace, how beautiful, how precious, what riches are hidden therein, what treasure, what joys, what delights." I accept all her teaching about the beauty of grace and the necessity of the Cross, but I feel I have problems enough without searching for more.

Monday, 26 August 2019

The day was unusual for a couple of reasons. The most important was that I spent hours putting together seven pages on a fundamental and crucial error in the majority verdict. I believe it puts a stake through the heart of the judges' case.

Unlike the prosecutor, the judges named precisely when the "offences" took place, i.e., immediately after Mass, after Pell and Portelli left the front steps in the five or six minutes of private prayer time of Max Potter the sacristan, who opened the sacristy door.

Much time has been spent on when Potter opened the sacristy door, on whether the two miscreants were not seen leaving the procession, on whether Portelli was always with me when I was robed. The significance of the altar servers' presence in the sacristy was enhanced by the evidence of Connor and McGlone.[1]

By their own evidence, the complainants remained with the procession until the toilet corridor, when they doubled back outside to enter though the south transept and go past the organ to the sacristy. After their alleged departure, choristers and servers continued within the cathedral complex, moving in different directions. The altar servers had a shorter distance to travel than the two who claimed to have fled and would probably have arrived at the sacristy before them.

---

[1] Jeffrey Connor and Daniel McGlone, former altar servers at St Patrick's Cathedral, Melbourne, testified on behalf of Cardinal Pell.

In other words, the two complainants could not have been in the sacristy before the time the procession took to arrive at the toilet corridor, perhaps four or five minutes, and would have arrived about the same time as or later than the servers. They simply could not have been there for five or six minutes when the sacristy was empty, before the servers arrived. Whether the sacristy door was unlocked or locked, they could not have been there.

All the difficulties about my appearing alone in the sacristy, within the five or so minutes after Mass, after their bolting away from the master of ceremonies and the sacristan remain.

I don't know exactly the legal significance of all this for the High Court, but it will be precious in the world of public opinion. It can be explained clearly and simply, and its effects are lethal for the judges' findings. It gave my spirits a boost, and I see the hand of providence at work in the judges' ineptitude. I feel confident in my reasoning but am keen to check it with the lawyers and to make sure Ruth has a copy before she goes to Sydney to talk with Bret Walker, the senior counsel.

We have a poor, mad shouter, a screecher and banger, who is apparently autistic and whom they leave alone until his fit passes. He let off a fierce denunciation of me and my crime, in colourful language, and consigning me to hell. It was not pleasant. However, I could hear one prisoner come to my defence.

As I lay on my bed before getting up, I was pondering Rose of Lima's call to us to seek trouble and suffering and my clear decision that this was not a suitable direction for me. Come what may, I have to cope with any disappointment and situation and deal with it appropriately as a Christian and, therefore, as a priest. I have to use my difficulties to try to come closer to Christ, and so I decided to add to my short list of aspirations or mantras (to use a non-Christian term).

So I pray now:

Nearer, my God, to thee.

Feast of St Monica, Tuesday, 27 August 2019

Today is the feast of St Monica, patron of so many mothers today, who never relented in her efforts to persuade her brilliant Manichaean son, with his partner (whose name we do not know) and son, Adeo-datus, to return to the full Catholic faith. In the city of Milan, led by the archbishop St Ambrose (no cardinalate in those days), Augustine did convert in 386.

St Monica died in Ostia, the port of the city of Rome, with Augus-tine and his brother present as they were returning to North Africa. As a Roman seminarian, I remember picnicking on the grounds next to what was billed as the house where she died. Holy Mother Church owes her and her prayers an enormous debt for the conversion of her son and his writings, which still nourish us today.

I wrote a couple of points of postscript to my pages on the fatal flaw, ending with the quotation from Kant which Friel keeps repeat-ing, "Truth is the daughter of time", because in this allegation the time opportunity is extinguished by the evidence of the complainers.

After saying my rosary while exercising, I phoned Tim O'Leary to tell him of my discovery, and he was delighted; Terry Tobin was a bit sceptical, but said he would study the report himself and then we could talk. Kartya was on her way to visit me when I phoned, so, with the help of a cooperative Mr Harris, I expedited the delivery of my text below to the property section. They gave it to Kartya and then announced she could not bring it into her meeting with me. Further dialogue ensued, and she was able to use it. This sort of obstruction is not unusual among warders I do not know and is strong in some quarters of the property office.

Kartya agreed with all my argumentation on my crucial point and said she and Ruth had recognized the issue when they were working together yesterday. She saw the same facts in a different context, i.e., how to convince the High Court to accept the appeal. I have no competence in this area, but I clearly see the significance of the issue for the media battle. Kartya and Paul don't see the situ-ation in these terms. Contrary to the conventional wisdom, Kartya cannot see the importance of this huge single tree because of her view of the entire forest. I was reassured that Ruth and Kartya shared my view of the evidence and would have been disappointed if it had been a surprise to them.

Kartya was surprised, and a little miffed, by the announcement in the media that I or we would appeal. I will phone Paul tomorrow and ask him to say simply that I have decided to appeal and the team is working on the grounds for the appeal. Kartya also replied that she would take Terry Tobin's request to come in with the lawyers and brief me on extracurricular activities. I received a strange card from Tess announcing "the extra-curricula pursuits are flourishing and about to bear great fruits that will have an extraordinary impact. The Immaculate Heart of Mary interceded on Thursday. The fallout will go far and wide and do great good." May the God of Victories be with us.

Tim O'Leary said there was a meeting of supporters today, perhaps of the group Tim McFarlane has called "the Council of Trent"! On a less important matter, Chris and Anne and Michael C[2] are all working to obtain some proper size gym boots: either my old ones or buying a new pair.

Sr Mary called for our paraliturgy and Communion—and a good chat. She had sent a message on Friday asking whether I would like to see her, but I received no such question. On Friday, Harris was away, and the senior officer was correct and cool.

My sad autistic friend gave me another serving of abuse this morning, but it didn't last long. So I pray for him the prayer of Francis of Assisi: *Pace e bene.*

And I make my own prayer of Psalm 9:14–15:

> *Have pity on me, Lord, see my sufferings,*
> *you who save me from the gates of death;*
> *that I may recount all your praise*
> *at the gates of the city of Sion*
> *and rejoice in your saving help.*

Wednesday, 28 August 2019

It was a typical and quiet day except that I had an unscheduled hour in the gymnasium, after my scheduled visit yesterday. My thighs are gaining strength, and I completed my seven and a half minutes on the treadmill more easily than yesterday and with a lower pulse afterward (down from 100 pm to about 84). The warder set up the table-tennis

[2] Chris Meney, Anne McFarlane, and Michael Casey.

table, so I could practice by myself, and toward the end I was hitting thirty shots without an error. Practice still helps, despite my age, as when I started on the ping pong I was embarrassingly inept.

The first exercise pen was flooded for my afternoon session after heavy rain in the early afternoon. This morning, I managed to phone Terry and Bernadette and received a couple of small disappointments. He had not searched out the reference for my large claim and, I think, wants to speak with me about "the Rome business". Charlie and the Queensland lady need to be hosed down, he said; and I replied that I didn't know what their information was, but my problems could be solved judicially or extra-judicially. Terry does not want anything to disturb the appeal to the High Court and claimed we don't want to be like [Nathan] Lyon (in the last Test cricket), who could not ask for a review because he had used his quota (and the review showed the batsman was out). I am not sure it is a perfect parallel.

I was a bit disappointed, as I thought Terry wanted to see me to report good extracurricular progress. In the evening, I reviewed Tess' card and saw Katrina was involved, which provided some extra reassurance. Terry had already spoken twice with Paul, who is coming to see me tomorrow.

I have received about fifty letters the past two days and am still moving through them. Bernadette's letter arrived with Terry's and Frank Brennan's reasons why I should appeal. Both were strongly supportive, but quite different in their reasoning, which I found interesting.

Terry's cold water doused my incipient optimism about being released before doing my full three years and eight months. This was not entirely justified, as I still don't know who is saying what on extra-curricular moves. My first reaction was to think that another three years in jail would be a huge waste of time, but from a Christian perspective, this thinking is mistaken. Jesus' Passion was not productive in any worldly sense, a painful "waste of time". However, Jesus' suffering was redemptive and can purify and vivify my suffering, if it lasts its full term. This suffering would be more productive spiritually than my taking things easily outside, but I hope that the prayers keep up for the success of my High Court appeal, and, more importantly for the Church, that I am exonerated by some substantial pieces of evidence.

There was renewed and shouted dialogue among the inmates tonight after lockdown, and my mad mate denounced me loudly for longer than last night. However, some unknown ally mounted a long explicit defence of my innocence. It is unusual that I have any defenders, and I have quite a few among the prison population. The poor man was weeping loudly.

Today is, as I foreshadowed, the feast of St Augustine, who died in 430 as bishop of Hippo in North Africa. Twenty years earlier, Alaric had sacked Rome, prompting the pagans to claim this was because the Romans had abandoned their traditional gods and Augustine to write his masterpiece *The City of God*. Augustine is fascinated by himself, but even more fascinated by the one true God of love, Beauty, so ancient and so new. He is one of the greatest preachers in all Christian history, and the many excerpts from his sermons in our breviary are always nourishing and interesting. His style, too, is quite distinctive, often punchy with contrasting language and examples.

Let me conclude with the second most famous quotation in the *Confessions*. (The most famous is "Make me pure, but not yet.")

Late have I loved you, O Beauty so ancient and so new; late have I loved you. For behold you were within me, and I outside; and I sought you outside and in my ugliness fell upon those lovely things that you have made. You were with me and I was not with you. I was kept from you by those things, yet had they not been in you, they would not have been at all.

Thursday, 29 August 2019

An unusually busy day by jail standards. After my morning exercise, Ruth, Paul, and Kartya called to brief me on Ruth's meeting in Sydney with Bret Walker on the strategy to be employed to convince the High Court to consider my appeal.

Ruth outlined some of the basic errors in the majority report and explained that they were working to establish that, in their reasoning, the judges reversed the onus of proof, also accepting the credibility of the complainant and using that to evaluate particular incidents. There were no significant differences among us on the evidence.

I explained precisely that my "fatal flaw" claim was based on the fact that the miscreants were in the procession and doubling back and could not have simultaneously been under attack in the sacristy. After a moment or so, Ruth acknowledged that I wasn't talking about the presence or absence of myself, Portelli, Potter, or the servers.

We had a lively discussion on what should be done when about the claimed extracurricular revelations. I still don't know what is alleged or promised, but explained emphatically that we should be active in the world of public opinion, not so much through social media, but through, e.g., *The Australian*. All agreed that we did not want to damage the prospects for the High Court Appeal and that any claims or revelations, e.g., my "fatal flaw", should wait until the appeal is lodged.

Ruth pointed out that J had identified me as Frank Little[3] and not as myself, which was also my recollection, but contrary to what Robert Richter had said to me on his jail visit. Robert is expected with Paul tomorrow morning.

Anthony Robbie[4] flew down from Sydney, and I obtained extra time so we met for nearly an hour. We went through the pros and cons of closing my apartment in Rome, and I decided we should sell the car. Anthony did not have much Roman news that I did not already know, except that Perlasca,[5] the money man, had been moved out of the Secretariat of State. This is good.

I asked Anthony R to suggest to Archbishop Fisher that Domus Australia[6] offer to celebrate a special Mass as part of the canonization celebrations for Blessed John Henry Newman. I had hoped to be present for this.

Kartya announced that Cardinal [Gerhard] Müller and Princess Gloria of Thurn und Taxis wanted to visit me. I explained who they both were and that their visit would generate a media circus. Anthony R thought such a visit would not be well regarded in Rome and will work to dissuade them. However, I will make it clear to Paul that I am not refusing to see them.

More letters arrived today, so that I still have not opened them. The prisoner who did not use his gym time yesterday decided to

---

[3] Thomas Francis Little was the archbishop of Melbourne before George Pell.

[4] Fr Anthony Robbie, a priest in the Archdiocese of Sydney, served as Cardinal Pell's secretary in Rome.

[5] Msgr Alberto Perlasca managed Vatican investments controlled by the Secretariat of State.

[6] Domus Australia is a pilgrim house in Rome owned by the Australian Catholic Church.

do so today, so I missed out. The phones were out of order for the whole day, but I obtained my afternoon exercise session.

My disturbed friend did not abuse me, and his mate Dave might have moved on. Certainly by now a couple of prisoners have been transferred out of the unit.

I also received permission to spend $50 extra a month on the phone and hope my August extra can be paid tomorrow so that next week I will be $100 ahead in the phone account.

One of my most regular correspondents wrote to say that my writings and teachings, not any personal counselling, helped her to retain her sanity when she returned to the Church after leaving the Pentecostals.

She wrote out for my consideration Psalms 37 and 57, and I close with verses 5 and 6 of Psalm 37.

> *Commit your way to the Lord.*
> *Trust in him and he will act.*
> *He will make your righteousness*
> *shine clear as the day*
> *and the justice of your course like*
> *the brightness of noon.*

Friday, 30 August 2019

During the morning, I was called out to the central common area to meet a couple of senior warders and hear Mr Harris, the unit commander, read out my monthly report. I remember that I could not have written more favourably myself. Harris recommended that I be transferred to an easier unit, and I was asked my opinion. Naturally, I was not opposed, but I didn't think the authorities wanted to transfer me at this stage, preferring to give me time out of my cell on each of my two visiting days. Visits will be preceded by a couple of hours in the garden area, and on the three other days, I will continue to have an hour in the gymnasium. It doesn't bring human company, congenial or uncongenial, but the garden is a pleasant area, vastly preferable to the grotty exercise pen.

My mad and sad friend is still with us, but he seems to have lost most of his mates and once again never commented on my misdemeanours.

Robert Richter called with Paul Galbally and strongly endorsed the reversal of onus argument for the appeal. I tried to find out more about the High Court judges. They did not esteem Maxwell highly and had already found against him in other case(s) and should not be too strongly hostile to a pushy, Catholic social conservative.

I urged the value of my crucial and fundamental error argument, meeting no dissent, and urged on Robert the importance of extra-curricular activities. Both insisted nothing should be done until the appeal is filed, while Robert claimed that a couple of friends had been running drugs in Southeast Asia for a couple of years and that he hoped their comeuppance would occur in a criminal court.

I explained that one dimension of my problem was that I didn't know what I didn't know. He repeated his claim that J identified the dean as myself, and I urged Paul to check the transcript. He and his wife are off to Europe for holidays tomorrow. He also mentioned in passing that after my jury he briefly considered retiring; but he changed his mind because there was work to be done, and he had since won a couple of cases in front of a jury. He was pleased when I mentioned that Boris Johnson shared his enthusiasm for Dr Johnson.[7]

I have added to the cards and photos on my shelves from what was sent to me. I have a splendid photo of Mother Teresa praying, face lined, eyes closed, hands clasped, a classic example of faith and strength. In addition to my English photo of the Milky Way, someone sent me a beautiful photo of red and white roses, one of the glories of God's plant creation, enhanced by human breeding and design. One cannot claim that the roses and the Milky Way represent the two extremes of creation as the human soul and the animal soul are higher forms of God's life than a rose, but these two images together, not far from Christ and the Cross, express something of the unexpected beauty and variety of God's creation. I remember walking through an aquarium, marvelling at the variety of beautiful fish and marvelling even more at God's ingenuity. We can only

---

[7] In his office, Robert Richter, who defended Cardinal Pell in his jury trials, has a large chair that once belonged to the English writer and lexicographer Samuel Johnson (1709–1784), whom UK Prime Minister Boris Johnson frequently quotes.

lisp and stutter about the mind of God, while his "heart" is an even deeper mystery.

A couple of verses of Psalm 35 capture something of this.

> *Your, love, Lord, reaches to heaven;*
> *your truth to the skies.*
> *Your justice is like God's mountain,*
> *your judgements like the deep.*
>
> *To both man and beast you give protection.*
> *O Lord, how precious is your love.*
> *My God, the sons of men*
> *find refuge in the shelter of your wings.*

Saturday, 31 August 2019

Today is the last day of winter, and, as is usual in Melbourne, it has not been too severe: I believe most of Victoria has received good rains (although I am not sure of this), and the snow fields still have good cover. The drought is bad in much of country New South Wales, while I am not sure about Queensland.

For some reason, we have no AFL finals matches, which will commence on Thursday, although I saw the last quarter of the VFL [Victorian Football League] qualifying final, when Richmond started the quarter over thirty points behind Essendon and won by two points. Butler, an AFL premiership player, scored three goals in about five minutes.

Last night I answered a poignant letter from Moya Hall of Ballarat East, who is dying with multiple cancers, but at peace, and replied to a woman who no longer prays and declared me guilty, narcissistic, and without remorse. I invited her to read Justice Weinberg's judgement and rebut it, and I invited and challenged her to pray once a day for a week: "Dear God of Love, if you exist, bring me to the truth."

I had a good workout for an hour in the gymnasium, increasing the exercise for my thighs and increasing the gradient slightly on the treadmill. I needed a siesta on the chair after my cold pie and sauce lunch, which still compares well with the other meals. My weight continues to be slightly under 115 kg [253.5 lbs], fully clothed, at least ten kilos [22 lbs] less than when I entered jail.

I am feeling well physically and adjusting to the fact that I will have to return to taking the novelties of each week as they come, liturgical, cultural, or sporting, setting to one side any lamentation for the times which lie ahead, whatever their length.

A Hornsby Heights woman from NSW [New South Wales] informed me that St Roch is the patron of falsely accused people. I cannot remember much about him, except that when I was in early primary school with recurrent throat problems, St Roch was the saintly throat specialist. As I haven't experienced throat trouble for about seventy years, please God St Roch's intercession will once again be powerful.

A Nebraska woman told me that Fr Gordon MacRae, imprisoned in the US for twenty-five years for paedophilia (and he claims unjustly), is praying for me. His prayers would be worth something. She also informed me that she is praying for me to St Thomas Aquinas, one of my intellectual heroes. I hope he doesn't mind that I prefer St Augustine's writing, but not for intellectual reasons.

I was also heartened immensely by the chief of staff of a well-known [New South Wales] NSW politician, a Catholic, announcing he has decided to receive confirmation because of my faith and dignity in this time of tribulation. Please God I continue to be worthy of such a compliment.

It is a venerable tradition that we try to honour Our Lady in a special way on Saturdays. When I celebrated daily Mass, I often celebrated a Votive Mass of Our Lady on Saturday.

Tony Macken, a regular correspondent, sent me a beautiful prayer Dante Alighieri placed on St Bernard's lips in the last stanzas of the *Divine Comedy*:

> *Virgin Mother, daughter of your Son,*
> *   more humble and exalted than any other creature,*
> *   fixed goal of the eternal plan;*
> *you are the one who has so ennobled human nature,*
> *   that he, who made it first, did not disdain*
> *   to make himself of its own making.*

WEEK 28

Hidden Power

1 September—7 September 2019

Sunday, 1 September 2019

I was well and truly awake for *Mass for You at Home*, despite my Saturday session in the gymnasium, and delighted to find Fr John Corrigan was again the celebrant. He did not disappoint. The music was somewhat different and better, and new images were used during the psalm. Also a plus. Fr John told the well-known story of the Hapsburg nobility, at their funerals, who are refused entry by the Conventual Friar when they list their titles and are only admitted when they confess to being mortal, sinful human beings. We enter heaven because Christ died for us, as even the saints go there with empty hands. So Fr John claims that when he arrives in heaven, he will announce, not that he is a country priest, but that he is a sinner in the love of God. In passing, the preacher acknowledged that there was a bit more to the whole situation than this, because we confront God as we are. Our small efforts are never enough, but chapter 25 of Matthew on the final separation of the sheep and the goats demonstrates that what we have done matters, even if it is never enough to earn the great prize. Even what we will have done, if it is good, was fuelled by Christ's redemptive victory.

I gave Hillsong a miss and returned to watch Joseph Prince, who told us God was not against wealth, but definitely against greed. John's Third Epistle reminds us that God wants us to prosper and be in health. We are the seed of Abraham, through the righteousness of faith, not through the Law. Joseph claimed, "I am the righteousness of God in Christ." Bless him.

Joel Osteen replaced his son as the teacher and explained that faith means being comfortable with not knowing. In fact, God has the solution before we have the problem. As long as we know who is in charge (God), we do not need to know how. Isaac was a bit disturbed when on the mountain with his father, Abraham, and no sacrifice; and lo, the ram appeared in the bushes.

Early on in the sermon and in passing, he informed us that Moses led two million of his people out of Egypt. I don't know of reliable estimates of the number of Jews in Egypt or of how many might have decided to follow him into exile. The number might have been considerable.

Two packets of letters arrived with a photocopy of sixteen articles sent by Tim O'Leary from Australia and overseas, nearly all of them of high quality and overwhelmingly supportive. This is comforting spiritually and psychologically, but also in an intellectual sense because it validates my own judgement of the trial.

I spent a good number of hours writing "Entirely Possible", which I hope to use after my appeal is lodged and to which I added a couple of points after my reading. Friel estimates statistically that if the ten obstacles to conviction are rated as likely to occur as not occur, then the odds of them coming up together are 1000 to 1 against. If we rate them as happening more slowly (25 percent likely for each development), then the odds against them happening together are 1,000,000 to 1 against.

Frank Brennan has written on the absence of opportunity for the crime, but not about the other side of the same coin, i.e., he did not centre upon the inability of the miscreants to be present.

A few lines from Psalm 27 will help me to conclude:

> *Hear my voice when I call, Lord;*
> *be merciful to me and answer me.*
> *My heart says of you, "Seek his face!"*
> *Your face, Lord, I will seek.*

Monday, 2 September 2019

Most of my letters remain unopened, perhaps four or five articles remain to be read, but my notes on "Entirely Possible" are finished. I gave them to Mr Harris to be placed in Property for Kartya to collect, but this evening he returned them to me, suggesting that I hand them in to be passed on to Property on the day she will come to collect them. He mentioned that one could never be sure who might read them if they were left overnight.

As the prisoner allocated did not want to go to the gymnasium, I had about forty minutes there before meeting for an hour plus with David and Judy.[1] Sonny is growing up, and the ups and downs of family life continue. We discussed when Margaret might come to visit, and both thought that Judy should also be present to help for the visit.

As I also had both my spells outside, it was a day of physical activity. Harris hopes the garden routine will begin on next Thursday, but permission was refused for Sr Mary to cut my hair! Harris will ask if a barber can come!

The day was overcast but not cold. David brought new gym boots, black with laces, and the same length as the prison issue, which is too small, but they might have more room, be higher around the toes. He also delivered Gerard O'Connell's book on the Francis conclave,[2] which Gerard had donated and sent, together with a book on the post–WWI AIF crew, which won at Henley in 1919.[3]

I spent the late afternoon writing up this journal and opening letters.

The money in my phone account was down to $3, so I boosted that by $15. My August $50 phone supplement was paid on Friday but has not moved through to credit as yet, and my September stipend of $190 will be paid this week.

A few of my correspondents were greatly encouraged by the pro-life rally in Martin Place a week or so ago against the NSW abortion bill. Probably some 5,000 plus attended, although Peter Hill thought the number was 10,000. Anthony Fisher, as our archbishop, was there, together with Glenn Davies, the Anglican archbishop of Sydney, and Eastern Christian leaders.

---

[1] David Pell is Cardinal Pell's brother; Judy is his wife.

[2] *The Election of Pope Francis: An Inside Account of the Conclave* (New York: Orbis Books, 2019) was written by Gerard O'Connell, Rome correspondent for *America* magazine.

[3] A rowing crew consisting of soldiers from the Australian Imperial Force (AIF) won the King's Cup at the Henley Peace Regatta held at Henley-on-Thames, England, in July 1919.

Miranda Devine remarked that (unfortunately) similar gatherings, dominated as Sydney's was by young adults, had not taken place in other Australian capitals and thanked me for my contribution to producing youth leadership and the institutions to sustain it. The leadership came from the Catholic leaders at Sydney University chaplaincy, University of Notre Dame, and Campion College. Thank God leaders are emerging in this time of adversity, because it could prove to be a long haul. The vitality, youth, and size of the protest almost certainly caused the premier to delay the final voting for some months, although the chance of ultimate victory is non-existent, and even useful amendments are unlikely.

An English family from Cheshire sent me the following prayer from Thomas à Kempis' *The Imitation of Christ* (3.36.3).

If at present you seem to be overcome and to suffer a confusion which you had not deserved, do not be sad at this and lessen your crown through impatience.

Rather look up to me in heaven, who am able to deliver you from all confusion and wrong and repay everyone according to his works.

Tuesday, 3 September 2019

Yesterday was the feast day of Pope St Gregory the Great, a Roman who became prefect of the city before entering the Benedictine monastery on the Caelian Hill near the Circus Maximus, going to Constantinople, the then home of the emperor, as *apocrisiarius*, or papal representative. In 590 he became pope and died in 604. He sent Augustine of Canterbury with his fellow Benedictines to give new impetus to missionary work in England and, with Pope Leo the Great, was one of the two greatest popes of the first millennium. For more than 150 years, Western Europe was suffering from the incursions of the barbarians, and the pope and bishops were assuming more of the burdens of civic leadership. Gregory was a writer and a preacher, a great leader, an excellent administrator, and a prolific letter writer. Some reports claim that he was often sick as he performed his many tasks. He is one pope and leader I admire immensely.

The day itself brought a couple of promising developments. Perhaps the most unexpected was Bernadette Tobin's news that John Finnis[4] from Oxford University had entered the fray to demolish the majority judgement. Terry Tobin is working on the English to make it more suitable for a newspaper and would like it published as soon as possible. This is another providential development as Finnis would have a legal standing, in his own area, comparable to or greater than Weinberg's.

I missed my session in the gymnasium as no staff were on duty there today, but met for less than half an hour by video link with Bret Walker, Ruth, and Kartya. After listening for fifteen minutes, I asked what time was available to us as I had about six points to make, of which two were important.

After I repeated my point about the impossibility of the miscreants being in two places at once, Bret replied that he and Ruth had been working on that point this morning. My second point was Christopher Friel's statistical estimate of the possibility of the ten obstacles or improbabilities being removed within five or ten minutes. Depending on the assessment of probability for each independent action (and some had a snowflake's chance in hell of survival), the odds against ranged from 1000–1 to 1,000,000–1. Bret didn't dissent, as I said that the statistics would need to be validated by an expert in the field. We had a brief discussion on what was in Maxwell's mind when he wrote the judgement. We were short of time, but I emerged none the wiser.

Sr Mary arrived about her usual time for the paraliturgy and Holy Communion. She knew of the ruling against her cutting my hair but believed she would be successful in our petition. My situation rarely arises in solitary confinement because so few prisoners are here for as long as I have been, and outside in the jail, designated prisoners cut the hair of the inmates. She will return to the topic when the jail boss Nick Selisky returns on Monday. When she urged me to keep asking every day, I explained my reluctance as I don't like harping!

My cell was searched, as part of the normal routine, by four tough and taciturn guards. As always, this was preceded by a strip search,

[4]John Finnis (b. 1940) is an Australian law professor and scholar at Oxford, known for his work in moral, political, and legal theory.

which I always dislike. No contraband was discovered, and I don't know what the lads thought of the religious images.

Sr Mary also brought me the names of thirteen new cardinals, which the Holy Father had created unexpectedly. I knew the Canadian Jesuit priest [Michael] Czerny, who had guided Turkson[5] at Justice and Peace, and have met the archbishop of Jakarta.[6] But very few from Western Europe, no archbishop of Paris, and no one from the United States. It will be interesting to hear George Weigel[7] on all this. I hope the First Eighteen is not receiving too many from the thirds; but I don't know enough about the newcomers. Why now? Is anything afoot?

Yesterday I wrote about the large youth-led pro-life rally in Sydney. Bruce Dawe, the Catholic poet from southern Queensland, is a consistent pro-life champion. Three verses from "The wholly innocent" follow.

> *I never walked abroad in air*
> *I never saw the sky*
> *Nor knew the sovereign touch of care*
> *Nor looked into an eye.*
>
> *I never chose, nor gave assent*
> *Nor voted on my fate*
> *Unseen, I came, unseen I went*
> *Too early and too late....*
>
> *Remember me next time you*
> *Rejoice at sun or star*
> *I would have loved to see them too*
> *I never got that far.*

---

[5] Peter Cardinal Turkson was president of the Pontifical Council for Justice and Peace.

[6] Archbishop Ignatius Suharyo Hardjoatmodjo, who became archbishop in 2010, was a current member of the Congregation for the Evangelization of Peoples and president of the Episcopal Conference of Indonesia.

[7] George Weigel is Distinguished Senior Fellow of Washington's Ethics and Public Policy Center, where he holds the William E. Simon Chair in Catholic Studies. His twenty-seventh book, *The Next Pope: The Office of Peter and a Church in Mission*, was published in July 2020 by Ignatius Press. He and Cardinal Pell have been friends since 1967.

Wednesday, 4 September 2019

No visitors today, professional or otherwise, but I did have an unexpected turn in the gymnasium, in lieu of my cancelled visit yesterday. My table tennis against the upturned other half of the table is improving, as I was able to hit fifty shots without an error a couple of times. My backhand, which I used to play most of my shots in the past, is still stronger than my forehand. Practice brings improvement even at my age.

My prayer routine continues unabated and gives an important focus to my morning—and in the evening. And I am sure it helps to keep me psychologically as well as spiritually stable against the temptation to lament my situation. The breviary readings are from Jeremiah, who continues to have a hard time of it.

Another batch of letters arrived, which are yet to be read (I am writing this late afternoon while the unit is quiet, although some poor wretch has been shouting and swearing off and on for most of the day).

Yesterday, one of my neighbours played some Mozart (on his radio or a CD, I know not which), and then some Puccini started, which he hastily cancelled.

Managed to phone Margaret this afternoon, and she was in good form, although troubled by itching; and I spoke briefly with Chris Meney, asking whether Sam knew any statistics, as I want to establish that Friel's odds and methodology are defensible.

This morning I managed to speak with Terry Tobin, who is keen for the Finnis material to be made available to the two barristers. He made no mention of any publication.

Quite a number of my neighbours in the exercise pen use a foreign language on the phone, so I suspect that a disproportionate number of overseas-born are in solitary with me. I am not sure what you conclude from this on criminality or drug usage. I have heard no one who gave evidence of much education. One conclusion beyond dispute is that I am not a typical prisoner!

Philip Gibbs (Anglican chaplain) called for a pleasant ten-minute chat. I learnt that the Anglican Diocese of Bathurst has been in financial difficulty and that the Sydney Anglicans have taken over, so that a new Evangelical Anglican bishop has replaced one from the High Church tradition.

One older (I suspect) nun from an enclosed ex-Catholic convent in Torquay (UK) wrote to console me, lamenting my situation and the state of the law in Australia. One of her friends explained that you could expect little else from a nation which cheated at cricket! I don't think she was joking.

David sent me some articles from Christopher Friel on the two judgements in my case and on the role of the jury. The articles are detailed and substantial, evidence to me of genuine competence in the law. He continues to surprise with his energy and ability, so that I should request Tim O'Leary or Michael Casey to try to discover more about him. He is not your typical PhD student, even in terms of availability of time. God is good. Helped by someone from Wales, whom I don't know, although he claims we were introduced briefly in Rome.

A day ago, Boris Johnson lost the vote on a no-deal Brexit. A House of Commons which has a Remain majority is determined to reject the popular vote of the referendum. Boris has said he will try to get the required two-thirds majority in the House to call an early election. Initially Corbyn[8] opposed this, because Johnson might win and carry though a No Deal! Boris is not done yet and could return to power with some sort of a pact with Farage's UKIP.[9] Tony Abbott[10] is in the UK saying it would be a disastrous blow for Britain, the worst since the invasion of the Normans, if she does not leave the EU on October 31. I'm inclined to agree and am not surprised he has spoken publicly, as he had written earlier along the same lines in *Quadrant*.

An Australian lady wrote me a short note saying, "We think of you everyday and we pray. Unfortunately there is nothing more that we can do", and she sent the following simple prayer.

---

[8] Jeremy Corbyn (b. 1949) is a British politician who served as leader of the Labour Party from 2015 to 2020.

[9] Nigel Farage (b. 1964) is a British politician who has served as leader of the Brexit Party since 2019. UKIP is the UK Independent Party, a British right-wing populist party, led by Nigel Farage since 2006.

[10] Anthony John Abbott (b. 1957) is a member of the Liberal Party. He was leader of the opposition from 2009 to 2013 and prime minister from 2013 to 2015.

Calm me, Lord, as you calm the storms.
Still me, Lord, keep me from harm.
May all the tumult within me cease.
Enfold me, Lord, in your peace.

Thursday, 5 September 2019

Paul Galbally unexpectedly arrived around 9:00 am, at least partially in response to my request to see him. He brought the John Finnis text, which I read through at his request in his presence. It is a tour de force. Paul understood that it had not been published, which surprised me. But if it hasn't appeared somewhere, then it should.

His basic thesis runs along the Walker-Shann-Tobin line that the majority decision reversed the requisite onus of proof, requiring the defence to prove innocence and requiring the prosecution only to demonstrate possibility.

He touched importantly on one basic flaw in the majority decision, pointing out that they rely on Potter's evidence to establish a hiatus of five plus minutes, but set all his other evidence aside as less than reliable.

Paul left the Finnis text below, and it arrived up around 4:00 pm, when I reread and marked up the argumentation. He is a formidable ally with an international reputation.

I spotted one error of fact on the last page (11), which did not invalidate or even damage any of his principal arguments.

The clearing of the sanctuary after High Mass on Sunday did not begin when the celebrant and procession left the sanctuary, but when the servers arrived at the sacristy, bowed, and were dismissed. I will phone Terry in the morning tomorrow and ask him to inform Finnis, as it is important that his text is faultless and offers no free kick to the opposition.

The hiatus or pause time was while the procession was moving from the sanctuary, down the centre aisle, and then outside the cathedral and back to the sacristy. Potter did different things after Sunday Mass, sometimes travelling with the procession of servers and choir, sometimes breaking off as they left the sanctuary and then

opening the sacristy door, either immediately or when his server
helpers arrived.

I am not sure Finnis understood how Potter varied his statements
as his activities after Mass were various.

Michael Casey arrived for a box visit, and they gave us nearly an
hour, rather than the scheduled half hour. He is well, and his work
is going well. Pabst has finished his book on the ALP and Catholic
social teaching,[11] and Michael is well pleased, saying it is a sophisticated piece of work. They are holding a number of launches in the
capital cities, and he is taking Pabst to meet Albanese,[12] the leader of
the Opposition and an ex-student of Cathedral College, Sydney.

I asked him to study both my written texts and give me some
comments on how "Entirely Possible" could be improved, whether
it merited a wider audience later, given the state of the discussion at
that stage, and under whose name it could appropriately appear. He
was not joining Tim O'Leary for a meal in the evening as he had to
be back in Sydney to celebrate Ruth's birthday. I phoned to wish her
well, but had to leave a message. Naturally, I asked Mike to pass on
my thanks to both his daughters for their wonderful support. Miriam
hopes to be a lawyer to battle against injustices like mine, and Rachel
is planning to call her son George!

In the evening, West Coast defeated Essendon in a one-sided AFL
elimination final. Despite their recent indifferent form, West Coast
are formidable contenders, boosted by Nic Naitanui's return as their
ruckman, who dominated the centre, and the Eagles regularly cleared
from the bounces.

I stayed up until past midnight to watch [Australian cricketer]
Steve Smith score a century and then 150. The Aussies have mas-
tered Jofra Archer, England's sporadic demon fast bowler, who is
bowling 10 miles per hour slower than a couple of tests ago, when
he felled Smith.

Tonight I pray with the Short Responsory of yesterday's Evening
Prayer.

[11] Adrian Pabst, *Story of Our Country: Labor's Vision for Australia* (Redland, QLD: Kapunela
Press, 2019).

[12] Anthony Norman Albanese (b. 1963) has been a member of the Australian Parliament
since 1996 and the leader of the Labor Party since 2019.

Guard us, Lord, as the apple of your eye.
Hide us in the shadow of your wings.

Friday, 6 September 2019

Today was a quiet day even by prison standards, without any professional or personal visits and no period in the gymnasium. Friday is usually not a gym day for me. David, the liaison person, called to tell me the proposal for me to go twice a week into the garden is going to the bosses next week and he anticipates no problem. Mr Harris, in charge of Unit 8, had thought the arrangements were in place, but . . . All moves slowly here, when it isn't stopped. Such is life.

On Friday, I try to do some small penance, so I do not eat meat, which is no problem here in jail, and do not have my chocolate with chamomile tea, which is my late-evening treat. I suspect the Desert Fathers went at their penances more seriously. At lunch, the boot was on the other foot, so to speak, as I forgot it was Friday, when we always have a salad with a bread roll, bun, and piece of fruit. I cut off a long slice of the tinned meat and ate it as a small penance (and it was—but very small). I will continue to agitate quietly, if I ever get the chance, for the reintroduction of a recommended Friday abstinence from meat.

Unfortunately, I am not feeling very "religious" or "spiritual" at this time, although I am not "bone dry". My rosaries while I am walking are a bit more distracted than normal, and my meditations are often dozy. I am still moving through the psalms, which is consoling.

Fr Danny Meagher, the Good Shepherd Seminary rector, who is a man of regular prayer, wrote an encouraging letter, bringing me news of the seminary and the recent ordinations and asking me to offer part of my sufferings for the good of the seminarians. This I certainly do, not forgetting the Redemptoris Mater seminarians also.

They saw themselves as accompanying Christ in his suffering, while looking toward the Risen Christ, and also understood that God was hollowing a space in their souls for his infinite presence. They believed they were chosen by God for their redemptive suffering. All was grace.

Danny then went on to urge me to relax, to sit back and give it to God. He urged me to look after my health and to continue reading and writing.

Most of the time in jail I am more or less relaxed, not confronting a series of stressful events. I don't resist God's providence, but feel it incumbent on me to do what I can to contribute to the efforts to clear my name—for the sake of the Church more than for myself. I pray while I am busy and striving and will continue to pray, in peace, I hope, when we have done all we can. I believe my lawyers and allies such as John Finnis can benefit from my contributions.

This morning I phoned Terry about the factual error in Finnis' document, to ask him to pass on this information and the reasoning behind it. He agreed and asked whether I was happy for him to send both my documents to Finnis. Naturally I was only too pleased.

In speaking with David, I learnt that Marg had had a fall, that it was one and a half hours before she was discovered and was sent to hospital. No breakages, thank God. She should be home soon.

I mentioned that I had no professional visits today, but the podiatrist did come unexpectedly to do my feet and, very helpfully, removed most of my two corns, one of which was painful every now and then. My larger court shoes have taken the pressure off the toe ends, and my new gym boots are big enough also (but only just), when I wear them for the gym.

Last night in Manchester, Smith scored 211, and the Australian team declared at 8 for 498. This should certainly be enough, and rain is probably England's best ally to avoid a defeat, by playing for a draw.

I have plenty to pray about and consider as I settle down for the next few months. The response in the breviary for tomorrow's opening psalm is appropriate.

Let us listen for the voice of the Lord and enter into his peace.

Saturday, 7 September 2019

During breakfast, the new senior officer brought me seven large envelopes of letters, which I accepted gratefully. When he asked whether I responded to them, I explained that I didn't because I had now received well over 2,000 letters and had neither the time nor the prison money to be able to afford to do so.

On phoning Terry, I discovered he had only received my second document "Entirely Possible". When I started to fuss and complain, he said he would contact Katrina immediately to remedy this situation. What he had received had already gone to Finnis.

Fr Frank Brennan's mother has just died, so I asked Bernadette to pass on my sympathy and the promise of my prayers to Frank and his father.

Frank is now Australia's best-known Jesuit. This reminds me that a Toowoomba correspondent informed me that the Jesuit superior general had announced for the second time that the devil is not a "person", but a myth or a symbol of the evil in the world. He is the same priest who explained that we cannot be sure what Jesus said because they didn't have tape recorders in those days. With leadership like this, especially if he is appointing like-minded provincials around the world, Holy Mother Church will need a serious miracle for the Jesuits to reverse their decline in numbers and recover widespread Gospel vitality.

At breakfast, after rain delays, England had climbed to 5 for 200, which is half respectable, but not enough (we hope).

The Brexit fiasco continues with the House of Commons ruling out a no-deal exit and so far refusing to call an election. Boris is visiting the Queen in Balmoral this weekend, and an election will probably be called next week when the recent legislation is enacted. A de facto alliance, or cooperation, between the Tories and Farage's Ukip still seems capable of achieving a majority. If a Brexit deal is not achieved, I foresee years of struggle for Britain's "independence" from the European Union.

With bad bush fires in southeast Queensland and northeast New South Wales, six or seven inches of rain anticipated in some parts of Tasmania, we had rain overnight, and it started to drizzle while I was outside this morning. I enjoyed my hour in the gymnasium, slightly increasing the weights for my arms and thighs and making it a little tougher on the treadmill.

Before opening the new batches of letters, I need to sort into categories twenty to thirty letters already opened.

Richmond eventually had a 47-point win over the Brisbane Lions after a slow start, grinding them into the dust. Dustin Martin kicked six goals. I then watched the cricket until about 11:30 pm, seeing England escape the follow on, scoring 298 and David Warner being trapped in front by Stuart Broad (LBW) for a third consecutive duck.[13]

With the AFL finals, the Test cricket, and the US Open in tennis, life is full of distractions. Watching and following sport is a blessing for many around the world and especially in Australia. Sufficient free time for workers as well as prosperity are necessary before a society can play sports widely and enjoy them. Some of the earliest sports clubs started in Australia as these prerequisites were met in the Australian colonies in the nineteenth century, especially those rich through gold. We thank God for all this, using some lines from Habakkuk's Canticle.

(God's) splendour covers the sky
and his glory fills the earth.
His brilliance is like the light,
rays flash from his hands;
there his power is hidden.

---

[13] Australian batsman David Warner was dismissed for leg before wicket (LBW) when English Stuart Broad bowled. In cricket, an umpire can rule a batter out if the ball would have struck the wicket if it hadn't been intercepted by the batter's body. A duck is when a batsman is out without scoring any runs.

WEEK 29

Conversions and Vocations

8 September—14 September 2019

Sunday, 8 September 2019

Unfortunately, I did not wake until 6:08 am and so just missed Fr John Corrigan's homily. As time goes on, I miss celebrating Mass more keenly, and watching the long Protestant services, with only a minimum of prayer televised and interminable preaching (of a high quality from California and Texas), makes me appreciate more deeply, even from a sociological point of view, the importance and role of the sacraments: ontologically fruitful, as ritualized sacrament and sacrifice. The acknowledgment of our sinfulness at the start of every Mass introduces another necessary element, which is rarely mentioned and almost never by Pastor Houston.

Joseph Prince was togged up in jeans and a black zipped-up jacket, with only a couple of rings, one on each hand. His theme was "Experience God's Sure Kindness to You", and he used chapter 14 of Luke's Gospel. We have only to come, because God is ready for us. The blind and lame are welcome, and those who come to the feast experience immediate forgiveness and eternal righteousness. Christ is our holiness so that we are saved forever in the Lord's name.

Joel Osteen's congregation in Houston, Texas, is less Asian than Prince's immense congregation. I wonder whether the third, raised, and distant tier are people or backdrop for the cameras. Not surprisingly, Osteen's congregation has a goodly number of African Americans. As always, Joel begins with a weak joke; then all rise, hold up their Bibles, and profess their Gospel faith. He has the same sober, good-quality suit and tie each week. The theme was "God Who Exceeds Expectations".

Joel many years ago went into a jewellery shop to purchase a new battery for his watch and finished up with a new watch and a wife. God did provide beyond his expectations. So God is merciful even for those of us with faith as little as a mustard seed. Joel's father, apparently also a pastor, used to have a print run of 10,000 copies for his books, but Joel's publisher decided to print 250,000 copies. I presume all or most of them sold or were distributed.

Songs of Praise featured the British ecumenical Spring Festival, which began in 1979 to gather Christians together for prayer and song. They featured a new composition about Christ's "Meekness and Majesty", which they hope will prove popular. I am no judge on these matters, but it was tuneful and the theology impeccable. We heard a church full of parishioners sing "Amazing Grace", which I wanted sung at the Sydney 2008 World Youth Day. No one seemed enthusiastic, although the reasons were a bit unclear, except that its origin obviously wasn't Catholic. I backed off quickly, perhaps too quickly, because I believed it was a hymn which most of the English speakers, at least, would have known and been prepared to sing. Few things are more useless than asking a congregation to sing a great new hymn without any preparation or practice. In fact, I thought our World Youth Day music was good.

I am writing this on Sunday evening after watching two hours of contemporary footage on 11 September 2001. We have a new shouter at the other end of the unit (not my denouncer), who is not very loud, but very angry and sometimes deeply anguished. Usually, those in this sad category are addicts, often damaged by ice [meth].

I was a bit despondent this morning, for no particularly good reason, but I took my two customary exercise spells, made a few phone calls, and learnt that Margaret was brought back to Mirridong [care home] from the hospital late on Friday night. Apparently, she is inclined to be a bit touchy, which is a good sign health-wise.

I opened twenty or thirty letters, but did not get any letter written. Something for tomorrow.

I should write one letter a day, to answer all the prisoners' letters (which I do regularly) and some others, perhaps those who are weekly correspondents.

One letter writer claimed that one jailed Christian, perhaps it was Cardinal Van Thuan,[1] wrote that letters received were like candles in the darkness. They are certainly an immense consolation to me.

Some further lines from the Canticle of Habakkuk (Hab 3:1–19), which we used yesterday, are appropriate.

> *For even though the fig does not blossom,*
> *nor fruit grow on the vine,*
> *even though the olive crop fail,*
> *and fields produce no harvest, . . .*
> *Yet I will rejoice in the Lord*
> *and exult in God my saviour.*

Monday, 9 September 2019

The pool in the first exercise pen was enormous due to overnight rain, with one of the wardens suggesting that I could bring my flippers when I claimed there was enough water for a swim. So I used the second area for both sessions, with the sky overcast but with no rain in the afternoon. In the morning, I managed to speak to Margaret, whose voice was a bit thick and muted; her mind was clear, and she said she was itching badly and likely to see a skin specialist in a couple of days.

Greg Craven[2] came to visit at 1:00 pm, although we had spoken of a 12:00 pm visit after exercise in the garden, which has not yet materialized. I was betwixt and between.

The end result was that we had a long hour visit in the box, rather than a contact visit. He looked well enough and was full of his customary energy and clarity of mind.

He thought "Entirely Possible" would best see the light of day when I am cleared, as it is quite personal. We discussed the composition of

---

[1] Francis Cardinal Nguyen Van Thuan (1928–2002) was bishop of Nha Trang in South Vietnam (1967–1975) and was appointed co-adjutor archbishop of Saigon in 1975. He was jailed by the Communist government of Vietnam in 1975, spending nine years in solitary confinement before his release in 1988. He was allowed to leave Vietnam for Rome in 1991 and was appointed president of the Pontifical Council for Justice and Peace in 1998.

[2] Greg Craven, a constitutional lawyer, was the vice-chancellor of the Australian Catholic University (ACU). He retired in January 2021.

the High Court (no Maxwells, he insisted), a hypothetical timeline, a decision to allow or not in September, and then an expedited hearing, whatever that means.

His wife, Anne, sent a message saying she was not sure which was the best thing going for us—Weinberg's judgement or the majority judgement! He shared completely our estimate of the state of play.

Greg confirmed that the Burke Fund had about $1.2 million in it, which pleased me, because my only concern was that the corpus should be producing good revenue. When I asked how this was possible with the university's conservative investment criteria, he professed not to know, but to be in admiration of the returns. Obviously, the four scholarships would be available for the Western civilization study tour this year.

I urged him to complete the purchase of the Rome campus of ACU during his reign and to encourage the Sisters, who are to have one of their twice-a-year council meetings quite soon, by saying the university will look for another Rome campus if this one cannot be purchased from them. He agreed that other suitable buildings are likely to be available in Rome, but I know he is very attached to this spot. The role of a financially embattled Catholic University of America in all this is another complication, although Greg insisted that he had rock-solid support from chairman and council for the Rome campus as central to the university's long-term strategy.

I asked him to pass on my thanks to his son Thomas for his splendid and encouraging letter. Greg has an extension on his term so that he is to finish at the end of 2022, *Deo volente*. His appointment as vice-chancellor was providential for ACU, and I continue to maintain, with no opposition expressed by my hearers, that the arrival of Notre Dame University in Sydney made the ACU powers (that be at that time) realise that a top-quality appointment was necessary for them to compete.

Only today I received letters from the Michigan Mercy Sisters in Sydney, with Sr M. Julian telling me about the excellent philosophy units she is teaching at Notre Dame (which has the best philosophy course, i.e., of the *philosophia perennis*, in Australia). Another letter is from a Notre Dame graduate who is to fly to the US for her postulancy in the Order. She was not practising her faith when she started at Notre Dame (she had not practised since the whole family lapsed during her primary school years), underwent a conversion, and is now profoundly grateful for the professional and religious benefits she received there.

The end of Psalm 28 speaks to us.

> *The Lord is the strength of his people,*
> *a fortress of salvation for his anointed one.*
> *Save your people and bless your inheritance;*
> *be their shepherd and carry them forever.*

Tuesday, 10 September 2019

The major event of the day was the visit of Sr Mary for our small paraliturgy, when she brings me Holy Communion. The small service she uses follows the elements of the Mass, omitting, of course, the Offertory Prayers and most of the Eucharistic Prayer, except the Our Father. It is a consolation.

The longer I am in jail, the more I miss being able to celebrate Mass or even attend Mass. Yesterday, news came through that Danny Frawley, captain of the St Kilda football team for nine years and a successful Richmond coach, died in an unfortunate car crash. He had previously suffered from depression. I knew him as a friendly teenager from my Ballarat years and especially when I was at Bungaree parish in 1984. His uncle Maurie was one of my closest friends, and my first cousin Msgr Henry Nolan was a firm friend of Danny's father, Brian. I arranged for Kartya to ask Peter Tellefson to ask Connie Powell to pass on to the family my sympathy and prayers. I so much regretted not being able to offer Mass for the repose of his soul and the consolation of his family. My own poor prayers are so inadequate in comparison with the Eucharist. May he rest in peace.

Mary did not have much news, although she has been unsuccessful in her attempts to obtain permission to cut my hair. She spoke with Selisky, but even he had to refer it upstairs. On top of this, they are reluctant to allow a prisoner to cut my hair in case he attacks me, according to Mary. The Australia-wide prison chaplains' conference had gone well, and Archbishop Comensoli attended the dinner and spoke. He promised he would say Mass at each of the eleven jails in the Melbourne Archdiocese, with Mary wondering whether he knows there are so many!

The non-event of the day was the cancellation of my time in the gymnasium because they were changing the door which opens on a basketball court. I am not sure whether this is the internal one I use or another outside. The extra exercise is good for me, and it is another hour outside my cell. Sr Mary feels strongly that I need a bit more human company, and I agree, provided the company is not hostile.

I spoke to the Tobins this morning to hear that Finnis' article has been posted on *Quadrant* online[3] and will appear in the printed October issue. Terry hopes for a decision on the eligibility to appeal sometime this year and, like everyone else, simply does not know when a hearing might follow.

It was a pleasant day, a bit overcast, for both my morning and afternoon sessions in the second exercise pen.

I spent some hours moving through the letters and still have about twenty left for tomorrow. Unlike most of my mail on other occasions, the US is the major source followed by Australia and then France. Letters come regularly from Britain and Ireland.

Fr Luke Joseph teaches Hebrew and Greek in the Wagga seminary and is parish priest of the small parish of Ladysmith. He is a deeply spiritual man, plainspoken and capable once in a while of being quite wrong, but not on this occasion. It was a wise, if blunt, letter.

As I am not suffering under the Nazis or the Communists and my situation is different, "there is less chance for vainglory as a result", he opined. He pointed out that writers of other periods had spoken of Jesus' shame and that I shared in this (this is a bit too generous). He continued, "You are suffering because of who you are and what you have stood for. In that sense you are suffering for your Catholic faith." I believe this is a fair and accurate comment, but not the whole truth.

He then went on to talk of that passage in chapter 2 of Paul's First Letter to the Corinthians, where Paul explained that the masters of this age had not known God's wisdom and crucified Jesus. Luke had long thought Paul was speaking of the Jewish leaders, but

---

[3] John Finnis, "Where the Pell Judgment Went Fatally Wrong", *Quadrant* Online, 9 September 2019, https://quadrant.org.au/opinion/qed/2019/09/where-the-pell-judgment-went -fatally-wrong/.

some commentators think he was speaking of the devils. The devils thought they were defeating Jesus by having him killed, but, in fact, they were doing what God required for Jesus' triumph and our salvation. "The same can be said in your case. What the devil might be doing out of hatred is turned by God to your benefit and to the benefit of the church." I might be helping the Church in Australia more by being imprisoned than I did when I was bishop and archbishop, he concluded.

God's ways are not our ways, and I only hope that, with greater or lesser enthusiasm, I can conform to God's will.

At the Annunciation, when Gabriel announced God's plan to Mary, she replied,

I am the Lord's servant. May your will be done.

Wednesday, 11 September 2019

Today was a beautiful early spring day: clear skies, but a bit nippy for both my outside excursions. I also managed an hour in the gymnasium, where I was able to hit 100-plus shots forehand and backhand once or twice without an error. Feeling very pleased with myself, I increased the gradient on the treadmill and the frequency of the thigh and arm exercises. I felt a bit sore around my right shoulder and under the arch of my right foot afterward, but I returned to my court shoes, with insoles, and laced them tightly. I suspect all this is of no account, but it probably shows I am close to the exercise limits for my aged body. Another possibility is that the right shoulder and arm might have been provoked by my table tennis prowess.

Some excitement in the unit this morning as the regular and usually subdued shouter turned vocal in a big way, shouting repetitive obscenities. The f-word was not only the refrain at the end of each verse, but punctuated the verses, also. Apparently, he was furious with some decision announced to him this morning; and when I went down to the gym, the squad were donning gas masks, and a towel had been placed at the foot of my cell door and all the other cells doors, presumably. No dogs had arrived by the time I was leaving, and all was quiet on my return. One doesn't ask anything more, but he was probably shifted.

Mr Harris went to bat at some senior meeting for me to receive a haircut, and his proposal, which was accepted, was that one of the nursing staff cut my hair, as has been done for other prisoners. I quickly responded that I thought all this was a good way forward. We shall see.

I am in two minds on how much I should push for a change of situation. It would help if I were able to have a couple of hours in the garden a couple of times a week. I don't know what it would be like elsewhere, as the guards here are regularly courteous, and I don't know what difference any request of mine would make. One of the two bosses might be tempted to enjoy my difficulties; but their first concern is my physical safety, and I don't know how to assess this.

I heard from Sr Sean Marie, who was with me in Rome, who has just been appointed as mistress of the seven postulants they [Sisters of Mercy in Alma, Michigan] have at the moment. An important role, and I believe she will do it well.

One regular correspondent informed me that Our Lady had appeared to five different visionaries proclaiming my innocence. I don't know how many, if any, of these events are truly supernatural, but I don't rule such a possibility out of court. In any event, whatever their status, it is better that these visionaries do not believe I am guilty. Life is stranger than we can suppose, as some distinguished scientist (Medawar?)[4] once explained.

I received a most encouraging note from a young Scot in Glasgow, who did his postgraduate studies in Sydney in 2010–2012 and who came regularly to the Sunday Mass at the cathedral. I remember speaking to him a number of times there and once in Glasgow, and he reminded me of another meeting at Domus Australia in Rome. He believes in my innocence, after studying the evidence, is grateful for what he received from the Catholic youth scene in Sydney, and assured me that many of his friends are praying for me, as he is.

A Pentecostal pastor from Hoppers Crossing wrote me a second letter of encouragement, explaining that, while "innocence before God is the most important thing, it is still vitally important for you

---

[4] Peter Medawar (1915–1987) was a British biologist, a Nobel laureate, and an author. He was known to admire and quote the British-Indian scientist J.B.S. Haldane, who famously said, "My own suspicion is that the universe is not only queerer than we suppose, but queerer than we *can* suppose."

and the community that you fight on to the High Court until justice is finally served." I agree with both propositions.

A couple of people have again sent me copies of St Teresa of Ávila's prayer that "God alone suffices", with one of them reminding me of her complaint to God after her most recent mishap when she fell in the mud: "If this is the way you treat your friends, it is no wonder you have so few." I have a foolish urge to add, "But I didn't say this—just quoted it!"

We must always remember God is good and do our duty, as David reminds us in Psalm 30.

> *Sing the praises of the Lord, you his faithful people;*
> *praise his holy name.*

Thursday, 12 September 2019

Today I didn't achieve as much as I hoped. They are giving me longer periods outside in the morning and afternoon, and this is a factor. The time in the sunlight is welcome, especially with weather like this morning, which was clear and crisp.

An unexpected phone hook-up with the lawyers Kartya and Paul this morning at 8:30 am. The submission has been drafted by Ruth and is awaiting Walker's changes and approval. They anticipate giving me this final draft tomorrow or Monday, and they hope to lodge the appeal on Tuesday or Wednesday. The prosecution then has three weeks to lodge its response. I asked Paul whether you can ask for bail when appealing to the High Court, with the unspoken underlying question as to whether it would be wise to ask. If little or nothing could be gained by such a request, what might be lost? Paul guessed the High Court would be able to grant bail given the extent of their powers, but could not comment beyond this.

I am still keen for 1000–1 and 1,000,000–1 against the odds to be quoted, and in the morning I attempted to phone Tim O'Leary to contact Michael Casey for Franklin's response.[5] As Tim was

---

[5] James Franklin is an Australian mathematician, philosopher, and historian of ideas. He is a professor at the University of New South Wales and the author of *The Science of Conjecture: Evidence and Probability before Pascal.*

unavailable, I phoned Chris Meney and established contact with my second call. "What is the methodology you used?" I asked, explaining that I understood arriving at 1000–1 against for ten factors with a 50 percent probability, but I couldn't arrive at 1,000,000–1 against for 25 percent probability.

Chris, whose first degree was in science, explained that it was simply a question of multiplying the one-in-four possibility ten times. My mistake had been to double the one-in-four each time rather than quadrupling it. At any rate, in this way, on the tenth step, the odds are more than 1,000,000–1 against. As I understand it, the methodology is very simple and uncontroversial. In the afternoon, I left a message explaining all this for Kartya and repeating my claim that these odds deserve at least a footnote! The methodology is so simple that I feel somewhat embarrassed for asking expert advice.

Fr Mark Withoos[6] called at my new Thursday visiting time of 2:30 pm, although my period in the garden immediately beforehand has not yet materialized. He looked well and in good spirits, reassuring me, when I explained that I was concerned for his future, that he had a good number of options. He had been up to see Margaret for a brief visit and found her well, if a little slow.

He spoke of developments in the Vatican, where a new external auditor has been appointed (who will be no good/use, he hastened to assure me), said that Batman and Robin would be gone from APSA[7] (although neither of us was clear on the identity of Batman or his helper), and claimed that Pentin has written another article on the Vatican's London investments,[8] while, most importantly, the pope has expressed publicly his concern over a €70 million loss over the last two years in the Vatican. If my earlier reports remain correct, this would be a significant understatement, perhaps explained by taking more revenue from Peter's Pence. In any event, it does not bode well.

I made sure Mark understood my fundamental trial point about the inability of the miscreants being in the sacristy at the time of their rape and the importance of the odds dealing with the ten issues. I was and remain keen that my supporters and friends are informed and consoled by this information.

[6] Fr Mark Withoos was Cardinal Pell's personal secretary in the Vatican.
[7] The Administration of the Patrimony of the Apostolic See (APSA) handles the Vatican's real estate and financial assets.
[8] Edward Pentin is the Rome correspondent for the *National Catholic Register*.

Another piece of disconcerting news was that a mutual priest friend is considering leaving the priesthood. I hope this does not come about. I am not sure why he is unhappy and uncertain about his vocation.

After lunch, I tidied up the final version of the family prayer my niece Georgie had requested. I will be interested in her reaction and will include the text in tomorrow's journal.

We do not live as though there is no tomorrow. We live and act as we love the many good things God has created, but remembering the final judgement we must pass and our final abode in the peace of God's presence. Today's readings have a responsory from John's First Epistle.

We are now God's children, but it is not yet clear what we shall become; all we know is that when Christ appears, we shall become like him, because we shall see him as he really is.

Friday, 13 September 2019

Today is the feast of St John Chrysostom, archbishop of Constantinople (d. 407), the "golden mouth", a great preacher and writer, part of an extraordinary flowering of talent in both Eastern and Western Christianity at that time. He died from exhaustion while in exile, expelled from his archdiocese. He was a tad outspoken and accused of comparing Empress Eudoxia[9] to Jezebel, a comparison which was not appreciated.

I sent off a number of letters today, one to Claudio Veliz on the death of Maria Isabel and one to my niece Georgie with the family prayer she requested, whose text follows.

God our Father, may we always thank you for the good things we have received.

Keep our faith strong so that we know you love us and believe that Jesus your Son, our Brother and Saviour, taught us what is important in daily life.

---

[9] Aelia Eudoxia (d. 404) was a Roman empress by marriage to Emperor Arcadius and mother of the future Emperor Theodosius II.

Keep us all together, young and old, in sickness and in health,
> even when we are apart.

Help us to continue to be strong and principled and persevere
> in love through every hardship.

Teach us to repent of our sins, to look beyond our differences
> and to forgive our enemies.

> We realise this is hard and pray for strength.

As the years pass, and especially when we are suffering, may we
> always strive for peace and goodness,

> so that we can be with You forever in the happiness of heaven.

Our Lady of the Southern Cross, pray for us.

St Mary of the Cross MacKillop, pray for us.

A quiet day, somewhat overcast for both my exercise sessions. No copy of the draft appeal arrived, although Patrick Santamaria and Nicholas O'Bryan[10] called on a social visit to inform me of the negotiations on a victim of Br X's. It is an ambit claim, where I seem to be peripheral, as X is a Christian Brother, who in this case offended in Melbourne.

Twenty or thirty letters still remained to be opened. The unit is fairly quiet, with only one muted complainant.

One Sydney regular wrote in to tell me of a lapsed Catholic who stormed into the office of a Catholic workmate, announcing, "I'm so angry about what they have done to Cardinal Pell I've gone back to Mass." Please God, she will continue if my appeal is successful. *Deo gratias.*

Another encouraging letter came from my long-term friend Michael Costigan, writer, ex-propagandist [Pontificio Collegio Urbano de Propaganda Fide in Rome], and former priest, who explained, or at least replied, to a devout Catholic woman in his retirement complex, who wondered how so many prayers were ineffective in my case. "God does not necessarily answer our prayers in the way we hope or expect or understand. Sometimes the answer comes in different ways. Perhaps on this occasion the answer came in the outstanding dissenting judgement of Judge Weinberg." God certainly writes straight with crooked lines.

---

[10] Patrick Santamaria and Nicholas O'Bryan are both solicitors with Galbally & O'Bryan, which has represented Cardinal Pell and other Catholic clerics.

Most of my letters are from people I do not know, although many from among the thousands are from friends and acquaintances.

I am proud of my contribution in Vox Clara[11] and grateful for the opportunity to contribute. A priest from Great Falls in Virginia was very generous. "Under your guidance at Vox Clara, you reorganized ICEL and produced a vastly superior translation of the Mass. The Mass and its rich theology may be the only way we will navigate through these desperate times.

"Now you are an involuntary monk, unjustly locked up in a secular monastery (well, I'm trying to put a nice spin on the things)." It was Pope Benedict who reminded me of the crucial role of bad, unworshipful and superficial, liturgy in the decline of faith and discipline and the spread of doctrinal and moral confusion. We have seen a considerable improvement in many parts of Australia in this area, even if Melbourne has slipped somewhat.

Geelong defeated West Coast in the AFL semifinal in a tough, typical finals match; and when I went to bed just after midnight, the Australian Test batsmen, apart from Marnus Labuschagne and of course Steve Smith, were departing regularly for miserable scores.

Psalm 68 is my prayer today.

> *This is a prayer to you,*
> *my prayer for your favour.*
> *In your great love, answer me, O God,*
> *with your help that never fails;*
> *rescue me from sinking in the mud;*
> *save me from my foes.*

Saturday, 14 September 2019

Today is the feast of the Exaltation of the Cross, a central element in the redemption. It is of course one thing to believe we are redeemed

---

[11] The Vox Clara Committee on English Liturgical Texts works with English translations of Latin liturgical texts so that they accord with the norms of the Church expressed in *Liturgiam authenticam* (28 March 2001) by the Congregation for Divine Worship and the Discipline of the Sacraments.

by the Lord's suffering and death, the necessary prelude to the Resurrection; another thing to believe that human suffering, my suffering,
can be made fruitful and redemptive through Christ's suffering; and
another thing, indeed, to embrace this. Our consolation is that the
Lord, at the prospect of his extreme suffering and when confronting
the mystery of evil, wished that he did not have to continue. Naturally,
many of the letters I receive console me with talk of Jesus' sufferings.

A beautiful day; warming up, so that I am not wearing my green
prison top, given that I have my white prison-issue T-shirt over my
singlet and under my shirt.

Obtained my hour in the gymnasium, and my progress continues, not spectacularly, but with small steps. I managed to score five
underhand basketball goals and increased the gradient again on the
treadmill. I am still fascinated by the improvements I can make with
practice, both physically and intellectually. My Sudoku expertise is
improving, though still at a low level, and even my ability to create
words from a set number of letters has improved.

When I was outside this morning, I managed to speak with Terry
Tobin on the new cheap landline Bernadette has arranged. Apparently, the High Court has handed down a judgement in the last couple of days, quashing the conviction of a murder suspect, condemned
on uncorroborated evidence. Terry informed my legal team, who
were grateful. Apparently, some legal luminary said that the claim
of this freed man was not as strong as my case. Terry also informed
me that he had sent my two documents to Finnis, who said that I had
got there before him (on exactly what point I am not sure). Terry also
was kind enough to say that "Entirely Possible" was accessible to the
general reader and could be understood.

I managed to speak with Ruth, as Michael was out, and she too
had heard the good news of the High Court's recent ruling. She said
that when someone sent a Supreme Court judge a copy of Finnis'
article, the judge said that was the third copy he had received.

Margaret answered her phone in hospital and was quite lucid,
explaining how she had rebuked Withoos for wearing his soutane
when he visited with Charlie and John Walshe. The ulcers on her
feet are bad, although the doctor was pleased with some improvement, and the itch has diminished, perhaps as a result of tablets. I
promised to phone tomorrow.

Fr John O'Neill, the redoubtable parish priest of Doonside, wrote to tell me of the ordination of Fr Jack Green, a former server in the parish. Three more servers are in fourth year in the seminary, and another has been accepted to begin at the end of this year. Remarkable fruit from a remarkable parish.

Eden Langlands, a Canberra seminarian and now one of the senior students at Good Shepherd Seminary, sent me a fine and well-crafted letter on behalf of the student body. He is a good friend, and I was very grateful.

Our muted shouter can be a much louder banger (on the door), but he is episodic, and we are not disturbed regularly or for any long time in the evening.

When I went to bed, I dipped into *The Oarsmen* by Scott Patterson, the story of the AIF veterans who won the 1919 Kings Cup at the Henley Peace Regatta against crews from the other Allied nations and Cambridge and Oxford Universities. To my faint surprise, I am thoroughly enjoying it as it recounts the stories of the Aussie crew members before, during, and after the Great War.

A couple of verses from the evening prayer in today's breviary are appropriate.

> *From bitter death and barren wood*
> *The tree of life is made;*
> *Its branches bear unfailing fruit*
> *And leaves that never fade.*
> *O faithful Cross, you stand unmoved*
> *While ages run their course;*
> *Foundation of the universe,*
> *Creation's binding force.*

WEEK 30

High Stakes at the High Court

15 September—21 September 2019

Sunday, 15 September 2019

This Sunday was unusual for a couple of reasons. I slept in and did not wake until *Mass for You at Home* was almost over, and when I rose to watch Joseph Prince and Joel Osteen, these were both lost to a live coverage of what was billed as the largest Australian marathon: forty thousand ran in Sydney today, but I did not watch their progress.

Hymns of Praise was based around an elderly group of women pilgrims walking the Cleveland Way in northeast England. It featured the Cistercian Rievaulx Abbey, which I visited with Chris Meney, when Jessica was teaching near York. Destroyed, of course, by that terrible Henry VIII and home at one time to six hundred monks, it was a centre of worship, culture, and commerce for four hundred years, founded in 1132. I suspect at least one of the churches where the community hymn-singing was filmed was Catholic, as they featured a couple of sentimental favourites from the last thirty to forty years, such as "For the Beauty of the Earth".

The weather was not as good as yesterday's, being overcast during my two outings and spitting rain in the afternoon. I took a quasi-siesta sitting in the chair, managed to get through to both Margaret and Tim O'Leary in the afternoon and to Michael Casey in the morning. No important news items, except that Friel has turned his energies on the legal proceedings, probably on the two Appeal Court judgements. He has unusual time and energy as well as formidable insight.

I spent a few hours moving through the letters, consoling as always. Naturally, many of them were from Australia, but a goodly number came from the United States and, surprisingly, from France. Articulate defences of my innocence have received wide distribution. As there was another bunch of thirty to forty delivered this morning, some still remain to be read tomorrow.

No sign of the draft appeal, which might have been delayed by the ruling of the High Court last week. I hope it arrives tomorrow.

One of my most frequent correspondents, and among the best theologians in that group, is involved in teaching the theology of the body. She expressed her admiration for the writings of Cardinals Arinze and Sarah,[1] saying that theirs is exactly what she needs as she is "living in a deceptively comfortable culture that can put the faith to sleep if I'm not diligent".

She then went to the heart of the struggle for the family, which I fear could be a harder struggle than the battle for the faith. Faith and family are intimately connected for most of us, and it is hard to know which is the chicken and which is the egg for both belief and unbelief. "We will never really reform the family in the world until we reclaim the genuine spirituality of the family, grounded in the Genesis story. It's like St John Paul gave the key to the treasure, but we threw it away and are trying to open the chest with a back hoe."

Letters of support come in regularly from priests in Australia, but also from priests in the US, Britain, Ireland, and France.

SBS had coverage of another large pro-life rally in Hyde Park [Sydney], where Archbishop Fisher spoke, together with Tony Abbott and Barnaby Joyce.[2] All three "grabs" shown were effective, on song [striking the right note], aimed at removing the worst extremes allowed by the bill.

I was searching for a prayer to end this entry today when I opened a letter from my most frequent Mentone correspondent, who believes that I will be fully exonerated "in the Lord's time" and that the Lord gave her Psalm 63 to encourage her. David is hard on his enemies but has some beautiful lines about God.

---

[1] Francis Cardinal Arinze (b. 1932 in Nigeria) was prefect of the Congregation for Divine Worship and the Discipline of the Sacraments from 2002 to 2008 and is cardinal bishop of Velletri-Segni. Robert Cardinal Sarah (b. 1945 in Guinea) has been Prefect of the Congregation for Divine Worship and the Discipline of the Sacraments since 2014.

[2] Formerly a leader of the National Party and a deputy prime minister, Barnaby Joyce is a member of the Australian Parliament.

Thus all my life I bless you;
in your name I lift my hands in prayer.
I am satisfied as with a rich feast,
and there is a shout of praise from my lips.
I call you to mind on my bed
and meditate on you in night watches,
for you have been my help
and I am safe in the shadows of your wings.

Monday, 16 September 2019

While I was outside walking and saying my rosary some time after 9:00 am, word came that I had a professional visit. It was Kartya, on her way to court, who came to give me a copy of the draft submission to the High Court. She had to leave quickly, so I started reading through it as I sat outside on a nice morning. Not a clear sky, as there had been heavy rain overnight, but not too bad. The document is closely written and tightly argued in legal language. I was delighted to discover that the knock-out blow was on the last page, where my point was laid out that the miscreants could not be in the sacristy under attack while they were still processing along the outside of the cathedral.

I then returned to my cell and worked methodically through the twelve pages of text which are allowed, preparing notes for the promised visit of Ruth and Kartya in the afternoon.

This was not quite finished when I was called for my midday meeting with Chris and Mary Clare Meney and their daughter Brigid. Chris and Mary Clare leave for a fortnight in Ireland on next Thursday. Chris, and indeed all the family, have been marvellous supporters all through this grim business. All the family are well. They, too, were pleased by the second successful pro-life rally in Sydney on Sunday.

Chris informed me that Michael Casey was dealing with Prof James Franklin, mathematician and scientist, on the compounding improbabilities from the ten factors mentioned by Weinberg. Chris had explained the time constraints, as they propose to hand in the appeal on Wednesday, and he anticipated a page would be delivered to Kartya in time.

Kartya explained that this had not happened as Franklin was concerned about the level of probability to be assigned to each factor, which was not my request. I repeated that what we needed was an agreed methodology for calculating the odds when the factors were placed together. I agree that the probability levels are controversial, but we can assign those conservatively. Later, after the Meney visit, I phoned Chris to confirm the limited nature of my request, saying that I simply wanted the methodology for a 50 percent probability and a 25 percent probability for all ten factors.

Ruth is reluctant to include any stats even in the notes, claiming, first, that it would be only an opinion. We agreed that mathematical conclusions are not opinions, but the levels of probability assigned to each factor are controversial designations or opinions. I repeated that I will work to progress the matter further—as I did with my phone call to Chris. Ruth also stated that she thought it would contribute new and inadmissible evidence.

I have little or no expertise on the criteria for legal admissibility, but I do know the effect in the media of a crisp, comprehensible argument or example. Everyone understands that if the odds are 1000–1 against, then there must be grounds for reasonable doubt; and if the odds are anywhere near 1,000,000–1 against, we have a jackpot.

A detailed examination of the majority judgement, which reverses the onus of proof, requiring the defence to prove that I am innocent, shows the extent of their incompetence. A retired senior judge said that the majority judgement was a disaster and the composition of the three-person juridical panel was a disgrace, while Ruth agreed with me that the majority case was more vulnerable than the prosecution case, not least by their identifying when the five- to six-minute interval occurred after Mass. They ignored Boyce's[3] concession at the appeal that the alb could not be parted, while at other times conceding to the defence more than to the prosecution. On occasion and by their own logic and conclusions on the evidence, they were unable to exclude reasonable doubt, as they claimed to do.

In the afternoon, I phoned Terry Tobin to tell him how pleased I am with the draft. Psalm 72 outlines the consequences of a bleak alternative.

---

[3] Chris Boyce is the senior counsel representing the prosecution.

How useless to keep my heart pure
and wash my hands in innocence,
when I was stricken all day long,
suffered punishment day after day.

Then I said: "If I should speak like that,
I should abandon the faith of your people."

Tuesday, 17 September 2019

The big news of the day was that the appeal to the High Court has been lodged. When I phoned the lawyers' office during my afternoon exercise, Sam passed on Kartya's message that it had been lodged with the court and she was now delivering a copy to the prosecution. When Sam answered that he hadn't read the documents, in response to my question, I took pleasure in emphasising to him that it is a splendid piece of work. The language and argumentation are legal, and it is not written for a newspaper, but its length and quality mean that it will be very useful for those interested and especially for my helpers and supporters.

Tonight, as I was watching the SBS news, it was announced that the appeal had been lodged. I am not sure whether the text will become, or should become, public, but I would welcome this, if it were legally appropriate.

In the evening after watching the SBS feature on Oxford as the royal capital during the English Civil War (1640–1649), I reread the appeal, which confirmed my estimate of its quality. One sad truth about the Civil War which I had not known was that the death rate in the British population was higher than in the First World War, worsted only by the Black Death. Muskets replaced the long bow for the first time, and most of those wounded died later through poisoning.

The gossip, which I believe was accurate in this case, was that St John Paul II, after he was shot, started to deteriorate from poisoning, but was saved by the intervention of a gunshot wounds specialist whom Cardinal O'Connor had contacted in New York and who flew into Rome quietly and did his good work without any publicity, and our great pope survived.

Sr Mary called for our paraliturgy and Holy Communion, and I brought her up to date with the news on the appeal and with the fact that nothing had changed in my own situation, except that they were arranging for me to chat with another elderly prisoner from Ballarat who will remain unseen in the next pen. I wonder how soon we can change this, if the chats go well.

I enjoyed my hour in the gymnasium, once again increasing my work rate slightly on the treadmill. More importantly, on one occasion, I hit an unbroken run of more than 200 table-tennis shots, which is a spectacular advance on my uncoordinated beginnings.

No new batch of letters arrived today, which enabled me to read and file into different piles all the letters received previously.

A couple of intercessions from today's morning prayer focussed my thoughts appropriately.

Our sufferings bring acceptance, acceptance brings hope: and our hope will not deceive us, for the Spirit has been poured into our hearts. It is through the same Spirit that we pray:
— Stay with us, Lord, on our journey.

Help us to realise that our troubles are slight and short-lived; they are nothing compared with the joy we shall have when we reach our home with you:
— Stay with us, Lord, on our journey.

Wednesday, 18 September 2019

The day was marked by the response to the lodging of the appeal. Early in the day, Chris Meney mentioned that the Australian legal writer Chris Merritt had written a trenchant article, broadly supportive of the appeal and pointing out the high stakes for both sides and for the Victorian legal system which follow from the outcome.[4]

Later in the day, Terry Tobin read me the article over the phone. I was encouraged. One consequence, however, is that the higher the stakes, the higher the pressure to close ranks and not embarrass the Victorian system. Please God, there will be enough integrity

---

[4] Chris Merritt, "A State's System of Justice Put on Trial", *Australian*, 18 September 2019.

in the High Court to avoid the sell-out that occurred in the Court of Appeal.

I wonder what Maxwell thought he was doing when he wrote such a shoddy piece as the majority verdict. How could he be so ignorant on a basic point such as the onus of proof? Did he have no regard for his reputation, for the fact that criminal law was not his area of expertise? As an archbishop, I had to speak on many topics where I was not an expert, so I worked to understand and justify what I would say publicly. I knew the limits of my knowledge and understanding, and generally I would run what I proposed to say past some expert. In this way, I picked up a goodly number of errors.

Terry was inclined to think Maxwell wanted one particular result and overestimated his capacity to achieve and justify this rationally. It is evidence of rot and incompetence at the heart of a state system when two senior judges of the Victorian Supreme Court err so publicly and, I dare say, so stupidly.

I am still keen to explore the possibility of asking for bail from the High Court, so I gave Terry and his senior legal friends three questions to ask. Is there any possibility such a request would succeed? Could making the request have damaging legal consequences for the appeal itself? Would such a request be stupid? Terry suggested that the High Court might refer the request back to the Victorian Court of Appeal. "To Maxwell?" I asked.

Had a couple of outings in the pen and an hour in the gymnasium, where a friendly guard allowed me to use a basketball, which other wardens claim is only allowed on Saturday. My table-tennis improvement continued, so that I had an unbroken run of 120 to 130 on the forehand. I toughened up the treadmill conditions slightly while lessening the weight for my thigh exercises and increasing the number of movements. My thighs are strengthening, so that I can rise from a regular chair without using my arms. This represents substantial progress comparable to my being able to walk up a flight of thirty-plus stairs with no pain in my knees. My balance has also improved so that I do not need to hold onto the bannister as I ascend. I am a little less adventurous when I descend, as there is much farther to fall, but I can descend without the help of the bannister.

I am writing this up at lunchtime, Thursday, as the time slipped past me with my Sudoku and penning a short note to James Gargasoulas, who is moving his cell to the other side of mine. He mentioned that he might be moving to another jail or facility.

Watched the SBS evening news as always, then Tony Robinson[5] as he completed his walk at the mouth of the Thames, then a double feature on the bomb attack in Kenya prior to September 11. Heaven only knows how close to the facts the film is, as I know nothing about the Kenyan bombing of the US embassy, but I can say the account has an air of verisimilitude.

Most of the daily batch of letters was read.

It is always useful for us, as it was for the Jews, to realise the strength and importance of God's providence.

> *It is you, my King, my God,*
> *who granted victories to Jacob.*

Thursday, 19 September 2019

It was a beautiful day when I was outside in the exercise pen this morning, although Sydney yesterday had 100 millimetres of rain (more than four inches for all Imperial Measure types like myself), and more is expected today. Unfortunately, not much fell on the dry inland areas, where some or many farms have been without income for three years.

Two wardens just knocked at the door to inform me Michael Gallacher and Michael Buck[6] had arrived and they were not on my list. They were happy to take off a couple of names so they would be able to see me. I believed I had put them on the list—mistakenly. When I checked, I found they were on Kartya's last list, which was still to be put into my visitors' file. I was checking an old and incompatible file! A bad mistake, but one these wardens were prepared to correct. A kind gesture.

By a coincidence, I had just prepared a new list for the coming weeks, so Sarah my niece and Tim O'Leary would be reinstated on the visitors' list.

---

[5] Tony Robinson, an actor and television presenter, walked the River Thames in Great Britain 200 miles from its source to the sea, exploring its history and influence.

[6] Both men are priests in the Archdiocese of Melbourne.

After a few quiet days in the unit, the worst recent shouter and banger and a somewhat less vocal companion have returned, after being I know not where for a couple of days. I think he is the same chap who rigorously denounced me, but he is more noisy than anguished and so less distressing, and he rarely if ever continues the commotion late into the night.

It was about 9:00 pm last night when I remembered that I had not taken a shower. I will work hard to avoid repeating this mistake, but all my prayers were said—and the three spells of exercise taken. To err is human, and to err more frequently goes, in my case at least, with ageing.

Another batch of letters arrived this morning, and the mess-up over the visitor negotiation reminds me that those letters in the penultimate piles have to be filed properly.

I have just spent twenty minutes outside. It was still a lovely afternoon, with a few more clouds than this morning; the building which is being constructed (the new police headquarters?) nearby has risen about eight stories during my nearly seven months in the klink. I wonder how many more stories will be built before I leave jail, or leave Unit 8.

The shouter was at the top of his form while I took my afternoon exercise, arguing fiercely with his mate; but his invective had not been enhanced by his spell away, being as repetitive and predictable as ever.

A great three-quarters of an hour with the newly ordained Fr Michael Buck, who lavished blessings on me from the most distinguished Anglophone saints, and Fr Michael Gallacher. They filled in with news that I had not heard, e.g., that Matthew Baldwin[7] was now working in the Secretariat for the Synod, an unlikely alliance. Apparently, he was asked to go there, despite the foreseen difficulties, as an "oblation". Charlie Portelli is the new secretary of the Melbourne Council of Priests with Brendan Reid as chairman. The clergy meeting for the archdiocese in Torquay was concluding today; Gallacher left early to visit me, and apparently there was the occasional moment of excitement as most of the attendees are young and orthodox clergy. One or two of the old perennials,

[7] Matthew Baldwin is a Melbourne priest who did his doctoral studies in Rome.

such as Paul Connell, experienced moments of light turbulence. With God's blessing, both of these priests should do fine work for the Church.

In the morning, I phoned to wish Judy and Bec well for their cruise out of New York. Bec was at school, but I accomplished my mission. To my delight, Georgie was also delighted with my family prayer, which has most of the Kerygma, describing it as "brilliant". *Deo gratias*. I asked them to call in at St Patrick's Cathedral in New York to pass on my best wishes and thanks (for his letters) to Cardinal Tim Dolan.

Psalm 43 reminds us what we owe the good God.

> *No sword of their own won the land;*
> *no arm of their own brought them victory.*
> *It was your right hand, your arm*
> *and the light of your face: for you loved them.*

Friday, 20 September 2019

A big day. Too many things happening, none of them particularly important in the history of salvation—haircut, arrival of letters and articles, and preliminary final of AFL between Richmond and Geelong.

Before breakfast, Mr Harris announced that a prisoner would arrive to cut my hair—an early and unexpected arrival because he was being shifted to another jail location today.

He was a young, slight, tattooed, and pleasant fellow, whose name might have been something like Mos, although one warden later claimed he was called Barak. My recall of names, unless repeated, is poor, so he might have been called Ross or Fothergill; but I don't think so.

He wasn't a professional barber, but he did a decent job, with Mr Harris providing some final pieces of advice. My sideburns are too long, but that is of minor importance. I remembered my smart-aleck response when altar servers would ask what I thought of their new haircut: "It's OK, but the face is the problem." I don't think anyone was badly offended.

A large batch of letters arrived, including one from Tim O'Leary, which contained John Finnis' reworked *Quadrant* article, Jeremy Gans' online "A Judge's Doubts", five articles on the appeal case by Christopher Friel, and sundry articles by, e.g., George Weigel, Raymond de Souza, and a typical and mordant piece by Fr George Rutler on "Penguin Dysphoria".

Apart from a break at lunch, when I watched the ABC *Garden Show*, I spent the remainder of the day until the evening news checking Finnis' published version and comparing it with the earlier version I had received, and then reading the Friel articles, typically dense while being as useful and insightful as ever.

Finnis' article will do a lot of good for my cause, and I was pleased and grateful that he had considerably reworked the Potter and sacristy sections. Terry mentioned that the published version was the fourth reworking. His is a now tighter impossibility version, and he devoted a paragraph to the impossibility of the miscreants being in the sacristy, being raped, while they are still in procession or breaking away, a topic which, he acknowledged, had not been treated explicitly in the appeal or earlier because of the ambiguity over when the five- to six-minute wait of sacristan Potter took place.

Frank Brennan noted that not one serious legal commentator had written in favour of the majority verdict. This speaks volumes.

The first preliminary final was a cracking game and brilliant spectacle, which Richmond eventually won comfortably after being 21 points behind at halftime. Tom Lynch kicked five goals. We might have seen the de facto grand final, as I believe these are the two best teams in the league.

I read my usual few chapters on the AIF crew preparing for the 1919 Royal Henley Peace Regatta. They have just rebelled against Steve Fairbairn, the very English Australian-born rower and squad coach, who was obliged to resign, ostensibly for reasons of age and health. The author made an interesting point, explaining that Fairbairn belonged to a rich pre–Great War generation of Protestant background, men and women who saw Britain as home. By way of digression, I had an aunt by marriage on my mother's Catholic side of the family, a wonderful lady, who talked of England as home until her death, about twenty years ago. She had only been to England a few times. Scott Patterson, the author, believed this Britain-first attitude changed radically with the men of the first AIF during the war, so that their first allegiance was to Australia.

My good friend the late Bishop Bill Brennan of Wagga made a parallel point, claiming that the old Protestant versus Catholic bitterness was never the same after the shared suffering of the war and after many Protestant men had met a Catholic priest for the first time in the Catholic military chaplains, who were highly respected by the end of the war due to their good work across the board. Some closing lines from Psalm 51:

> *Give me again the joy of your help;*
> *with a spirit of fervour sustain me,*
> *that I may teach transgressors your ways*
> *and sinners may return to you.*

Saturday, 21 September 2019

Another "busy" day by jail standards, with a second preliminary final in the AFL and a Rugby League final of some sort in which the Melbourne Storms beat the Parramatta Eels 32–0. And a documentary on Hitler.

Mr Harris was in charge today, so my morning and afternoon times in the exercise pen were somewhat longer than a half hour. The day was warm, but overcast, and it had rained before my afternoon outing; so we had the customary puddle in the first pen. I changed out of my green prison top because of the warmth in my cell, but I needed more than my shirt.

Had a good hour in the gymnasium with two chatty guards, who enabled me to have the customary Saturday basketball and to play table tennis. This double was a first. I eventually threw three goals underarm with the basketball and passed three hundred shots unbroken on my backhand in the table tennis and over a hundred on the forehand. I don't use my feet to move, so I would be rather useless in a game, given my slowness and poor balance. Boredom is a small price I pay on the treadmill, so I now hold on by alternating hands, with a change every minute. This improves my balance, helps pass the time, and still enables me to pray my aspirations sporadically. I am becoming stronger.

The Collingwood versus Great Western Sydney preliminary final was not a great spectacle, and the first half was the lowest scoring first half since 1928. The Magpies came home very strongly in the last quarter, which began with them about five goals down, but fell four points short. The grand final will be very different from a Richmond-Collingwood clash, the two clubs with the largest following. West Sydney would not average 15,000 spectators a match in Sydney. As someone who wrote off Richmond's chances of being premiers early in the season, I now believe the Tigers could crush the Giants on next Saturday. But the newcomers have surprised on two weekends in a row, so I hope they don't continue in that vein next week.

I watched the second half of the Rugby League final with my usual low level of enthusiasm.

The documentary on Hitler took us through to the mid-1920s, when he had consolidated his leadership of the Nazi party. A recent article in *First Things* claimed that the Nazis were worse than the Communists, being founded on hate rather than resentment, and also claimed they were more modern than what they saw as an old-fashioned Communism. This surprised me, although there is no enormous difference between them in their evil consequences. The Communists who switched sides in Germany to join the Nazi party were dubbed "roast beef" Nazis, because red inside and brown outside, just as one wing of the Greens were like watermelons, red inside.

I have heard recordings of Hitler speaking, and, despite my limited comprehension of German, I too was fascinated by the intensity and flow of language. Fr Con Finn, SJ, was an Irish Jesuit on the formation staff at Corpus Christi in Werribee, who had studied in Germany before the Second World War. On one occasion, he went to hear Hitler speak, intending to stay only briefly, but he remained there fascinated until the end. I wonder at what stage the spirit of evil entered into Hitler, and I would not be surprised if he had been actually in the possession of the devil. The twentieth century had more moral monsters than any other century, e.g., Hitler, Stalin, Lenin, Mao, Pol Pot, whose capacity for evil was increased exponentially by scientific and technological progress. And as scientific progress continues, the dark side will continue to draw on these forces to disastrous effect.

In times of trouble, we should always turn to the Lord, as Psalm 43 reminds us:

Awake, O Lord, why do you sleep?
Arise, do not reject us forever!
Why do you hide your face
and forget our oppression and misery? . . .

Stand up and come to our help!
Redeem us because of your love!

WEEK 31

Blessings of Sport

22 September—28 September 2019

Sunday, 22 September 2019

I woke up at eight minutes to 6 am and so was able to watch *Mass for You at Home* celebrated by Bishop Terry Curtin, who preached a sophisticated and appropriately nuanced sermon on how we cannot serve both God and money. They had one good hymn I didn't know, composed by the Australian Jesuit composer Christopher Willcock. Brad Roswell again did a reading, while the congregation was once again a small group of rather elderly women. I know the Mass transcends its surroundings, but the congregation betokens a church in decline.

Joseph Prince was a repeat of what was proclaimed a classic 2007 performance. I didn't realise he had been preaching for so long, and he does not seem to have aged much. The amphitheatre then was much smaller. He preached on Noah and his ark, which he described as a symbol of the Messiah. He claimed that Isaiah spoke of the suffering Messiah, but I doubt if this is correct. Isaiah certainly spoke of the suffering servant, but I don't believe even he linked the Messiah to suffering, much less a redemptive death. Even in 2007, Joseph was snappily dressed with a couple of rings and a couple of pendants from the chain around his neck, visible because of his open-neck shirt. Once again, it was a good Christocentric sermon.

Joel Osteen spoke of the woman who was a hoarder with a house full of trash which the civic authorities forced her to throw out. Our hearts and minds and souls can also be submerged by guilt and worry, etc., but God calls each of us to be a masterpiece, wonderfully made.

Only God can give us beauty for ashes. It was only once at the end of the half-hour sermon that the word "repentance" was mentioned. Even God cannot do much with our guilt if we refuse to repent, although he always loves us. Sin does not get much of a run, either, in these sermons.

When I discovered the *Compass* program was about the first Anglican clergyman to take a same-sex partner, I decided to switch the TV off and wait for *Hymns of Praise*, which featured Whitby Abbey, where the English bishops decided to follow the Roman, not the Celtic, dating for Easter at a synod in 664. Apparently, St Hilda from the nearby convent, who was in charge of both the men and the women in the monastery, according to the narrator, was influential in the synod, also. I didn't realise that Captain Cook was born in Whitby, nor did I realise he was heavily influenced by the Quakers, who were influential there in his childhood (as the program claimed). He is one of my heroes, but I had thought of him as irreligious, not hostile, and not following the Anglicanism of his youth.

Clara Geoghegan[1] is now working with the Australian Christian Lobby and sent me excerpts from a recent speech by the thirty-year-old Martyn Iles, their managing director. The speech was unpolished, but perceptive and prophetic, i.e., it diagnoses accurately what is happening and what is likely to continue unless it can be diverted and until the forces of decency, which are still considerable, can impose a bit more equilibrium by regularly asserting the voice of reason. Iles is pessimistic about this approach because "logic and argument no longer mean diddly squat to a new generation."

His speech was occasioned by the ongoing political struggle in New South Wales to legalise explicitly, not just as a de facto practice, pretty well every form of abortion. Martyn points out that the opponents of life have become more brazen, no longer interested in denying abortion is an act of killing.

A Greens MLC[2] explained that sex is for enjoyment, which sometimes produces unwelcome consequences such as a baby. Abortion

---

[1] Clara Geoghegan lectures in Church history and spirituality at the Catholic Theological College in Melbourne. In February 2020, she became the executive secretary of the Australian Catholic Bishops' Conference.

[2] A state parliamentary member who belongs to the Greens party.

is another form of contraception. The unborn child is genetically distinct from the mother, but the vital issue is that the woman herself is able to decide what is to be done. Because she has decided, the decision is good.

In these circles, the argumentation has gone past relativism. Rarely do they speak of my truth and your truth; rather, they respond, "Yeah, I know that might be true, but I don't care." What matters is "what I want and feel". They claim to be empowered as only God is empowered, so they are furious, regard it as akin to blasphemy, when someone claims they are wrong.

Iles quotes Jeremy Rifkin, an economist who explains that these new atheists do not see themselves as guests in someone else's home, no longer feel they must conform to a set of preexisting cosmic rules. It's their creation; they are the architects, and they make their own rules. They don't even feel obliged to justify their rules.

As evidence of this view, Iles cites Michel Foucault, an archpriest of postmodernism. Truth claims are power claims, which repress and victimise people. Therefore, Foucault urges the people to run from these claims, not to engage with them.

Against this, Iles sets up St Paul as an exemplar who relied, not on his own power of argument, but on the power of God for salvation. Without God's power in this new generation, more so perhaps than in any period since the pagan Roman Empire, we cannot win this struggle. Without God's power and his tools, all will be lost.

I certainly agree that God and Christ should be brought into the debate regularly, as another, the most reasonable argument. The Son of God is described as *Logos*, the Greek term for the word "truth", "reason". My differences from Iles, to the extent they exist, represent the different approaches of the Evangelicals and the broader currents of the Catholic position, which explicitly includes and embraces the *philosophia perennis*, ancient wisdom, ancient words.

Psalm 9A speaks on this.

> *But the Lord sits enthroned forever.*
> *He sets up his throne for judgement;*
> *he will judge the world with justice,*
> *he will judge the peoples with his truth.*

Monday, 23 September 2019

A somewhat overcast day, not cold, with some showers. I curtailed my afternoon exercise when the drizzle recommenced.

Early in the morning, Paul and Kartya called to see me. I anticipated that a visit was due, but it was a surprise to see them both at that time. Kartya brought a copy of the document delivered to the High Court, and I went through and checked the changes from the draft. All strengthened the document. Ruth incorporated one out of three precisions I suggested, but nothing was lost by all this.

When I enquired about the possibility of bail attached to my appeal, Paul replied that bail is not available to those already serving a sentence. He also thought it would be unwise to request that my case be expedited, as the High Court chooses its own pace. So we don't know when leave will be given or refused or when the case might be heard. February or March next year is one conjecture.

David and Sarah visited, as Judy and Bec are already on the East Coast of the US. Sarah has just returned from an international meeting in Vienna devoted to identifying the important questions to be asked about the future. She didn't feel it was as useful as the earlier meetings of the series.

The Brownlow Medal[3] count was televised this evening, and the medal was won by Nat Fyfe of Fremantle for a second time. From country West Australia, he boarded at Aquinas College in Perth. In year 11, he was playing in the school thirds, but after he turned the corner personally and in his football in his last year of school, he wrote to the football coach on the eve of a trip to the East Coast seeking special consideration. He was chosen as number twenty-three on the list. He spoke eloquently and with good sense. I am not surprised he is team captain, and I suspect a thoroughly decent human being with a strong Catholic flavour.

The letters continue to arrive, and I continued to open and read them during the Brownlow count.

An unknown supporter in Chartres, France, sent photos and an article about Our Lady of Orcival, sometimes known as Our Lady

---

[3] The Charles Brownlow Trophy is awarded annually to the best and fairest player in the Australian Football League according to votes cast by the field umpires after each game.

of Irons, who is patron of prisoners. Above the main entrance to the thirteenth-century Romanesque church, we find handcuffs and chains placed there by liberated prisoners. It seems as though relics arrived in the ninth century, but pilgrimages could date from the sixth century. I think a few prayers to Our Lady under this title would not go astray.

An Irish journalist from Shankill, Dublin, wrote to explain that she "was appalled at the blatant disregard for facts", with journalists apparently brainwashed by the #MeToo movement, "a modern version of the Salem Witch Trials". However, my story is reaching every corner of the earth, through the alternative media, both online and in print, she claimed.

A regular supporter from Kingaroy, with a dash of the poet and mystic in her heart and mind, asked me to imagine myself "covered in prayer talc from all the prayers you've been saying and imagine the traces of prayers for you making their way to you, falling upon your soul like glitter from the sky".

A good friend, a retired secondary-school principal, wrote of the challenges for good and ill facing the Church today and expressing her belief that "your suffering is instrumental in gaining these positive signs of hope for us." Please God, it is so.

Another writer from Connecticut in the US gave me some beautiful quotations from Pope Benedict.

Without truth, without trust and love for what is true, there is no social conscience and responsibility, and social action ends up serving private interests and the logic of power. . . .

. . . Fidelity to the truth . . . alone is the guarantee of freedom.[4]

Tuesday, 24 September 2019

A quiet day after the two sets of visitors yesterday. The weather was a bit better, but still overcast with no rain.

I enjoyed my hour in the gymnasium, although I was not able to break Saturday's ping-pong records, with 190 consecutive shots on

---

[4] Benedict XVI, Encyclical Letter *Caritas in veritate* (29 June 2009), nos. 5 and 9.

my backhand and over 100 on the forehand. On each visit, I raise the treadmill requirements a notch. My balance is not perfect, but improved, and my thighs continue to strengthen.

Last night in bed, I finished reading Scott Patterson's *The Oarsmen*, the account of the Australians winning the King's Cup for the eights[5] at Henley in 1919. The beautiful setting of Henley, the absence of terrible violence—but not the absence of spiritual and psychological wounds from that violence (WWI)—the excitement and the escape of sporting competition must have been a wonderful relief and release, especially for the soldier spectators. For the competitors, where the weeks of hard training and community living exacerbated their scars of body but especially of mind, the races would have reminded them of the costs of all human achievement, even of the less important events like sporting competition, and of the fun, excitement, and, indeed, exhilaration of a racing eight, perfectly balanced and powered relentlessly over the water in deadly serious, but harmless, competition with other crews.

Sr Mary called as usual for our prayers and Holy Communion. Our time was cut short by fifteen minutes, to her displeasure, but she was delighted by the fact that I had received a haircut "after weeks of high-level negotiations", as I explained. She was not sympathetic to their reasons for not allowing me a couple of outings a week in the garden. She also informed me that on last Tuesday afternoon, not long after leaving me, the ABC announced that my appeal had been lodged that day. It was no state secret, but still good going on their part.

St Thomas More also wrote a prayer for good humour.

Grant me, O Lord, good digestion, and something to digest.
Grant me a healthy body and the necessary good humour to
sustain it.
Grant me a simple soul that knows how to treasure all that is
good
and that doesn't frighten easily at the sight of evil,
but rather finds the means to put things back in their place.

---

[5] Eight-oared crews.

> Give me a soul that knows not boredom, grumbling, sighs and
>   laments,
>   nor excess of stress, because of that obstructing thing called "I".
> Grant me, O Lord, a sense of good humour.
> Allow me the grace to be able to take a joke, to
>   discover in life a bit of joy,
>   and to be able to share it with others.
> Amen.

Wednesday, 25 September 2019

A big day in the big world outside as the Supreme Court in Britain ruled unanimously that Boris Johnson's prorogation of Parliament was unlawful. In the US, Nancy Pelosi, leader of the Democrats in the House of Representatives, announced that they would commence or try to commence the impeachment process against President Trump, because of a conversation with the new president of Ukraine (the ex-comedian with no political experience), where Trump allegedly threatened the president with economic reprisals if he did not commence investigations into the activities of Joe Biden's son in Ukraine. Trump has promised to publish the full text, and the president of Ukraine has denied there was anything improper in the conversation.

I think it unlikely that the attack will do Trump any long-term damage, unless someone has tampered with the evidence. He would be unlikely to release a text which shows he is guilty. I think Trump is better than any likely alternative for a couple of reasons. China is a dictatorship which is exploiting the free-market system, using or ignoring its conventions and obligations when it suits. It also persecutes the Muslims in western China and Catholics in many regions. It needs to be opposed and its rise slowed, although this places Australia in a difficult position between our great ally and our largest trading partner. A world dominated by China would not be an improvement on a world where the US is predominant.

Boris Johnson's path might be more difficult. I hope Britain leaves the European Union with a substantial increase in freedom for action. A majority in Parliament want to remain, while the country has voted to leave—the Establishment versus a mixed bag of deplorables. Labour under [Jeremy] Corbyn wants a second referendum, but the party is not adopting a position for or against Brexit. Corbyn would be a disaster. In fact, he is one of Boris' most valuable assets. As the Parliament is deadlocked, an election seems the best and just option.

Johnson and Trump are more like the rulers of old in their private lives, rather than the "respectable" politicians who have led the Anglosphere for most of the last century. Johnson is the first prime minister to have his current partner or mistress move into Downing Street. I'm not even sure if she qualifies as a partner. But I am still a Boris supporter.

The seventeen-year-old Swedish climate extremist Greta Thunberg has addressed the United Nations. She has sparked the student climate strikes in some Western countries. Entire ecosystems are collapsing, she claims. Leaders have stolen her dreams and her childhood with empty words. How dare they do this, she emoted.

The situation is more than slightly ridiculous, systematic of a Western world which wants to have the capacity to ignore natural masculinity and femininity, redefine marriage, exalt abortion, and no longer recognizes the proper and limited range of options for children. How dare world leaders do this to her generation, destroying their hope! When the natural law is explicitly rejected, its natural contours no longer respected, fear certainly enters into the vacuum, and it is usually accompanied by ignorance. The climate change industry provides billions of dollars for its champions, and changing course would destroy the livelihood of a goodly number. The truth will out, but we have few signs that the end is nigh!

I managed to write five letters and bring my journal up to date. Except for today's (Wednesday's) entry, which I am writing on Thursday.

I had an hour in the gym, which I enjoyed as always, reaching about 230 uninterrupted backhand shots and over 100 on my forehand.

We seem to have only one banger and shouter, although when he becomes agitated, the pathos, volume, and violence of his language indicate a sick and uneducated man. Then he suddenly falls quiet, and we are undisturbed by him most of the time.

The weather was decent with no rain falling while I was outside. I spoke to David, but Margaret did not answer.

A woman from Kladno in the Czech Republic wrote to encourage me and left me with this quotation from Genesis 22:8 (Douay Rheims translation).

And Abraham said:

God will provide himself a victim for an holocaust, my son.

Thursday, 26 September 2019

During my morning exercise, I was able to catch Terry at home with Bernadette. He had been enquiring about bail, and apparently those in jail can apply for bail to the High Court, but a positive result is highly unlikely. When Lindy Chamberlain[6] was feeding her baby in Darwin jail, she was not allowed out on bail.

Apparently, Keith Windschuttle published another article in *Quadrant* online yesterday, dedicated (I think) to the timing impossibility. And today, or on Tuesday, Andrew Bolt had a piece in the *Herald Sun* along the same lines, where he announced that he had gone to the cathedral to walk the route himself. All this is useful and consoling.

The voices claim that the chief justice is irritated and angry that she has come under such attack. This surprising reaction, I believe, is evidence that she didn't fully understand what she was about. Certainly, one of her few comments at the trial referring to the chasuble was evidence of hypersophistication or a basic misunderstanding. Maxwell's view of his contribution, for he apparently wrote the majority judgement, still remains a mystery to me. How could a Supreme Court judge reverse the onus of proof?

---

[6] Cardinal Pell's case has been compared to that of Lindy Chamberlain, who in 1982 was convicted of murdering her infant daughter, Azaria, on a family camping trip in 1980. The case was attended by extraordinary levels of controversy and media attention, arising from the Chamberlains' claim that Azaria, whose body was never found, had been taken from their tent by a dingo [Australian wild dog]. Despite the evidence supporting this claim, the Chamberlains became the object of considerable public hostility, fuelled by, among other factors, public suspicion of their Seventh Day Adventist faith and their alleged lack of emotion in public appearances. Their appeal to the High Court of Australia in 1984, on the grounds that the jury's verdicts were unsafe and unreasonable in light of the evidence presented against them, was dismissed. In 1986, a further item of clothing Azaria was wearing at the time of her disappearance was discovered at Uluru. This new evidence led to a judicial inquiry, which resulted in the exoneration of the Chamberlains and the quashing of their convictions in 1988.

Terry reported that Fr Paul Stenhouse was unwell, very tired, and has been tested for leukaemia. I gather, too, he has been in and out of hospital during the last six months. In the recent issue of *Annals*, he announced that after 130 years it would not continue to be published next year. Paul alone has ensured its survival for many years and has done a heroic job. Where are our young Catholic writers? Young priest writers? I sent a request that he include an article of mine, perhaps under a pseudonym, before the end.

The letters continue to arrive, averaging about seventy-five a week at this stage. The abbot and forty-six monks from Our Lady of Clear Creek Abbey in Oklahoma sent me a fine letter, promising regular prayers and enclosing Sir Richard Lovelace's poem "To Althea from Prison", which I will use to conclude this entry.

A regular correspondent from Dallas in Texas is a walker and marathon runner (if I remember correctly) who has walked the Camino de Santiago de Compostella, where I once celebrated the Sunday Mass in Spanish but preached in English. Many of the large number of walkers are not technically "pilgrims", because they no longer have Christian faith, although many are searching for peace and meaning and perhaps truth. I acknowledged them and their quests in my sermon and eventually received a letter of thanks from a Scandinavian (as I recall) who was present, grateful his quest had been acknowledged.

My correspondent has deep faith and meditates regularly; she also regularly prays for me. She explained that sometimes toward the end of her daily walk, when she was "prayed out" and finding it almost impossible to meditate (which was not too often), she would pull out her hymn sheet and start singing one of her favourite hymns. "Suddenly I'd feel ok again. I'd be picking up my feet and smiling and the doldrums would be gone. In addition to the magic of music, I think the oxygen intake required for singing perked up my whole body." So she enclosed for me a double-sided song sheet ranging from Beethoven's "Ode to Joy" to the "Pange Lingua".

I haven't started singing in my cell, but sometimes when my meditation is a low-quality struggle, I do like to hum the beautiful tunes (nearly all of which I know) as I pray the equally beautiful words of the hymn. Perhaps this helps to explain St Augustine's claim that the one who sings prays twice.

Now to Sir Richard Lovelace.

Stone walls do not a prison make
Nor iron bars a cage:
Minds innocent and quiet take
That for an hermitage.
If I have freedom in my love,
And in my soul am free,
Angels alone that soar above,
Enjoy such liberty.

Friday, 27 September 2019

While today is the feast of St Vincent de Paul, the readings of the day conclude St Augustine's excerpts on the obligations of the shepherds (bishops and priests), while the readings from Ezekiel continue. I have long admired the Augustine sermon 46 on the shepherds and used a small quote from it on the card produced to mark my consecration as an auxiliary bishop. The shepherd is there to feed the sheep, not himself. Being a bishop is fraught with danger, unlike being one of the baptised. Being a Christian is a benefit for oneself, but being a bishop means being at the service of the sheep, which is not an easier road and for which each bishop must render an account to God. Augustine acknowledges their existence and rebukes the wicked shepherds.

In this same sermon 46, Augustine writes of the struggles and sufferings each Christian must endure, but which will not be beyond their strength. However, we have no escape from some sort of suffering.

The bishop of Hippo tells his congregation: " 'The Lord chastises', scripture says, 'every son whom he accepts.' And do you say, 'Perhaps you will be exempt'? If exempt from suffering chastisement, then exempt from the number of his sons. 'But', you will say, 'does he chastise every son?' Without doubt he does chastise every son as he chastised even his only Son.''

Augustine was speaking these truths to his own Catholic congregation in Hippo, which was most likely a smaller group than the Donatist Christians. They knew of slavery and strife and the enduring hostile presence of the diminishing percentages of pagans. This teaching is true, but it is stiff medicine, especially today, when we are surrounded by painkillers and counsellors, able to withstand anything but discomfort.

Tim O'Leary called yesterday on his way to his beach house at Fairhaven, as school holidays have commenced. He is another one who has been a marvellous support, not least by his photocopying and sending me so many articles. Young Paddy is at the University of St Andrew in Scotland and was in their rugby team to play Edinburgh University. Unfortunately, they were beaten 63–0 in front of 10,000 people. Obviously, in earlier years the scores have been closer. I asked Tim to send Prof Jeremy Gans of Melbourne University a copy of "Entirely Possible" for his perusal, but not for publication or attribution.

My most frequent correspondent from Singapore suffers from headaches and often asks Mother Mary to remind her to offer such hardships for some soul in Purgatory or someone who needs to be redeemed. She then continued very wisely: "God is not fussy. He will take all that we can give him for souls."

Much closer to home, another regular correspondent from Carlton told me how impressed she was by a recent talk given by a visiting author and businessman from the US. Apparently, the buzz word among many American corporations to characterise the age in which we are living is VUCA, i.e., volatility, uncertainty, complexity, and ambiguity, and the speaker believes a new culture of leadership is needed to revitalise the Church. He might be right, but it depends on what he means. As Pope Emeritus Benedict rightly observed recently, we don't need another Church.

My problem is with the note of ambiguity as typical of this age. Neither Trump nor Corbyn nor Xi Jinping nor Identity Politics nor the #MeToo movement—none of them is characterised by ambiguity. Nor are the neopagans who have dismantled much of the inherited foundations and framework of our social conventions on human life, sexuality, marriage, and family. Nor are the revitalised and radicalised Muslims ambiguous. Nor are the climate change totalitarians; nor are the increasingly confident anti-Christians, at least in Australia. Trump, not known as a man of faith, has slowed down the anti-Christ in the US, and we hope Prime Minister [Scott] Morrison will do the same here in a very different way. The danger, long term, is for the ignorant imposition of policies by those who are not interested in claims to truth. Those espousing ambiguity are likely to be the first to be overwhelmed, even if they acknowledge the importance of truth and reason.

Let me end by returning to my Singapore friend.

God is not fussy. He will take all we can give him for souls.

Saturday, 28 September 2019

Today is Grand Final Day in the AFL, where my Richmond team with a history of over 130 years is playing the Great Western Sydney Giants [GWS] with a history of eight years. The Giants' first coach was Kevin Sheedy, a loyal Catholic and ex-Richmond player, who asked me when I was in Sydney to become the club's patron. I was unable to do so for a couple of reasons. Most of Western Sydney is outside the Archdiocese of Sydney, and I was a Richmond fan. The matches I saw in Sydney involved the Swans, but I was only a fellow traveller for them, and my first loyalty remained with the Tigers.

Sydney is not interested in any sport in the way Melbourne is obsessed with Aussie Rules, so while football progress has been good with the Giants, due to a lot of AFL money and the wisdom of men like Sheedy, the growth in the supporter base has been much slower. Nor are there many expatriates from AFL states living in Western Sydney, who have contributed mightily to the Swans' base. The landings at Gallipoli in World War I were a good idea, poorly executed. An AFL base in the working class west of Sydney is a fine idea, with the Giants achieving more early success than the Anzacs did on the Turkish coast, but it will be a long, hard struggle off the field. Continuing success will be important, because everyone loves winners, especially in Sydney.

So far today (it is 1:30 pm) I haven't received any new batch of letters, which enables me to catch up and stabilise my situation.

I used my hymn words for meditation outside in the exercise pen, and it went well. It was a help to prayer, although once again I did not sing aloud! Mr Harris asked whether I wanted to go outside this afternoon or watch the football. I opted for the latter, and he wasn't surprised. The three televised matches a week have been a boon for me, and I have watched most of them, except when it was an ugly or boring game.

Richmond thrashed GWS by eighty-nine points in front of 100,000 people. After an even, low-scoring first quarter, the successive waves of Richmond players streaming down the ground completely vanquished and demoralised the opposition. Marlion Pickett, twenty-seven years old, who was a guest of Her Majesty for a couple of years, gave an inspired performance, with more than twenty possessions, one goal, and a few magic moments. Shaun Grigg retired early to bring Pickett in under the salary cap. Today was his first AFL game.

I have watched more football this year than at any time of my life and enjoyed this victory as much as I did in 1980 when the Tigers crushed Collingwood. There are likely to be more premierships over the next three or four years. Dynasties don't last forever, but the next few years should be good.

Why is Melbourne more obsessed with sport than Sydney, with regularly larger crowds of spectators even when we are speaking of the same game, e.g., cricket? More spectators in Melbourne came to see the New South Welshman Steve Waugh's final innings than in Sydney.

The beaches are not as attractive an alternative in Melbourne, and their transport system to and from the complex of ovals and courts is much better. I also believe AFL is a more attractive spectacle with a wider range of skills and humanity on display than in rugby. Fewer mums are opposed to AFL than rugby and, unlike the soccer in Europe, many women, young and old, and families come to AFL matches. One Italian friend said that soccer there is a favourite escape for men who are unhappy with their wives! The AFL, like soccer, has devotees in every class of society, unlike the two rugby codes which are divided along class lines, with a thug's game played by gentlemen and a gentleman's game played by thugs (although I see nothing gentlemanly about Rugby League).

Sport is better than civil strife and revolution, and we are blessed by a society which provides the free time and facilities, the health and the wealth for these amusements. Neither is there violence as in the pagan Roman amphitheatres; and sport is much better for children than terrorising them with uncorroborated fears about climate change.

For all these blessings, Lord, these worldly escapist pleasures, make us truly grateful.

WEEK 32

Vatican Investigations

29 September—5 October 2019

Sunday, 29 September 2019

I awoke at twenty to six, so I was able to watch *Mass for You at Home* celebrated by Fr Justel Callos. He gave an interesting sermon on Dives and Lazarus, accusing Dives of insensitivity, of ongoing uncaring as he ignored Lazarus. He pointed out that even when we are not rich, we can still be wrapped up in ourselves, insensitive to the needs of those around us.

The program usually features some footage from town or country while the hymns are being sung. Today we had some fine shots of the streams of living water, flowing down the Pilgrims' Way entrance to the south transept of St Patrick's Cathedral, Melbourne. They featured the beautiful figure of the Lamb at the source of the fountain. Yesterday in the breviary, we had an excerpt from chapter 47 of Ezekiel about the four rivers of life flowing from the four sides of the Temple out into the countryside, producing fish and fruit, giving life even in hard times. This Old Testament passage provided part of the inspiration for this beautiful monument, ideal for Australia, where even in Victoria the general population understands the danger of drought, our absolute dependence on water. *The Age* provides everyday information about the amount of water in the Melbourne water supply, something that has not been done in the past in Sydney, because of the heavier rainfall there and a significantly larger water storage capacity.

Joseph Prince was kitted out nattily in a black leather jacket with three rings. His sermon was typically lively and Christocentric, and for the first time in my limited experience, he denounced the pride of life and lust, the sins of the eye and of the flesh. We are to love either God or the world, remembering God gives us an incomparable and undefiled inheritance. We need to be more than neutral Christians, not like the tribes of Reuben, Gad, and Manasseh, who had little enthusiasm for the capture of the Promised Land.

Joel Osteen urged us to fight against discouragement: to persevere, to be like King David, who ascended to the throne because he wanted it badly enough. We should resemble Bartimaeus, the blind man, who was not deterred by those who wanted to keep him away from Jesus. Faith without works is dead, and what God has put in us is worth fighting for.

Songs of Praise was held in Nottingham, which has six hundred or eight hundred caves under the city, where the Catholic Mass was celebrated in times of persecution. Robin Hood is the best-known citizen of Nottingham, and I was surprised to hear he was a devout Christian, who was captured while he was at prayer, perhaps weak from fasting. A church full of worshippers who were in good voice for a couple of old favourites, such as [Charles] Wesley's "O for a Thousand Tongues to Sing" and "Praise Ye the Lord". A tonic as always.

The day was a bit overcast, no rain during my two outside exercise periods. I managed to contact Marg, by phone, who was as delighted as I was by the Richmond victory. When speaking to Anne McFarlane, her son-in-law David Bell said it was a boring match. I replied that I thought it was magnificent. Anne had a brief period in hospital with asthma while she was at Torquay for the weekend. Please God she will be OK.

A batch of letters arrived, including an envelope of articles from Terry Tobin and a couple of opinions from Greg Smith, SC,[1] formerly deputy crown prosecutor in New South Wales and attorney general, on the possibility of applying for bail. Apparently, it is not quite as hopeless as I had been led to believe. Perhaps an application for bail or expediting my case might be the way to go.

In the evening, I watched what turned out to be a 2012 documentary on the use of satellite technology to identify sites and buildings in

---

[1] Greg Smith, the former attorney general (2011–2014) of New South Wales, is a senior counsel (SC), a designation that has replaced Queen's Counsel (QC) in some Australian states.

the Roman Empire not visible to the human eye. I learnt of a string of Roman forts and settlements across North Africa from Egypt to Morocco, which monitored travellers and shepherds as they moved in and out of the empire, something like customs officers as well as guarantors of peace and prosperity.

The site of Portus, the great port of the city of Rome, had been identified, but the satellites found a canal running parallel to the Tiber up to Ostia and the site of the ancient and immense lighthouse of Portus, 150 metres by 30 metres [492 by 98.5 ft], three stories high, one of the wonders of the ancient world and situated not far from the present Fiumicino Airport. The satellite also pinpointed the bridge the Romans of Trajan's time made to cross the Danube for the invasion of Romania, another prodigious feat of engineering for the time. Apparently, the invading Roman army numbered sixty thousand troops. The Pax Romana was eventually real in most parts of the empire for hundreds of years, but it was built and maintained at great human cost. Psalm 50 follows on from these various musings.

> *A pure heart create for me, O God,*
> *put a steadfast spirit within me.*
> *Do not cast me away from Your presence,*
> *nor deprive me of your holy spirit.*

Monday, 30 September 2019

I was rather pleased with myself to discover, and I wasn't looking for the quote, that a week ago after GWS defeated Collingwood I wrote, "I now think Richmond could crush GWS next Saturday", before admitting that the Giants could also surprise us. For once, my intuition was correct. My day started very pleasantly as the senior warden brought in for me a copy of the Sunday *Herald Sun* with thirty-two pages on the massacre. I have often remarked that my move to Sydney and then overseas [to Rome] from Melbourne saved me at least an hour a week of reading time, which would previously have been spent on the "footy" news.

The day was overcast, but with no rain. Neither was it cold. The highlight was the visit of Gabriele and Anna Turchi, who drove down from Sydney with their children to see me. I had a meal at their place each Tuesday night before we went together to the Neo-catechumenal weekly meeting. They are loyal friends, and even their young daughters have defended me at their schools. Most of the Neo-Cat national catechists who met together in Italy recently sent their best wishes and the promise of their prayers, as did Kiko and Fr Mario Pezzi, co-leader. My Sydney friend Carlos has been in hospital during the last fortnight. Unfortunately, the owner of the Turchis' house and his architect were recently there measuring up the site for redevelopment. However, Gabriele said they will enjoy it as long as they can.

I have been pondering the wisdom of requesting bail from the High Court pending my appeal—in the light of Greg Smith's advice. I informed Galbally and said I would pass on my documents for him to distribute to my legal team, together with a few words from myself to them. One important question is whether and how much harm it might do to my case. I don't believe I could appeal on the grounds of ill health, but an appeal on the grounds of impossibility, the impossibility of the miscreants being present during the alleged crime time, would at the minimum excite some public interest. So, too, would a request to the prosecution to support the application for bail!

It will be interesting to see what sort of logical and legal response is possible and forthcoming from the prosecution to the claims not only of Weinberg, but of Finnis, and now Windschuttle and Bolt. I feel convinced that the possibility of bail application merits discussion. When I phoned Paul this afternoon, he said he could call in tomorrow morning, and Mr Harris said he would arrange for me to be able to pass my letter and the documents to him.

Only a few letters arrived today, but I didn't manage to write any letters.

One unknown friend from Grantham, UK, sent me a card with a Constable painting of the sea, information that a Mass had been offered for me, and the following lines from Psalm 139:

> *If I take the wings of the dawn*
> *and dwell at the sea's furthest end,*
> *even there your hand would lead me,*
> *your right hand would hold me fast.*

Tuesday, 1 October 2019

Today was an unusual day by my prison standards, as I was not able to eat some of my lunch until 2:30 pm. The salad lunch arrives around 11:15 am.

I had my usual Tuesday hour in the gymnasium and used the time well. I am now able to walk on the treadmill briefly without a hand on the bar, and for some time I have been able to continue holding on with one hand alone. In other words, my balance is improving, although I am careful. The improved balance is also evident as I climb the stairs out of the gymnasium without holding onto the bannister. Once again, though, I am careful.

At midday, I was taken to see the doctor, who said nothing about the results of my recent blood test. All must be well. I asked her to examine my back to see why I had had a small amount of blood on my singlet [T-shirt] for a couple of days. She could find no cause for alarm and no cause for the blood. I had reported that I had an intermittent toothache. She muttered something about it not being a cavity. My blood pressure was 123 over 78. Although I am now used to the lower blood pressure, these low readings might help explain my lethargy in the mornings. But as I explained to Sr Mary, who brought me Holy Communion today, I have been lethargic for forty years.

I was then taken to my professional visit from Paul Galbally, after I had picked up the advice from Greg Smith, SC, former NSW attorney general, and my two-page letter to my legal team on the possibility of asking for bail from the High Court, pending the appeal. Paul conceded he was wrong in claiming that you cannot ask the High Court for bail, as he was informed by Ruth after he had spoken with me. He will send my letter and Smith's advice to the team for examination, but Bret's view previously was that nothing would be gained by asking for bail and no one has been successful when asking for the process to be hurried up. He feels the High Court will recognize the special features of the situation, without saying so publicly, and move ahead expeditiously. Paul and I agreed that it will be interesting to see the prosecution's reply. Paul thought they would try to fudge the issue.

Another question is who will represent them in the High Court. Ruth is adamant that it won't be Boyce. Paul also pointed out that if the decision goes against Ferguson and Maxwell, they will carry that burden for the rest of their careers. As one blogger on the *Quadrant* website commented, it is scary to have the state's two most senior judges making such mistakes and wrongly assigning the onus of proof.

Paul also brought a piece of very good news as the Victorian legal authorities have allocated $390,000 toward the cost of the first trial, where the jury could not agree. We had applied for $800,000, apparently, but could not guesstimate how much we might receive. At any rate, as we used to say, $390,00 is better than a kick in the pants.

An Irish correspondent sent me the text of "St Patrick's Breastplate", which concludes:

> *Christ in the heart of every man who thinks of me,*
> *Christ in the mouth of every man who speaks of me,*
> *Christ in the eye that sees me,*
> *Christ in the ear that hears me.*

Wednesday, 2 October 2019

October is an important month in the life of the Church and, therefore, in the pontificate of Pope Francis, as in October we have in Rome the Synod on Amazonia, which has a population of around four million Catholics, and a meeting of the German bishops, a meeting whose status is in dispute. What are the powers of a national church in a single, worldwide Church under the successor of Peter?

Cynics and many others fear that the Amazonia Synod will be used to break the discipline of an unmarried clergy in the Latin Church by allowing the ordination of older married men to the priesthood in this isolated spot, while insisting that the discipline can be maintained everywhere else. Although South America is not a stronghold for women's rights, and neither is Amazonia, the fear is that the diaconate for women in some form will be attempted.

As most of the parish clergy in East and West for the first Christian millennium were married (although urged to live as brother and sister, a system apparently policed by the women), the reintroduction of a married clergy is not a threat to doctrinal order. I fear it would damage our vitality even further, as the Protestants with their married clergy are weaker than we are. Therefore, I do not support such a change.

For similar reasons, I do not support the reintroduction of women deacons, although there were non-ordained women deacons in the ancient Church in the East and West. Disruptive elements would use such a change as a step toward women priests.

Another important procedural point is that pastoral and, even more importantly, doctrinal changes with universal implications and consequences should not be introduced surreptitiously through local synods, in this case, for a tiny number of Catholics (fewer than the Catholics in Australia and about one quarter of the Catholic population in each of Mexico City and San Paulo). I also heard a couple of years ago that the Brazilian bishops had told the Holy Father privately that they do not want a discipline change in mandatory celibacy of the priests.

The retired Cláudio Cardinal Hummes is in charge of the Amazonian apostolate and has been pushing for the changes on celibacy during the whole of Pope Francis' pontificate.

In Germany, the situation is potentially more dangerous, as the "orthodox" bishops, who belong to the school of St John Paul the Great and Pope Emeritus Benedict, are outnumbered. Two underlying dangers at least are not too far below the surface.

What criteria will the German bishops use in judging, e.g., what changes are possible in the areas of life, marriage, family, and sexuality? Do they appeal ultimately to the apostolic tradition, or is that subordinate to modern and better understandings?

Walter Cardinal Kasper[2] famously differed from Pope Benedict, urging that the local Church had a logical priority over the universal Church. Will this line of argumentation be carried further, so that the German bishops assert their capacity to teach morally in a way which is contrary to the tradition and, more particularly, different from the teaching in, e.g., Poland and the majority of the Church, and different from the teaching of the pope as the ultimate guarantor of the apostolic tradition? The Catholic Church is not a federation, loose or tight-knit, on either an Orthodox or Anglican

---

[2] Walter Kasper (b. 1933) is a German cardinal, theologian, and author who served as president of the Pontifical Council for Promoting Christian Unity from 2001 to 2010.

model. Pope Francis has already written a personal warning letter to the German bishops, which has received scant publicity, and it will be important that he follows this up with whatever firm action is required. It is to be hoped that Catholic instinct and right order will reassert themselves among the German bishops. Let us pray that this is so.

My meditation technique of humming the words and tune of some beautiful hymns is proving valuable, enabling or provoking fewer distractions and easier prayer. *Deo gratias.*

A senior warden, with a crown on his epaulette, brought the good news that from tomorrow I am to be allowed in the garden for two hours twice a week before my outside visitors arrive. Mr Harris had explained that he was pushing for this. A couple of verses from a Stanbrook Abbey hymn fit the bill today.

> *O fathers of our ancient faith,*
> *With all the heav'ns we sing your fame*
> *Whose sound went forth in all the earth*
> *To tell of Christ, and bless his name. . . .*

> *You told of God who died for us*
> *And out of death triumphant rose,*
> *Who gave the truth that made us free,*
> *And changeless through the ages goes.*

Thursday, 3 October 2019

A pleasant day in many ways, but especially for three reasons.

I passed my first couple of hours in the garden, walking for two spells of between twenty and thirty minutes. I am not allowed at the far end away from the main prison building, supposedly because that area is visible to nearby apartments. There is an office block parallel to the garden with at least some people working inside.

The garden seemed to be bare, more than I remembered from my first and only visit with Chris Meney. No roses were in bloom, and the only flowers were under the central rotunda, orange flowers at the end of long green stems. The plant shape resembled that of

Agapanthus [lily of the Nile], but the flower itself was different. I will attempt to discover the name.[3]

It was the first warm day of summer reaching 29–30°C [84–86° F], but a beautiful breeze sprang up as I was resting on a park bench in the shade next to the visitors' centre. I took some material Joseph had sent me to read after my walks and rosary, but I never got to it as both guards (in succession) seemed open, or even keen, to chat. Apparently, some of those in solitary confinement come to enjoy their own company and become slow at chatting. The first warden had a Baptist background, while the second had no religion, although he knew quite a bit about different aspects of religion. I was able to inform him there was no evidence Jesus ever married Mary Magdalene, as he thought, and he was prepared to concede that Jesus the "man" had existed.

Two or three senior officers called, murmuring pleasantries, with one suggesting that my twice weekly visits to the garden might be increased. On some days, it will be hot, but the seat in the shade is a bonus, and psychologically the time outside should be a boon. I'm not expecting increased time soon.

When I returned to my cell, I found a regulation large prison brown paper bag full of goodies from the canteen. Apparently, according to the warden, the prisoner next door had been moved on, and the warden offered the loot to me. With an allowance of $140 a month, I am not sure how the prisoner could have afforded such a treasure of chocolate, crisps, dry biscuits, sauces, salt and pepper, shampoo and conditioner, cordial, corn flakes, etc.

I took about half the contents and returned the rest with a note that it might go to another prisoner, suggesting Gargasoulas, as he is the only one I "know" through letters, only a few of which arrived today.

Immediately after my time in the garden, I spent forty minutes with Fr Anthony Denton, who has just returned from a six-month (or so) break overseas, which he enjoyed immensely. I was pleased to find him in good form, as he considered a couple of priestly work options, different from his Beaumaris parish. His brother Fr Francis was the first priest after my incarceration to send me a beautiful letter of support.

---

[3] The plant is *Strelitzia*, more commonly known as a bird of paradise.

My gymnasium workout yesterday went well, as I twice managed to continue beyond a hundred with my forehand in the ping pong and went well beyond two hundred shots once on my backhand. So, too, on the treadmill, I found I could continue for a minute or so without a hand on the bar and also increased the speed for the last thirty seconds. All this represents a small improvement, while my weight dropped a further kilo [2 lbs].

Psalm 16 has something for all of us.

> *I am here and I call, you will hear me, O God.*
> *Turn your ear to me; hear my words. . . .*
>
> *Guard me as the apple of your eye.*
> *Hide me in the shadow of your wings*
> *from the violent attack of the wicked.*

Friday, 4 October 2019

Today is the feast of St Francis of Assisi, one of the most remarkable saints in two thousand years, whom I did not know well until I was into my priesthood. It was on this day in 2013 that I accompanied Pope Francis on his first visit to Assisi as a member of the C8 (as it was then), the worldwide council of papal advisers which would be expanded to become the C9 through the addition of Pietro Cardinal Parolin, the secretary of state. The pope was not long elected, and my most vivid memory of the day was his embracing each of a large group of profoundly disabled adults and greeting each nurse who accompanied the sufferers. Without any doubt, the Holy Father has the gift of empathy and sympathy.

Assisi lies in one of the most beautiful pieces of countryside in the world, the Umbrian region, an ideal location for a saint who so loved God's creation. Would Francis have been as eloquent in the Mallee?[4] Whatever of that, we thank God for him, another unplanned and unexpected flowering of God's providence. The good God is always with us even in unpropitious times and circumstances.

---

[4] Mallee, in Victoria, Australia, is a flat, low-lying region with sandy, mostly infertile soil and a hot, dry climate.

After the movement and excitement of the two previous days, today's routine was only punctuated by a visit from Paul and Kartya. The weather had changed again, so that it was overcast and some light rain fell as I was out for my afternoon exercise.

Kartya brought copies of Roman newspapers, sent her by Fr Anthony Robbie, announcing the dramatic financial news from the Vatican, where five people have been suspended, including Tommaso Di Ruzza of the AIF,[5] the supervising financial body, and the monsignor [Maurizio Carlino] who had been [Giovanni] Cardinal Becciu's secretary.[6] My brother, David, had received a call from Fr Robert McCulloch,[7] reading from Italian reports, and Danny Casey confirmed the story when I phoned him. The picture is unclear to me, but a property valued at €200 million [$240 million] is mentioned in one report. I need to await further information, but this is good news, provided it is a serious attempt to confront the corruption which exists and they have the necessary evidence. I will encourage Tim O'Leary to provide as much information as he can.

Fr Damien Heath, a Ballarat priest about ten years older than me, spent many years as a missionary in Peru, South America, and I once asked him how life there differed from Australia. He replied that it was as different as Chaucer's *Canterbury Tales* is from Galsworthy's *The Forsyte Saga*. I think it was a useful and clever answer, although it didn't factor in the indigenous populations in South America explicitly, and I also suspect that the same analogy could be made (more accurately?) between Australia and Italy.

My copies of *The Spectator* arrive late to prison, when they arrive, so only in the last week have I read a copy of *The Spectator* of

---

[5] Tommaso Di Ruzza was director of the Vatican Financial Intelligence Authority (AIF) from 2015 to 2020. He was suspended from service in October 2019 during an investigation into the purchase of luxury real estate in London by the Secretariat of State.

[6] Archbishop Giovanni Becciu was the substitute for general affairs in the Vatican's Secretariat of State from 2011 to 2018, when Pope Francis made him a cardinal and the prefect of the Congregation for the Causes of Saints. In 2020, after Cardinal Becciu was accused of improperly using Church funds to purchase a London property, Pope Francis requested his resignation as prefect and removed his prerogatives as a cardinal, including participation in future papal conclaves.

[7] Fr Robert McCulloch is an Australian priest with the Missionary Society of St Columban who worked as a missionary in Pakistan for thirty-four years. He is the procurator-general of the Columban Fathers at the Vatican.

14 September, which contained a review by Mark Glanville of Tobias Jones' book *Ultra: The Underworld of Italian Football*.

Soccer is an obsession in Italy, in a more limited section of a larger population, as AFL is in the southern states of Australia. The Ultras are football hooligans, often violent and tribal, penetrated especially by the forces of the ultra-right. My team Roma, which I follow because my Roman Neocatechumenal friends are "Romanistas", are generally left-of-centre politically, while their Roman foes, Lazio, are certainly linked to the right; a number of their supporters still give the Fascist salute when a goal is scored. Their chants are often politically incorrect in the extreme, racist and anti-Semitic. Both sides blaspheme profusely.

One group of Ultras comes from Cosenza in Calabria, I Nuclei Sconvolti (The Deranged Nuclei), and they have always rejected Fascism. One of their leaders was "U Monaco", Padre Fedele, who used to lead the chanting at the game from a floodlit pylon. He encouraged them to help immigrants and the homeless with soup kitchens. After cooperating with a well-known female porn star to raise money for Rwanda, he was accused by #MeToo of raping a nun. He replied, "Today is the most beautiful day of my life, because I feel closer to Jesus Christ, persecuted and crucified." He was defrocked, and only later was his accuser shown to be a serial liar. In an ancient Catholic culture, the clash between good and evil is often played out in explosive technicolour.

St Thomas More is one of the most un-Italian of men, but his prayer against greed is "on the money".

O my sweet Saviour Christ, whom your own wicked disciple, entangled with the devil through vile wretched covetousness, betrayed: inspire, I beseech you, the marvel of your majesty, with the love of your goodness, so deep into my heart that ... my mind may set always this whole wretched world at naught.

Saturday, 5 October 2019

A rather nondescript day, overcast but not cold, which was brightened by my midday pasty, heated up in the microwave and doused with tomato sauce from my newly obtained supply, and by a productive hour in the gymnasium. I fell just short of two hundred shots on my backhand and cannot remember exactly how many hits I made on the forehand, although it was over one hundred. The basketball was out, and I managed to score three goals. I just managed to finish my 7.5 minutes on the treadmill when I had to return upstairs.

Watched the horse racing for an hour or so, but in a rather perfunctory way. I didn't bother to watch a couple of more important races.

This morning I spoke by phone to Tim O'Leary, who had been in West Australia during the week. He promised to collect and send me recent articles and spoke of the Vatican finance scandals. I am keen to obtain more and accurate information. Phoned Chris Meney in the afternoon, thinking he might be home, only to find him in Galway, Ireland, at 6:45 in the morning. Jane has joined him and Mary Clare, and they are going to Clare today. They had already visited Msgr James O'Brien in Ballyhea, and he was glad to see them, sending me the volume from his last liturgical conference.

We have enjoyed comparative quiet in the unit for some days, but we have a gentleman fairly close who shouts occasionally but, last night, took, not to banging, but to knocking loudly. It is now about 6:20 pm, and he (if he is the same one) is shouting, with another joining in sporadically. Sad and incoherent, rather than angry or anguished. But the tone can change as the episode continues.

Five or six letters arrived today, after a big number yesterday, which I have not finished reading. Michael Buck sent me a copy of his three speeches around his ordination, and they justified the good reports I had heard. He used his talk at the dinner to explain his ordination card, which featured Durante Alberti's *Martyrs' Picture* of the Trinity[8] in the chapel at the Venerable English College in Rome, where the college community gathered to sing the Te Deum when news came of the death of one of their forty-four ex-student martyrs. I didn't realise that the adjective "venerable" was attached to the college because of these heroes. He emphasised that there was no exact parallel with Australia, not even with the "Peoples' Republic

---

[8] The painting, created in 1580, shows the Trinity with two English martyrs: St Thomas Becket and St Edmund. Blood from Christ's wounds is falling onto a map of Britain and stirring up a fire.

of Victoria", but he felt an hostility in society toward the Church and was uneasy.

I have already mentioned that those who write to me are a self-selecting group, most of them serious Catholics, orthodox believers, who are not fantasists. Just within the last week, I have received a couple of letters from Germany and one each from Scotland and the US, all the writers uneasy about the future political climate. A German publisher wrote that the people there are shocked "by the anti-Catholic atmosphere in Australia" and think "we are on the way to suffer similar hostility against the Catholic Church in Germany." A German professor of medicine thanked me for my writings, lamenting that "it does not help the boat with lost orientation to move the lighthouse." He then gave me a quotation from St Teresa of Ávila which I did not know: "Lord, I do not ask for a lighter burden; I ask you for a stronger spine." Whatever of the future, we should continue the political struggle to defend the Church, as we are free citizens in a democracy. We are not yet hobbled like the citizens of Hong Kong, and we have every right, under heaven, to resist (by peaceful means) being placed in extreme conditions, being put to the test for our Christian convictions. Without a sea change, I cannot see any socially conservative Catholic as prime minister in the foreseeable future, and Tony Abbott was partly a victim of this new age. The selective and superficial Catholicism of politicians like Daniel Andrews, and Malcolm Turnbull to some extent, even helps them implement their un-Christian ambitions. The Trudeaus also come to mind.

We should remember that things could be worse and that in many ages they were. The works of E. H. Plumptre's hymn "Thy Hand, O God, Has Guided" should console us.

> Thy hand, O God, has guided
> Thy flock from age to age;
> Thy wonderous tale is written,
> Full clear, on every page;
> Our fathers owned Thy goodness,
> And we their deeds record,
> And both of these bear witness,
> One Church, one Faith, one Lord.

WEEK 33

Preparing for the High Court

6 October 2019—12 October 2019

Sunday, 6 October 2019

We moved to summer time today, as I learnt from last night's television, and I still managed to wake up for the 6:00 am *Mass for You at Home*. Fr Justel Callos was the celebrant, and his sermon message was just for me: "If you are tired of waiting for something, trust in the Lord."

Joseph Prince was well togged out as always with jeans and a grey zipped-up jacket, high zipped-up black boots, and three rings. He was in good form as he spoke on his theme of "How to Pray and See Results".

Joseph started with the confrontation between Elijah and Baal, but Jesus changed this old world with the Cross. He closed the book of vengeance and made us righteous through his death. There was one acknowledgement that Jesus calls us to repentance, but he has drenched us with blessings. It is not clear what we have to do, beyond acknowledging Jesus as Lord.

Joseph is not heavily into heaven and hell, death and judgement, but is not as affirming as Joel Osteen, who urges us to call in help, hope, and opportunity. We will eat the fruit of our words, which therefore need to be positive, not derogatory. Let the weak say "I am strong" and call in help and energy. Don't call in bad things about yourself; call in what you want to be, and it will come. Book success in every season.

Geraldine Doogue[1] had a half-hour *Compass* program on the coming Plenary Council, and most participants linked it to the sexual

---

[1] Geraldine Doogue is the presenter of the Australian television program *Compass*, which focusses on issues related to faith.

abuse crisis. I was apprehensive about the program, but it was not as bad as I feared. All the participants, except one who had left, loved the Church and wanted her strengthened. Some would change her radically. What was most disappointing was the absence of discussion about the main challenges: no discussion on the call to repent and believe, the challenges to faith, family life, sexuality, life. A lot of the discussion, in other words, missed the point.

Geraldine Doogue pointed out that the sexual crisis exposed deep flaws in the Church. Much that was shameful was revealed, and she encouraged [Brisbane] Archbishop [Mark] Coleridge to agree that the Church was hovering between life and death and fighting for survival. What leader could publicly agree with such sentiments, even if they were partially true? The decline in faith and morals goes back to the 1960s at least, and the paedophile crisis is only one example and cause which is hastening the decline.

The leadership of the Church came under substantial attack, and Robert Fitzgerald and Francis Sullivan ran their usual arguments. For Robert F., the leadership model in the Church is illegitimate and in need of massive reform. Francis S. urged the introduction of women deacons and a more inclusive policy for same-sex-attracted persons and claimed that the areas in Church life with "oomph" were lay-led. None of this was new or surprising.

What was most disappointing were the views of the president of the Australian Catholic Bishops' Conference, who claimed the bishops had failed in a colossal way and made catastrophic mistakes. It would be an overstatement to say that he continued this tradition in the program, but he did not help, did not provide leadership to steady the ship and rally the believers, but followed the bait thrown out, took the easy path. The path to renewal lies in a return to the sources and the kerygma, not in imitating the Uniting Church. The bishops broke the back of the paedophile crisis nearly twenty-five years ago with *Towards Healing* and the Melbourne Response.[2] Offences fell radically from the 1990s. It was the bishops who set up the Truth, Justice and Healing Commission, where Sullivan was

[2] *Towards Healing* was the official response in December 1996 of the Australian Catholic Bishops' Conference to the problem of sexual abuse. The Melbourne Response was the policy the Archdiocese of Melbourne adopted at a public forum in October 1996 in response to the problem of sexual abuse.

executive officer. These facts need to be acknowledged as well as the many disastrous mistakes. The Church did not come to grief through doing what the Gospels urged but through not doing as she should have. The Church takes her message from Christ and the apostles and listens so she can teach and serve more effectively.

Prime Minister Gillard struck a mighty blow for the anti-religious forces by calling the Royal Commission,[3] which was reinforced by much of the media and did a mighty service for the victims and for the Church, which was forced to confront her sins and crimes, often luridly rerun many times by the press. Unfortunately, the Royal Commission became more anti-Catholic as it progressed, and the televising of the hearings produced something like the Soviet Union show trials.

Sometimes leaders have to be defensive when the only alternative is capitulation to untruths or partial truths. And standing up to the prevailing secular hegemony can be uncomfortable or worse. The extent to which we have a crisis derives from the fact that we contradicted the best in our Christian and Catholic culture through our crimes and sins. We need evangelists and prophets, not facilitators.

The crisis has caused a lot of hurt, much of it below the surface, which is not confined to the victims, who are vocal and well-organized, and the bishops do have to tread carefully as well as justly. The Massgoers, those who have remained loyal to the Church in spite of the scandals, need to be reassured that the leadership is not following the line of the Sydney *Morning Herald*, *The Age*, and the ABC. Of course, the bishops are not setting out to do this, but they need to demonstrate that to both sides, while supporting justice for all involved.

In these threatening times, we must always remember God is with us and in our daily struggles. Psalm 119 reminds us God is victorious.

> *There are shouts of joy and victory*
> *in the tents of the just.*
>
> *The Lord's right hand has triumphed;*
> *his right hand raised me.*
> *The Lord's right hand has triumphed.*

---

[3] Julia Gillard (b. 1961) was the prime minister of Australia and leader of the Labor Party from 2010 to 2013. She established the Royal Commission into Institutional Responses to Child Sexual Abuse in 2012.

Monday, 7 October 2019

Today is the feast of Our Lady of the Rosary, instituted by the austere, reforming Dominican Pius V to commemorate the important naval victory of the Christian fleet over the Muslims in 1571 at Lepanto. The pope believed the victory was helped by many Catholics praying the rosary to Our Lady, and the feast was known as Our Lady of Victories.

The Muslims no longer are a threat to the West in the way they were for a thousand years, but their capacity for terrorist violence will remain for the immediate future at least. The SBS, a somewhat unreliable guide, announced that US forces are leaving the Kurdish-controlled area of northeast Syria, abandoning the Kurds to a proposed Turkish offensive. The allies of the US must always beware.

I enjoyed my second two-hour spell in the garden, taking two twenty-minute exercise periods and chatting with a couple of wardens. It was not warm, and in fact I felt slightly cold. Naturally I enjoyed it.

Monday is my weekly contact visit day for an hour-long visit, usually preceded by a strip search, which I now handle better than when I arrived. They did not enforce the worst indignities, so I was grateful for that small kindness.

The hour with Terry and Bernadette Tobin passed quickly and very pleasantly, although they didn't have a great deal of news. I recounted my Sunday experience with the tub containing my possessions from the property section, which had twenty or thirty more letters which had not been sent on to me. I complained, and everyone was at a loss to explain it. I suggested everything be passed out to my lawyers, and they could identify the letters for me and send them back here. I did find an article from Caitie on the dumbing down of US universities[4] in an express post envelope from Bernadette, who explained this was the second copy she had sent. The warder prudently suggested that the tub and its contents be left here and that I speak with the commandant Silensky (I keep mistaking his name).[5]

---

[4] Greg Lukianoff and Jonathan Haidt, "The Coddling of the American Mind", *Atlantic*, September 2015.

[5] Nick Selisky, general manager of the Victoria Department of Justice and Regulation.

In fact, he and another senior officer did call this morning. He suggested many of the letters were hostile and therefore kept from me, but I doubt that was true for most of them. At any rate, a senior officer will examine them all and report to me. Silensky conceded that the quality of staff varied, and all agree I should receive my mail.

I managed to write four letters yesterday, two of them to prisoners and one to the two young Dominican Sisters who were professed for the Ganmain convent today. I offered all of my prayers today for them. All the Sisters there have been great supporters, writing and praying regularly.

I felt rather tired and a bit disgruntled this afternoon for no sufficient reason. I will try to go to bed earlier tonight. I rarely put out the light before midnight, but we are not woken by the siren until 7:15 am, more or less. This is not a place for old-time Prussian efficiency—thanks be to God.

Only a few letters arrived today. A verse from Psalm 16 seems appropriate.

> *I am here and I call, you will hear me, O God.*
> *Turn your ear to me; hear my words.*
> *Display your great love, you whose right hand saves*
> *your friends from those who rebel against you.*

Tuesday, 8 October 2019

It was a beautiful spring afternoon as I took my exercise, clear and fresh, although it started to rain lightly when I returned inside.

Today saw the successful resolution of the problem of my undistributed letters. It proved to be a storm in a teacup, resolved, at least in part, by Mr Harris' intervention, although I was quite clear in my mind that I would reject every attempt to pull the wool over my eyes.

The day began badly when Mr MacLean (with Mac, the Scottish spelling), a senior officer with three pips, arrived in my cell to explain that the letters I had not received were either hate mail or contained photos of children. This claim could have been described in many ways, but I replied that I had read some of the letters, mentioning

Caitie's article and some cards, which did not fit into these categories. He quickly retracted, saying that he had not read all of them and would get an officer to do so. That was OK by me.

I then wrote to him a one-page letter repeating these facts and explaining that I did not want to escalate the matter but wanted only to receive the letters, which were my due, and I would be grateful to know the number of hate letters and photos. I slipped out a note to Mr Harris, requesting he look at the letter before I sent it, but heard nothing.

When I was leaving for my hour in the gymnasium, MacLean was at the desk, so I hailed him and said I had a letter, which I retrieved for him. He said he would read it and get back to me.

Eventually after lunch, he returned, saying there were no hate letters, but photos and cards with gold paper or religious objects, and then giving me about fifteen to twenty letters, asking me to choose what I wanted, and limiting my choice for photos to six. I put aside what I did not want, while he approved my selection except for a group photo outside Lima, where World Youth Day volunteers had constructed the Cardinal's Steps [an outdoor path] on a hillside— dust in summer, mud in winter—in an immense new shanty town for migrants from the mountains. Heaven only knows how bad their previous conditions must have been for them to flee to these. Many did have work in Lima, however. The photo was confiscated because the group contained one child.

All was resolved and no blood was shed, but when I discussed the situation with Sr Mary, she remarked how powerless most of the prisoners (three-quarters without year-twelve qualifications) would be to fight their corner successfully.

The loot included the original article Caitie had sent me on 30 June and the second copy Bernadette had sent a fortnight ago, as well as photos of Rachel Casey's baby-shower parties.[6] I will now be able to heal the small hurt Caitie felt in my not commenting on the article.

I spent an hour in the gym, playing quoits for the first time in decades. Much room for improvement. In the ping pong, I did not

[6] Rachel Casey is the daughter of Michael Casey, former secretary to Cardinal Pell, 1997–2014.

reach 200 shots on my backhand or 100 on my forehand. Regularly solving my daily (easy) Sudoku.

A lady from George's Hill in Dublin sent me a beautiful card with Vermeer's *Woman Holding a Balance* on the front. A great painter, Vermeer was one of the first to paint the middle class, rather than saints or aristocrats.

Her message was:

Praying and hoping the scales of Justice swing in your favour this time!

Wednesday, 9 October 2019

Another day successfully negotiated. The medical staff had given me a new hose or attachment for my sleep apnea machine yesterday, so that worked well. They also promised a new adapter and connection, which is loose and needs to be coaxed into position to achieve sufficient current for the machine. The machine is a blessing, as I felt better on the first morning after I used it many years ago, due to the unbroken sleep.

My time in the gymnasium went well, although I often feel tired and lethargic in the mornings. For some reason, I sensed that my reflexes were sharper this morning from the moment I started my ping pong. So it proved to be, as I scored 290 unbroken shots on my backhand and about 150 on my forehand, both personal bests, as they now say.

I received three new books, two on history, one on Catholic social justice theory and the ALP [Australian Labor Party], and two copies of *The Spectator*. While phoning Kartya this afternoon, I discovered that she had delivered the prosecution reply this morning and the books and magazines, but they had not arrived to me. I asked Mr Harris if he could expedite matters, and he promised to do what was possible. It would be useful to read the document before Paul and Kartya come tomorrow to discuss it. Paul said the document was disingenuous and did not deal with many of the issues; because it cannot! Kartya was very cross with the prosecution's approach and also recounted that the chief prosecutor's name, not Boyce's, was on the document. One senior lawyer predicted that if she appeared in the High Court, she would be slaughtered as the young boys had been slaughtered by Herod in the massacre of the innocents. Kartya knew the reference, of course, but we wondered who was innocent.

In some dioceses, priests were ordered not to preach on my case, so one or two or more, such as Brendan Purcell, preached on John Fisher or Cardinal Newman, while the congregation drew its own conclusions.

In April this year, *Annals* ran Fr George Rutler's article on Newman and myself.[7] Newman was sued for libel by a disreputable Neapolitan friar, Giacinto Achilli, who, after a history of sexual offences, eighteen in Malta alone, had formed a No-Popery society to denounce the Whore of Babylon.

The case ran for five days in 1852, concluding with a guilty verdict against Newman, who received the nominal fine of £100 [$136]. He received donations for his huge legal expenses, perhaps £2 million [$2,726,335] in today's values, and letters of support from many countries.

Later in that same year, Newman wrote to his sister Jemima, "I cannot help saying that educated men and judges have more to answer for when they do wrong, than a vulgar prejudiced Jury." Who could disagree with such a general proposition?

May my faith always remain strong up to and beyond the High Court ruling on my appeal, so that "the intimate sense will never fade away, will possess me more and more, of the true and tender Providence which has always watched over me for good and the power of that religion which is not degenerate from its ancient glory, of zeal for God, and of compassion towards the oppressed" (J. H. Newman).

Thursday, 10 October 2019

Today was a solid working day for me after Mr Harris finally obtained the prosecution reply to our appeal this morning, after it had floated in limbo somewhere in the prison for twenty-four hours. It is

---

[7] For another version of this article, see George W. Rutler, "What Newman Can Tell Us about the Cardinal Pell Verdict", *Crisis*, 14 March 2019, https://www.crisismagazine.com /2019/what-newman-can-tell-us-about-the-cardinal-pell-verdict.

unimpressive. Paul yesterday used the term "ingenuous" to describe it, but my choice for a one-worder was "mendacious".

While it was only ten pages, I had not finished reading it when I was called for my two hours in the garden before my visit. It was coldish, requiring a cardigan after I finished my twenty minutes' walking and rosary; so I finished reading the document rather than chatting with my single guard (sometimes there are two). There is not much colour in the garden apart from the red-orange flowers under the rotunda, but the roses are budding and not too far from blooming. I have taken to watching the ABC gardening show, when I am not exercising, between 11:00 and 12:00, and am learning a lot. I would like to have a nice garden near the seminary and am looking to see how many of my old-fashioned favourites, more suited to southern Victoria, might be planted usefully in Sydney. Roses are still my favourite flower. The show features many lovely gardens from the different regions of Australia, although my preferences derive from my childhood rather than favouring Australian native plants or Italian or Middle Eastern models.

I was much taken by the Japanese gardens I saw, and at one stage floated the idea of planting a significant number of fruit blossoms on the lawns at St Patrick's Cathedral, now locked in by an iron fence; but as I could not find one supporting voice, my project lapsed. I was particularly proud of the English cottage garden developed at my residence at Gellibrand St, Kew, but it was axed, on cost grounds, soon after my successor moved in. One aspect of the TV show which surprised me was the number of repeats, even in the few months I have been watching.

I should return to this gardening digression with a word or two about Sydney, where I lived at Cathedral House, without my own residence. In front of the house, we have a magnificent jacaranda tree, which we have featured in cathedral photos. I think I wrote about jacarandas in my Sunday *Telegraph* column, and a correspondent wrote from Brisbane recounting how the Queensland University featured their jacaranda in their centenary celebrations and by the year's end it had to be removed. The letter urged me to have our jacaranda tested, which we did, and it passed the test. However, I planted another directly in front of the house entrance, so it would be able to take over when the older one dies. It is growing steadily.

I also planted two or three on either side of the back entrance, and one of these remains. The only other horticultural blow I struck at St Mary's in Sydney was to insist on the replanting of two ancient and very tall palm trees, which were slated for destruction as we restored the footpath and cast-iron fence on St Mary's Rd. Demolition would have been cheaper, but both palms are now thriving near the restored Chapter House, the oldest building in the complex (1840s).

The Langrells called in the afternoon, as Jessica (Sr Mary Grace) was home from Canada for Tom and Billie's wedding. We had a great chat, and the wedding, joining two strong Catholic families, was a wonderful celebration religiously and humanly. After Lauren's death, they are returning to some normality, and this wedding and grandchildren (hopefully) will help the healing.

I spent the day preparing eight pages of points for my meeting with Paul and Kartya tomorrow, and in the evening, when I had finished, I celebrated with a Kit-Kat and a whole small bottle of Coca Cola (not my usual half bottle) as I watched the last half of Monty Don's[8] program on some magnificent Islamic gardens in Iran and Morocco and then the next instalment of *The Name of the Rose* by Umberto Eco,[9] a fabulous writer, a Catholic atheist who loved Western Catholic culture but did not believe in God. I wonder whether he had a mother of strong faith.

A few disparate lines from Gerard Manley Hopkins will serve as our prayer.

> *Glory be to God for dappled things—*
> *For skies of couple-colour as a brinded cow; . . .*
> *Landscape plotted and pieced—fold, fallow, and plough;*
> *And all trades, their gear and tackle and trim. . . .*

> *He fathers-forth whose beauty is past change:*
> *Praise him.*

---

[8] Monty Don (b. 1955) is a British broadcaster on subjects related to gardening, especially on the BBC series *Gardeners' World*.

[9] Umberto Eco (1932–2016) was an Italian novelist and cultural critic best known for his 1980 novel *The Name of the Rose*, a popular historical mystery.

Friday, 11 October 2019

True to their word, Paul and Kartya arrived around 9:30–10:00 as promised, after I had completed my half hour in the exercise pen, which I must volunteer to clean. It was not warm but pleasant with some clouds.

I phoned the Tobins, and Terry was home, which I did not expect. He had a list of points for discussion on the case, and to my surprise he had obtained a copy of the prosecution's reply.

I made a number of basic points, one of which was that we should not place all our eggs in one basket, by proving exclusively that an important issue of law was at stake, to the exclusion of the facts and injustices of the case.

Terry agreed, explaining succinctly the legal point at issue. Does a person accused of paedophilia now have to prove his innocence against any complainant, even one who is unable to produce any corroborative evidence and must confront hostile evidence (a reversal of the onus of truth)?

The second point to be stated is that a flagrant injustice has been perpetrated by the guilty verdict.

Terry mentioned that a mutual friend had prepared a couple of pages, which he was inclined to send to the barristers. I felt that nothing was to be lost (except perhaps the barristers feeling miffed about "interference"), but I don't know whether anything emerged from this quarter.

I was going to request that Terry pick up my journal booklets to take back to Sydney, so the typing could commence. As Terry was already in Sydney, Bernadette volunteered to perform this task as she was coming to Melbourne tomorrow. I was to inform Kartya that this was my wish, as I believe the Tobins would be able to prevent any breach of security.

I passed my eight pages to Paul, who read them through, and we discussed the issues as they arose in the prosecution document. As I anticipated, they were "over" all the issues, and we agreed that my legal arguments were correct. The only exception to this was a tentative disagreement between Kartya and myself on whether Potter claimed he was in the procession of 15 and 22 December.

Bret was most unimpressed by the prosecution document, saying that it would not impress High Court judges and that he was preparing a strong statement exposing the inadequacies. Apparently it was a significant point in our favour that they described the argument about B denying that he was assaulted as "ingenuous". The team was vexed by this, as [Bret] Walker is a top jurist who is not ingenuous. I expressed my ambition that our document should smite the foe mightily, and Paul assured me that this would be done.

For some reason that was not explained to me, Kartya was keen for the document to be filed earlier than Tuesday. However, I thought this boded well, although they were anticipating differences and delay on which documents are to be provided.

In the morning, I expected that Bret would sign off over the weekend, but when speaking with the solicitors this afternoon, Kartya said Walker had already approved the document, which she would bring for my examination tomorrow, to be lodged early on Monday. This is wonderful news, provided I am happy with the end product, something I anticipate as our discussion all ran the same way.

A prayer from Thursday's breviary points in the correct direction.

> *Lord, in answer to our prayer*
> *give us patience in suffering hardship*
> *after the example of your only begotten Son,*
> *who lives and reigns for ever and ever.*

Saturday, 12 October 2019

It was quite a warm day—probably around 20°C [68°F]—so that I was briefly tempted to take off my green prison top when I was outside mid-afternoon. In the morning, I did ask for a broom to clean up the second pen; Mr Harris said OK, but the broom never arrived. As I returned to the cell, he mentioned that he had forgotten to give me the broom to clean my cell (which I had done yesterday). I clarified that I had been talking about the exercise area, and the topic lapsed.

In the afternoon, the exercise pen, which develops a huge puddle after rain, had been scrubbed out by a young prisoner who volunteered to do so, as Mr Harris explained, unprompted. The end result was excellent, as the grot on the ground was gone. No harm was done by any of this, which is typical of my time in prison.

I had expected to see Kartya in the morning with our Applicant's Reply to the sad nonsense of the prosecution. In the early afternoon, I had arrived at the lift to descend for a professional visit, when we were halted and I was returned to my cell while the guard discovered what was happening. It was explained that Kartya had decided she did not need to see me, provided she could be sure I received the document today, which, the warder added, would be with me within a half hour. And so it was.

Later in the afternoon, when I was speaking on the phone to Terry, he delivered a message from Kartya, who had called at the jail in the morning but had been discouraged from seeing me because it was a visitors' day and I would have been seen by prisoners and/or visitors if I had descended for the visit. She did not persist in these circumstances.

The system is geared to be at least partially inefficient, so that the right hand does not know what the left hand is doing, as part of the punishment procedures. Generally, there is not much malice, at least in my experience, although some officials enjoy exercising power and being obstructive. Working in the Vatican was a useful preparation for the run-arounds imposed in jail.

The Applicant's Reply is very much a lawyer's document prepared for the High Court, which demonstrates no interest in providing a few gems for the media. It is closely and tightly argued and is, I suspect, a forensic masterpiece something like the dissection of a corpse. It seems Walker has written most of it himself, as the document moves at a high level in precise, sometimes complicated language.

I produced three drafts of a final sentence, which I will ask to have added at the end of the document, for the sake of the general populace and setting out the stark claim of a grave injustice, demonstrated on factual as well as legal grounds.

In the afternoon, I watched some of the horse racing from Randwick and especially from Caulfield, which featured the Caulfield Guineas [race]. As I explained to my sister on the phone, it took me back to Royal Oak days, when we followed the races closely.

In the evening, I watched the next episode on Hitler, featuring the invasion of Poland and the defeat of France, where his victories united a formerly dubious German people in support behind him.

This was followed by a film on the Madras mathematician with little formal education [Srinivasa] Ramanujan, a genius who went to Cambridge University before the First World War to work with Godfrey Hardy, an English mathematician, and John Littlewood, leaving behind in India his young wife. Just before his early death from tuberculosis, he was made a Fellow of both Trinity College in Cambridge and the Royal Society. He was a devout Hindu believer, who claimed his mathematical insights (for want of a better word) came from God. Hardy was an atheist whose chaplain had told him that God was like your kite in the sky, which you pulled on in need. His kite never flew.

But he did believe that the mathematical truths or principles which explained the universe were there to be discovered by us and were not the invention of any human genius. Scientists should be invaluable allies in the defence of truth, even if only physical and mathematical truths in their beauty, as an essential building block for civilized communities and as a prerequisite for belief in God. If there is no objective truth, there is no God. And if we cannot know objective truth, we are in a pretty pickle, condemned to speak only of appearances, to swapping intuitions and being unable to resolve our differences rationally.

Ramanujan was not a Christian, and I am not sure he was a monotheist, but we profess:

> *There is none like the Lord,*
> *there is none besides you.*
> *There is no Rock like our God. . . .*
>
> *For the Lord is a God who knows all.*
> *It is he who weighs men's deeds. (1 Sam 2:2–3)*

WEEK 34

Miscarriage of Justice

13 October 2019—19 October 2019

Sunday, 13 October 2019

Sunday had an unusual beginning, as I did not wake up in time for the televised Mass and was even slightly late for Joseph Prince. As always, he had his high black boots and, on this occasion, wore a tight-fitting black suit with a shirt and tie. He is certainly no John the Baptist, but he loves Christ, even if his message is incomplete. Today he spoke about prosperity in every area. He lamented the division between the Southern and Northern Kingdoms [of Israel] in the time of Jeroboam (931 B.C.), urging the important connection of humility and full knowledge. Joel Osteen was displaced by Channel 10's coverage of the Bathurst car race.

Songs of Praise came from multiracial Birmingham with some excellent community singing, using hymns announced as old favourites, as I am sure they were. I knew only one of them, "How Great Thou Art", but I wasn't surprised the others were much loved.

I am regularly using my list of hymns for my meditation, humming the words to myself. I found it easier, and I lapsed into fewer distractions. It seems to be something like the monks chanting the psalms at regular intervals during the day. For years I went to Tarrawarra [Abbey] for my annual retreat, partly because I found the chanting of the psalms a congenial way of praying.

When I phoned Terry during my morning exercise, we agreed on the following wording of a sentence to be added at the end of our Applicant's Reply: "The findings of the Court of Appeal are founded on fundamental legal error and 'factual' assertions which are false and even impossible. This results in a grave miscarriage of justice."

Terry will suggest this wording this afternoon to Kartya in preparation for our discussion tomorrow morning. The words add nothing
to the legal argument but draw on it to provide something for friends
and foes in the media to seize upon.

The second reading in the breviary today is from St Cyril of Alexandria, who was active in the Council of Ephesus (431), defending
Mary as *Theotokos*, "the God-bearer", whom we call "Mother of
God", asserting the strict unity of the divine and the human in the
person Jesus Christ.

Cyril compares the building of the Temple in Jerusalem to the
building of the Church, present in many places, in the New Dispensation. Just as the prophet Malachi promised peace to all those who laid
the foundation for the rebuilding of the ancient Temple, so too the
peace of Christ will come into the souls of those who work to build up
the Church, so "they will find it easy to save their souls and to devote
themselves completely to the pursuit of virtue."

One or two correspondents have written wondering how so many
prayers around the world have not so far resulted in my exoneration.
God works at his own pace and allows human events to progress
along their own paths—generally, except when a miracle occurs. I
do believe God is still with his Church in Australia and with me and
that God believes in ultimate justice and in the importance of my
exoneration for the life of the Church.

My health and equanimity have been real since I went to prison,
and spiritually, too, I have not felt on the edge of an abyss, although
occasionally I do slump a bit. I am sure God has brought me this
peace that Cyril of Alexandria was speaking about, through the love
and support of my family, friends, and loyal supporters, not all of
them Catholics or even Christians, and especially from their regular
prayers and penance. Years ago, a family friend was dying, leaving a
loving wife and children. When I visited him in hospital and mur-
mured something about praying for a miracle, he interjected. "No,"
he said, "the miracle has happened because I accept my death."

I have learnt a lot from various SBS programs since I have come
here, despite the relentless left-of-centre propaganda. A few days ago,
they announced breathlessly that the glacier on Mont Blanc was melt-
ing at the end of the northern summer, never mentioning of course
the trees from previous warm periods buried in the ice of the Alps.

Tonight Michael Portillo was travelling by train in Ukraine from Kiev to Lviv to Odessa, which was founded, I discovered, by Catherine the Great in the second half of the eighteenth century. I have fond memories of my trip to Ukraine with Bishop Peter Stasiuk and some Australian bishops in 1998 to visit the Ukrainian Greek Catholics. This prompted one memory in particular of a Greek Catholic country parish priest, a married man, somewhere in western Ukraine, who was building a new church and seeking donations for the church bells. I rose to the bait, so somewhere in the countryside, we have such a bell, called George, which will, please God, continue to call the faithful to worship for many decades.

A priest from Galway, who had known his own problems, gave me the words of a little prayer he had "formulated one dark night".

Dear Jesus, all I can do is trust in you and ask your grace, day by day, to follow your way. Mary, I need you. Amen.

Monday, 14 October 2019

Good weather today, genuine spring weather for my couple of hours in the garden. I walked for 15–20 minutes on two occasions, chatted a bit with the guards, and read some material on the late Jim Macken[1] and on Philip Lawler's[2] estimate of Pope Francis. Quite a few birds were flying around initially, like sparrows, but plumper and browner. Most disappeared after a while, but the bird song continued through nearly the whole period. The gardens are not like the Ballarat Botanical Gardens, but they are such an improvement on my grotty exercise pens. I did manage to obtain a broom this morning and swept the second pen, which is now much cleaner, although the walls also could do with some work.

Soon after 9:00 am, I phoned my lawyers to discover the fate of my suggested final paragraph. Ruth had spoken with Bret, and the reply

---

[1] James Joseph Macken (1927–2019) was an Australian lawyer, judge, and human rights activist.

[2] Philip Lawler (b. 1950) is the editor of *Catholic World News*, the first English-language Catholic news service on the Internet.

was simply that the content of the statement had been settled and no additions were possible. This reflected a decision, but gave no explanation. I suspect he was busy with other things, that the document had been formatted exactly into five pages, and that he had signed it already. I was more annoyed than disappointed, because while the addition added nothing to the legal argumentation, it would have served a public relations purpose. I agreed, but asked Paul to convey the message that I was disappointed.

In the afternoon, when I was more sanguine, I informed Terry Tobin, who pointed out that the few lines could be issued as a statement if and when the document became public.

Terry in his turn had a piece of good news which he had read from an article on page 3 of *The Australian*, where a couple of notables from Western Australia had announced that those accused of crimes which had inflamed the public should be able to choose between trial by jury or trial by judge. I was named specifically as one of those who did not have a ghost of a chance of a fair trial by jury, or some such phrase. I need to see the text before I comment further, but it is good news.

The decision of the Supreme Court in Britain to intervene in the prorogation of the Parliament controversy shows that even the highest judicial authorities are influenced by their predispositions and by the climate of the times. The voicing of public disquiet about my position is to be welcomed, in my view, not only as supporting the objective truth of the situation, but as a counter to the waves of hostility and prejudice. A number of writers and visitors have claimed that more people are conceding that I was wronged, with quite a few saying my individual innocence doesn't avail much, as one man should "die" to requite the sins of his people.

Tonight, the ABC *Four Corners* had a balanced and informative program on the penetration by Communist China of some Australian universities through the Confucius Institutes. One in four students at Sydney University is Chinese, and their government-backed organization has the biggest group on the student council this year and provided the president, a first for a Chinese Australian. The official Chinese university groups are used to keeping tabs on the Chinese students. It is good to see the ABC making a useful contribution. Andrew Hastie, the Western Australian member of the Federal Parliament, an ex-soldier who warned about increasing Chinese influence, recounted the story of Melos, a much smaller island and community than we are, who opted for neutrality during the war between Athens and Sparta and was destroyed by the victorious Athenians after the war. [Prime Minister] John Howard showed the way we should follow into the future, and he was respected by the Chinese. He was keen to cooperate as much as might be appropriate with China on trade, but he made it quite clear that our allegiance was with the United States and that we are committed to the ideals of a free and democratic society.

Psalm 58 says something for me and perhaps for Australia.

> *Rescue me, God, from my foes;*
> *protect me from those who attack me.*
> *O rescue me from those who do evil*
> *and save me from blood-thirsty men.*

Tuesday, 15 October 2019

Today is the feast of St Teresa of Ávila, known in many non-English speaking countries as Teresa of Jesus. She was a sixteenth-century Spanish Carmelite nun, another Spanish spiritual luminary like Ignatius of Loyola, John of the Cross, leaders of the Catholic renewal or Counter-Reformation in Spain (although the Protestants were never strong there), who was a reformer and mystic, a mighty force for God. It is interesting that her own convent in Ávila only accepted her strict reforms to community life early in the twentieth century.

She was also a remarkable spiritual writer, and Fr John Masso, who brought Opus Dei to Australia and was a good friend whom I visited in Pamplona when he was dying, gave me a copy of her masterpiece, *The Castle*, whose exact name I forget.[3] I struggled through without liking it, perhaps because it was too "Spanish", with Teresa constantly emphasizing her own unworthiness, but more probably because, for my liking, she linked progress to Christ too strictly to suffering. Seventeen or so years ago, I was much less open to putting a lot of emphasis on such an essential link. I always believed in

---

[3] *The Interior Castle* (1588).

redemption through the Cross, and one Australian archbishop years ago lamented on television my "crucifixion Christianity". But I had much less enthusiasm then for seeing that as the only or best Christian journey for us.

In today's breviary reading from *The Book of Her Life*, she wrote: "A man can bear all things provided he possesses Christ Jesus dwelling within him as his friend and affectionate guide. Christ gives us help and strength, never deserts us and is true and sincere in his friendship." She then continues on to emphasize that prayer must always be Christocentric, even high contemplative prayer. St John Paul once got into trouble in Sri Lanka for teaching this and warning against a mysticism which voyaged into the abyss, into nothingness.

A letter arrived today from a priest friend (who also had a spot of serious bother). He wrote that he was forced back to fundamentals by his troubles, shedding a lot of baggage and being all the better for it.

Like most other adult Christian believers, I can attest that Christian faith is an enormous support in times of trial because God always loves us, but also because our deprivations or decline or tribulations can be joined to Christ's for some good purpose. This gives meaning and purpose. The secular alternatives are to see suffering as brutal and without meaning, best confronted by a Stoic determination to act honourably. But even this needs to be rooted in something deeper, e.g., the public estimation of good people or of successive generations.

Paul and Kartya called to discuss the lodging of our reply and explained that accompanying documents are to be submitted by 9 November, and soon after that we shall learn the date when leave to appeal will or will not be granted by the High Court. This is usually through some sort of hearing. If successful, Paul believes the court will move expeditiously to judge the matter, whatever that means. Perhaps a hearing in February.

Sr Mary called with her Filipino assistant Mel to bring me Communion and to tell me she will be away next week. As always, she brought me Sr Mary McGlone's sermon, this week on the Ten Lepers. For the first time, I was not highly enthusiastic, although it was still a good, thoroughly prepared sermon.

So I pray.

God our Father, for what we have received, so much good, so many blessings, make us truly grateful.

Wednesday, 16 October 2019

Today I received about twenty-five letters on top of the twenty-five I received yesterday, and a couple of them, from Fr Brendan Purcell and Katrina Lee, contained about fifteen to twenty articles on the case, the synod, the Vatican finance scandals, and the looming threat from the Germans.

Yesterday, I organized a mass of letters and paperwork into the appropriate folders after they had lain in a penultimate mess before the final sorting. This took me some time. Today, I embarked on opening and reading the letters and quite a few of the articles. Not surprisingly, many of my correspondents are deeply concerned about the state of the Church at the moment and worried how the synod and the German meeting will go.

My earlier confidence about the unlikelihood of a schism remains, but the odds against have shortened. Cardinal X is a man of hot air and is likely to fold under stern resistance, but those Germans around him might be made of sterner nationalist stuff and insist on their ability to do better than Jesus, reshaping teachings on sexuality, marriage, family, ministry, morality (even on life issues), so pushing the apostolic tradition into an inferior subordinate position more appropriate to its "lack of sophistication".

A month ago, Phil Lawler in Rome had an interesting article on the possibility of a schism, an article which only arrived to me today from a regular American correspondent.

Lawler argues that the possibility of a schism is remote, but Pope Francis has spoken calmly about such a prospect, saying he is not frightened by it, something Lawler believes is frightening in itself.

Many German members of their "synod", where half of them are laity, are openly planning to challenge Church doctrines, and [Rainer] Cardinal Woelki of Cologne, the leader of the orthodox party, has expressed his fears of a schism, so that the German church is the first cause of concern. Not surprisingly, the *New York Times* has been writing about the prospect of a schism by the John Paul and Benedict followers in the United States, the Gospel Catholics. Nothing about Germany.

I believe Lawler's diagnosis is correct when he points out that the topic of schism has been raised by the "busiest and most aggressive online defenders" of Pope Francis, who "recognize that they cannot engineer the radical changes they want without precipitating a split in the Church. So they want orthodox Catholics to break away first, leaving them free to enact their own revolutionary agenda."[4] This won't happen.

Especially in the Amazonia Synod, the more immediate danger is that important doctrinal changes might be introduced on, e.g., the nature of revelation, the uniqueness of Christ, the call to baptism and conversion, while loud protestations are made that no essential change, much less distortion, has been made to the apostolic tradition. Another variation of this sleight of hand could be to advocate the ordination of *viri probati* as elderly married men in this remote area, which has 80 percent Protestants in some parts, where some priests are like Bishop Erwin Kräutler, the retired Austrian-born missionary with no enthusiasm for conversion or baptising the indigenous, and where there is little enthusiasm for Mass-going and no money to support a married clergy—to advocate such ordinations in this tiny church, while claiming that the discipline of mandatory celibacy for other Latin-rite clergy is to remain in place generally. Another exception might be the Pacific Islands. The ordination of married men, young or old, must be faced squarely across the world and decided on the grounds of prudence and spiritual productivity. Jesus and Paul and John were not married, so there are good scriptural precedents for a celibate clergy as well as the history of spiritual achievement in the Latin Church. And I suspect the overwhelming majority of young priests want the discipline to be maintained. Priestly celibacy, lived faithfully, points eloquently to the supernatural.

We must pray for Wisdom to do her work in these two synods and in the Holy Father.

Alone with none to aid her, [Wisdom] is all powerful, herself ever unchanged, she makes all things new: age after age she finds her way into holy men's hearts, turning them into friends and spokesmen of God (Wis 7:27).

[4] Phil Lawler, "Who Benefits from All This Talk of Schism?", *Catholic Culture*, 17 September 2019, https://www.catholicculture.org/commentary/who-benefits-from-all-this-talk-schism/.

Thursday, 17 October 2019

The highlight of the day was the visit of my successor in Sydney, Archbishop Anthony Fisher, who had been in Bendigo on Wednesday for the consecration of their new bishop, the Ballarat-born Shane Mackinlay, who was dux of St Pat's, Ballarat, when I was living across the road with Bishop James O'Collins. Please God, he will help turn things around or at least slow the rot.

Anthony had been in Rome last Sunday for the canonisation of Cardinal Newman, a celebration I had hoped to attend. In opening the synod, Pope Francis spoke of the cardinals today suffering for their faith: Barbarin and I are the most likely candidates. The archbishop had spoken on Newman and conscience, and Tracey Rowland on Newman and education. After the talk, she responded to questions, and with typical indiscretion (as I asked the archbishop to tell her), at one point she said I had done more for Catholic education than anyone (for some period unknown to me). The whole audience of 600 to 700 people, almost entirely Anglophone, immediately gave a sustained burst of applause. I was deeply touched. He also reassured me that three cardinals had said to him explicitly that no one in Rome, whatever their stance, believed that I was guilty. He wasn't able to add any news about the financial scandals in the Vatican but was intrigued by the developments.

I am still not entirely sure what is going on, although the new procedures are working to some significant extent, as the IOR [the Vatican Bank] would not provide the €100 million [$1,316,718] without clarification and authorization. In the bad old days of a decade plus ago, the pouring in of good money after bad would have (and did) go on under the surface, undetected for much longer.

It is not surprising that initially the Secretariat of State refused to be audited and that, when this was required, it sacked the external auditors and then removed Libero Milone, the [Vatican] auditor.

I don't know how much is due to Vatican incompetence and to Vatican criminality, but Peter's Pence is involved, and the losses would certainly amount to tens of millions of euros. Mincione,[5] the

---

[5] Raffaele Mincione, and Italian businessman living in London, was the owner and manager of Athena Global Opportunities Fund when the Secretariat of State invested millions of euros through the fund.

erstwhile partner from whom they separated, invested €40 million [$48 million] and finished up with €160 million [$195 million]. I don't know whether this included his 2 percent annual commission for eight years, which gained for him €16 million [$19 million].

I am not sure what the explanation is for the forced resignation of Domenico Giani, head of the Vatican police, ostensibly because the circular [memo] about banning the five suspects from the Vatican was leaked to the press. Giani had shown kindness to me, but he had led the raid on Libero Milone, the auditor, using physical violence on a door and a safe (when keys were available, it is claimed) to intimidate. It could be that the party of the new *sostituto* [deputy secretary of state] feels that Giani was much too close to the former *sostituto*, [Angelo] Cardinal Becciu. Apparently the atmosphere in the Curia continues to be bad.

I was organized for my thirty-minute meeting with Archbishop Anthony, preparing a list of what I thought were eight points, only to discover we had no sixth point.

We discussed the Australian Plenary Council for next year, and he was happy to accept a few thoughts from me on "getting back on mission" produced by Catholics for Renewal. A strategy is needed for the forces of righteousness if only to limit the division and confusion and to avoid too much of the Church lurching off in the wrong direction as a result of such a gathering.

The two West Australian (WA) legal authorities who spoke of the necessary option of trial by judge rather than by jury in certain contentious areas were the former WA governor Malcolm McCusker QC and criminal lawyer Tom Percy QC. They explained that judges have to give reasons, while a "hangover" from the Middle Ages exempts juries from this. It was Percy who named me explicitly, saying I "never had a ghost of a chance in front of a jury".

It was this last claim, Terry Tobin felt, that explained the presence of Justice Peter Kidd, head of the County Court, on a Channel 10 program, *The Project*, which discussed my case in anonymous terms. Kidd felt that the system balances out, and Waleed Aly, the commentator, asked about judges required to pronounce sentence when they do not agree with the guilty verdict. Some felt Kidd's participation was ill advised.

Late at night, news came through that Boris Johnson and the EU had struck a deal, conveyed with the SBS London correspondent's barely disguised discomfort. There is no certainty the British Parliament will approve such a deal.

Let us hope that the author of Psalm 106 had the Vatican today in mind when he prayed:

> *He (God) stilled the storm to a whisper;*
> *all the waves of the sea were hushed.*
> *They rejoiced because of the calm,*
> *and he led them to the haven they desired.*

Friday, 18 October 2019

One small disappointment yesterday was that I did not have my two hours in the garden. The unit warders had to transfer one or more difficult prisoners—it was raining off and on—and ... I didn't make a fuss, but I shall be vigilant in the future about my entitlements.

My sleep apnea machine has not worked for a couple of nights due to a faulty cord connection. About ten or more days ago, I alerted the medical section to the looming difficulty and have been trying for some days to find out how far the proposal had reached. Despite my efforts, the best result I achieved was a roundabout message that they hoped the new cord and connection would arrive this week. So this morning when I was in the yard, I phoned Anne McFarlane to enquire by phone with ResMed whether the cord was available for the model which I carefully identified through its numbers.

In the middle of the afternoon, I finished up with two cords. The medical section eventually produced a cord which actually worked, and Anne had purchased another one and dialogued so effectively with the prison authorities that it arrived to me some hours after she delivered it. This was little short of a miracle and a considerable achievement.

In the morning, a dozen letters arrived including a large envelope crammed with photocopied articles from Tim O'Leary, as he had promised. I had some recollection of his mentioning two envelopes, so there could be more to come. I still have articles to read from earlier deliveries; I never anticipated being under some time pressure while in jail!

Chris Friel continues to write, mainly analysing the judgements of the appeal. He has homed in constructively and imaginatively on two questions I identified, but where I felt I did not progress far in my understanding.

Why was [Justice] Weinberg so noncommittal on the majority's absurd timing for the hiatus? I wondered whether he felt the majority would try to remedy the defect if he pushed the issue while leaving their mistaken verdict in place. I am hampered by ignorance of the protocols the judges must follow in considering the drafts or final versions of the verdicts of other judges. This tentative and crude hypothesis of mine seemed unsatisfactory even to me.

Friel believes Weinberg deals with all or most of the issues on the impossible hiatus, so "demolish[ing] the majority with a mattock" but not spelling out the theory's futility, "so he is obviously treating them (majority) gently", guessing that the majority are leaving "an independent judgement on the whole of the evidence" to the High Court.

I have only two additional comments on this first question. Friel correctly places great importance on Potter's evidence, while saying next to nothing on the evidence, their evidence, that the miscreants could not have been in the room before the servers because they were still in or leaving the procession. Even a credible witness cannot be in two places at once.

My second additional comment here is that the majority's precise identification of the time of the offence, as distinct from the imprecision of the prosecution, especially with the jury, is fatal for their cause, evidence of incompetence.

My second question is this: What did [Justice] Maxwell, who allegedly drafted the majority judgement, and [Justice] Ferguson think they were doing? If in fact they ignorantly reversed the onus of proof, this is an extraordinary error for Victoria's two most senior judges. Friel's theory is less simple (and therefore less plausible?) and more cynical. "They are just making the argument for the Crown as best they can so that in the end the truth will prevail", i.e., with the High Court.

The other event which was notable was an unpleasant incident while I was walking in the exercise pen and saying the rosary. Suddenly I was spat upon (or this was attempted) through the screen of the window between the two pens, which should not have been open. It was totally unexpected and accompanied by crude obscene abuse which identified and condemned me as a rock spider, etc. I was angry, paused, and went back to the window, glaring at him and saying, "How dare you come threatening me." He beat a hasty retreat out of view and then returned to his abuse.

I said nothing more and did not identify myself, although I did pray for him. I remained quietly in the pen for another half hour, but when the medical staff brought my evening medicine, I asked to have a word with the warder who put me in that area, complaining that the aperture was open and that this was the third occasion (and by far the worst) in a row where I had been abused, probably by the same man. I said I would not take my exercise again if he was next to me and abusive. The warder acknowledged that the screen should have been closed, but claimed (truly) he had only been in this unit yesterday and today. Later Mr Harris apologized, as he had forgotten to close the opening.

It was ironic because while meditating on the crowning of thorns mystery as I prayed the rosary, I had thought how I was no longer too much hurt or upset by most abuse. But this did upset me for a while. Today is the feast of St Luke, the author of my favourite Gospel, and the afternoon Scripture reading is from 2 Timothy 1:8–9.

Take your share of suffering for the sake of the gospel, in the strength that comes from God. It is he who brought us salvation and called us to a dedicated life, not for any merit of ours but of his own purpose and his own grace which was granted to us in Christ Jesus.

Saturday, 19 October 2019

Today was a quiet day, rather cool but clear in the morning, overcast and a slight drizzle as I took my afternoon exercise. In the early morning, about 8:30 am onwards, I think, no one seemed to be in the next pen, while in the second session the other pen was occupied but quiet. I was able to phone Anne McFarlane to thank and congratulate her on her unusual achievement, facilitated I suspect by Mr Harris, who understood the importance of getting things right medically (with my sleep apnea electric cord).

I also phoned Tim O'Leary, who was watching *The Sound of Music* with his son Joe, to thank him for so many articles which I still haven't finished reading. Tim asked whether I had read the two pieces from Xavier Rynne on the synod, which I did subsequently. Tomorrow I will ask Tim to get George Weigel to advise Xavier that he should remain anonymous.

Danny Casey and Anthony Robbie had also sent some articles on the financial scandals in Rome and their aftermath. Fred Martinez in the *Catholic Monitor* and Claudio Meloni [medium.com] on "The London Palace and the Scam to the Vatican" (I don't know either of them) have produced two lurid, romanticized articles which probably contain many truths but are inaccurate in some respects, oversimplified on their supposed factions, but evidence of the disharmony and disarray in the Vatican at the moment. Neither said explicitly that amidst all the sound and fury and the clouds of deceptive smoke and fog, it is now much harder for gross incompetence and corruption to continue. Much is still concealed. But ongoing corruption is impeded, when it is not eliminated. The two fundamental problems are the annual deficit, which is now structural, and the looming shortfall in the pension fund. While they are public knowledge, the scale of the deficits and losses are obscured, and I am still not sure how much progress has been made to remedy these two threats.

It is also heartening that a number of the articles highlight the central role of the erstwhile *sostituto* in the financial affairs of the Secretariat of State (whether he was the authorizer rather than the architect of the disasters is unclear) and his central role in the cancellation of the external audit and the removal of the auditor. One lurid press report claimed he is about to be thrown under the bus, but I shall believe that when I see it. Cardinals are not like laypeople except in Australia.

The Caulfield Cup was run in Melbourne, and the richest horse race in the world, the Everest, took place for the third time in Sydney. This sprint of 1200 metres [three-fourths of a mile] seems too short for it to become a great favourite with the public, apart from the dwindling number of aficionados. One wonders how the industry can continue to afford the prize money, $14 million for the Everest and $5 million for the Caulfield Cup, although it helps, as with the financial losses in the Vatican, if you only mention the amounts briefly and quickly. In the evening, England defeated the Wallabies soundly in the rugby union World Cup quarter finals in Japan, although the Aussies were not disgraced. Both sides fielded a goodly number of top class players whose families originated in the Pacific Islands.

I enjoyed my hour in the gymnasium, throwing four goals through the basketball ring (a spectacular improvement) and continuing my excellent form in the ping pong, scoring over 100 unbroken shots on both backhand and forehand sides of the table. I even reached over 250 shots on my forehand a couple of days ago. "Excellent" in my self-description is a relative term. Unfortunately, my right knee is swollen spectacularly after a too-exuberant use of the weights for my thighs. But I am still quite mobile and have no pain.

I did maintain my daily prayer routine despite all this worldly activity, topped off by another program on Hitler as the tide turned against Germany on the Eastern front, in Sicily and North Africa in 1942–1943, and then in Normandy in 1944. Hitler's evil arrogance and military stupidity gave immense advantages to the Allies, while he continued his surreal daily routine of luxury and escapism at Berchtesgaden, increasingly dependent on drugs. He was taking seventy pills a day as well as injections.

I should conclude this section with a prayer for the Church—

Especially that the damage from the Roman Synod can be limited and contained and that the rise of China will not result in a terrible war or in a Chinese hegemony in Asia and the Pacific with or without war.

The lessons of history are not entirely reassuring.

WEEK 35

Vatican Finances

20 October 2019—26 October 2019

Sunday, 20 October 2019

For some time we have been quiet in the evenings with no bangers or shouters. But tonight at 5:45 pm, we had an outbreak of almost demented shouting with one fellow proclaiming in a childish voice that he wanted to go home, another shouting to him to "shut up", others asking "Who are you?", while a couple of others just banged loudly as their contribution to the excitement. Then, after five or ten minutes, it subsided and ceased as suddenly as it had arisen.

My regular correspondent Gargasoulas has written to say that he is being transferred to Unit 10, where he will be able to mix with the others, some of whom he knows, and one or two terrorists. He will be able to do a bit of cooking, be out of his cell, and phone during the day. Naturally, he is delighted with the prospect, and after his three years in solitary, I am pleased for him. He told me he is not appealing, so he has a long road ahead of him. He promised to continue writing to me if I replied.

I managed to wake up in time for Mass on Channel 10 celebrated by Fr Thang Vu, who I suspect is not long ordained. He was pleased with himself for celebrating the Mass, his English was intelligible but somewhat halting, and he followed his sermon text closely on this Mission Sunday. He spoke briefly, but it was a Gospel message, and he celebrated with sincerity and dignity. He did not explore that sentence in today's Gospel which I find one of the most disconcerting in the New Testament, when Jesus himself asks, "However, when the

Son of Man comes, will he find faith on earth?" (Lk 18:8). My efforts, such as they were and are, were designed to help us today to plead not guilty to that implied charge, but the scale of the secularism in the Western world is unprecedented in history as the old pagans were nearly always polytheists. This was probably true even in Confucian China. And we don't know how the Son of Man will react if and when he finds little faith, except that he will be merciful. It is interesting that devotion to the Divine Mercy has joined the devotion to Jesus' Sacred Heart as very popular among the devout.

Joseph Prince's session was again a rerun, this time from 2010, the second one I have noticed. Naturally, he appeared younger, but only slightly so, and his hair was curly with less hair oil. Only a couple of rings, no high black boots, jeans, and a grey block jacket. The auditorium was much smaller, the song was belted out in a haze, and he was shouting more than he does now.

The romance of Christianity is to be dead to the Law and alive in Christ Jesus, who is all God and all man, a slightly misleading claim. Jesus is true God and true man, with two natures in one person. Justification and sanctification cannot come through the Law, and Jesus through his redemption is like a close-relative redeemer, who saves us when we are in trouble with our mortgage. It is OK to be rich, because Jesus is rich and wants to help us, and the streets of heaven are paved with gold.

Joel Osteen gave a truly excellent sermon of homely Christian wisdom, urging his congregation to disregard the disgruntled and dividers, those who stir up trouble. Be calm, be respectful, and be gone from such types. We have to stay grateful, not become poisoned; be like the good sons of Noah, who covered their father's drunken nakedness. We should repent of our sins, mind our own business, and have success in every season. I am not sure that Jesus promised Joel's reward, at least not in every season.

Songs of Praise told good stories of Christian service on the Isle of Sheppey near London and gave us the usual wonderful community singing of such hymns as "Love Divine" and even "The Lord of Sea and Sky". England in many ways is a pagan place, often a secularist trendsetter, especially for the Anglophone world, but it has many pockets of faith, of bedrock resilience like the Catholic resistance in France, if less exuberant.

As today's antiphon reminds us:

The Cross of the Lord is become the tree of life for us.

Monday, 21 October 2019

During the two hours in the garden, the big news was that the first rose had bloomed, in red and gold, like the colours of ancient Rome's army and my Italian football team, Roma. In the days when I travelled frequently by air, I had the Roma colours in the ribbon on my suitcase. A number of other buds are close to blooming, which will add some variety to the place, where the only burst of colour is on the orange flowers under the rotunda, whose name no one I have asked knows. The boss of the jail called in while I was outside, asked how I like it (very well indeed), and wondered whether I would water the garden. Why not? I replied.

It was cloudy and quite cold, so I put on my cardigan as I sat on the veranda and read one of Lord Jonathan Sumption's Reith Lectures.[1] As the forecast predicted, the sky cleared in the afternoon, and it was pleasant out in the pen.

My knee is a little less swollen than it was, but I have no pain, although I am a bit "proppy" when I walk. All in all, not as bad as I feared, although I have asked for a Voltaren refill and suggested the physio might have a look at the knee.

I learnt that the prisoner who spat on me did worse to some other prisoner (I don't know what that was), and the senior officer in the unit moved him out, presumably to somewhere worse; and I don't know where that might be.

While the blooming rose is a bonus, the blessing of the day was the visit of Prior Benedict Nivakoff (nee Jeremy Adam) of the Norcia old rite monastery in central Italy, which was twice struck by earthquakes three or four years ago.

We had a great chat, and I was delighted to hear his news that the destruction of the old monastery and their shift into the deserted

---

[1] Jonathan Sumption is a former justice of the UK's Supreme Court. Commissioned and broadcast by the BBC, the Reith Lectures are annual radio addresses given by current leading figures.

monastery in the hills had been a blessing to their community, which now numbers nineteen, including four novices, two of whom are German.

I wasn't surprised to learn that no government reconstruction had started on the monastery in town over the burial places of Benedict and Scholastica. This is a disgrace, as it had been promised. Apparently, the town is struggling back to life within its ancient walls, and the hotel Seneca has reopened and is waiting for my return! The brewery is again in production, and on my liberation I must try to obtain my regular supply in Australia, with some Amarone red wine (if the price is not prohibitive).

I enquired about how much of their library had survived and was told that about half was still usable. Pope Benedict had made another donation of books, as had others. If they had not been so well served, I had considered leaving my library (now in Rome) to them; but this is not necessary. My preference is to have the books back in Australia.

We spoke in Italian to discuss the situation of the Church in the Vatican: the two synods and the financial scandals there. He was probably more pessimistic than I. He wondered whether our Plenary Council in Australia might be similarly dangerous, and I replied that one aim must be damage control. Until recently, I had never turned my mind to what should be done now we have this event, and I am coming to think that the bishops, or a number of them, should strive to exercise leadership: identify one or more unifying projects, while making clear that all at the council will be expected to listen to the voice of the Spirit, found first of all in our revealed tradition, and that no doctrines incompatible with the apostolic tradition will be endorsed and taught. In other words, the aim of the council will be to renew the actual Church in Australia and not to replace her. Benedict had no problem with this.

I also mentioned that it was becoming increasingly unlikely that I would have a vote in the next conclave, as the Holy Father seems very well, and I have turned seventy-eight. And of course if my appeal is not successful, all this talk is irrelevant. But I do have an ambition to live long enough to speak at the next preconclave meeting on the life of the Church and the type of pope needed.

I sent my regards to the community, especially Fr Cassian, and was dismayed to learn that my priest friend James, who lived as a hermit outside Norcia, had been moved on by the bishop. Benedict did not know where he was. Finally, I asked him to pray that, through some imprudence or foolishness or uncharity, I would not impede or damage the good fruits that God might will to come from my imprisonment. I was touched by his visit, while he was here visiting the small new traditional monastery in Tasmania. The universal Church is wonderfully rich, and even their archbishop, Renato Boccardo, is being kind and friendly towards them.

In this evening's Scripture reading, we have Paul writing to the Colossians (1:9–10).

We ask God to fill you with the knowledge of his will, with all the wisdom and understanding that his Spirit gives. Then you will be able to live as the Lord wants and always do what pleases him. Your lives will be fruitful in all kinds of good works.

Tuesday, 22 October 2019

A quiet and uneventful day, which saw me take my exercise in the pen in the morning as well as an hour in the gymnasium, although I wasn't allowed out in the afternoon as the exercise areas were being painted. That will be an improvement, I anticipate, because the walls were dirty.

I was lethargic in the morning, as is sometimes the case, but managed to score my three goals with the basketball and score above 100 for an unbroken series in ping pong for both forehand and backhand. Given the parlous state of my right knee, which is improving slightly, I did not do my thigh exercises on the weights. The gymnasium is always a good psychological break, and exercise slows the decline and aids sleeping. Thanks be to God I have slept well on nearly every night since arriving here.

As Sr Mary was away, her Filipino assistant, Mel, came to bring me Communion. She is a kind and pleasant woman, who should do good work among the prisoners. Already two of them have spoken to her about becoming Catholics.

Spoke to Bernadette and Terry for more than fifteen minutes this morning, on two calls on their landline, which means the call can be made without destroying my budget. I urged Terry to read Friel, especially on my two questions about the contrasting judgements of the appeal. Bernadette and Terry were both in admiration of my prison journal, and Terry felt that it should all be typed up—rather than some sections only, which might be better suited to publication.

Nuzzi's book on the Vatican finances[2] appeared at the weekend, and *The Australian* gave it coverage. It seems Nuzzi has access to accurate information about the annual structural deficit (€75–80 million in two years); about a big loss for the year by the APSA [Administration of the Patrimony of the Holy See], which allegedly has hundreds of properties unoccupied; and about looming problems with the pension fund. Peter's Pence revenue has also fallen. Nuzzi has never been completely reliable, but he could be genuinely opposed to corruption. I must ask Fr Robbie to send me out a copy of Nuzzi's book, which dovetails nicely with the news of the London property fiasco and Mincione's spectacular profit. As so much of the Catholic establishment in the US has been alienated, sources of extra income will be difficult to find; and I don't know who in the Vatican has the capacity to lead a thorough reform, let alone the will to do so, which would require the unambiguous long-term support of the Holy Father.

Removing thousands of suspect and illegitimate accounts from IOR, the Vatican Bank, has obviously reduced activity and revenue, while spectacular property losses over decades (now public knowledge) and refusal to implement appropriate investment policies and techniques have worsened the losses. I don't think there is any imminent chance of bankruptcy, because the Vatican has no authorized loans or debts, although the activities of the Secretariat of State might still be hidden. For decades, the Vatican has shrugged off allegations of financial corruption and incompetence, something which is better accomplished when the books are being balanced or in profit. With mounting annual deficits, the chickens might finally be coming home to roost.

I continue to move through Adrian Pabst's *Story of Our Country*, the ACU-sponsored, through the PM Glynn Institute,[3] account of

---

[2] *Giudizio Universale* (Universal Judgement), a book by Italian journalist Gianluigi Nuzzi, was released on 21 October 2019.

[3] The PM Glynn Institute is a public policy think tank at the Australian Catholic University.

the ALP [Australian Labor Party] and Catholic social teachings. A fine piece of work by a scholar who knows his field. And I also managed to send off three letters, two to prisoners.

Today I opened a letter from a prisoner in jail in New Zealand, who said his situation was exactly the same as mine and who sent me a copy of a prayer, the "Rune of St Patrick". A section follows.

At Tara today in this fateful hour
I place all heaven with its power,
and the sun with its brightness
and the snow with its whiteness . . .

and the sea with its deepness
and the rocks with their steepness,
and the earth with its starkness;
all these I place,
by God's almighty help and grace,
between myself and the powers of darkness.

Wednesday, 23 October 2019

Today was quite warm, probably near 30°C [86°F] in the afternoon. Summer is on the way, and much of northeastern Australia remains in extreme drought conditions, probably the worst in living memory (and this is not a climate change fanatic's exaggeration). Please God we are not in for a thirteen-year drought like Australia experienced in the medieval warming.

Passed nearly two hours in the gymnasium as something was "on" in the unit, perhaps a difficult prisoner transfer. Met all my goals, managing to top 100 shots on backhand and forehand in the table tennis and scored four goals (underarm) in the basketball. The knee is improving, but I again refrained from using any weights for my thighs.

Kartya called this morning to bring me up to date, and I discovered the documents had to be with the High Court on November sixth, and not the ninth. We had a small victory over the prosecution, who previously (in my opinion) continued to run the line that there was no legal issue central to the appeal and continued to want us to provide masses of irrelevant documents on the facts, at our expense. The High Court registrar ruled that they (the prosecution) could produce them if they insisted, but at their own cost. It was a good decision. Kartya also deposited more newspaper reports on the Roman financial scandals, with Danny reporting that [Óscar] Cardinal Maradiaga from Honduras had entered the fray to denounce the accusations as another bad deed of the anti-Francis forces. The Holy Father doesn't need enemies when he has allies as colourful and unwise as the Honduran cardinal. None of the five charged are major players, so it will be interesting to learn what becomes the central focus of interest.

Yesterday, I finally received from the prison property section the September number of *Annals*, which is ending this year after 150 years of publication. This will be a loss to Catholic life and to journalism, a fact that is immediately evident from the quality of this issue.

Two magnificent articles dealt with my case, "Falsely, Matilda", by George Weigel from the US, and "A Blight on the Whole Criminal Justice System", by Anthony Charles Smith, a retired non-Catholic barrister of thirty years' experience from Queensland.[4] Both dealt with the issues and evidence, but their main claim was that I was not so much on trial as the Australian criminal justice system, especially in Victoria.

Weigel has written many times on the theme and began by repeating his amazement at the lack of corroboration for the "utterly implausible" allegations. He surprised me by claiming that the hostility towards me in Australia for decades has "no analogue to it anywhere else in the Anglosphere" and that this has produced the distorted lens which reversed the onus of proof.

His central message is "George Pell is an innocent man who was falsely accused, and he has been unjustly convicted of crimes he did not commit. It is not George Pell who is in the dock now, but the administration of justice in Australia." He believes this statement

---

[4] George Weigel, "Falsely, Matilda", *Catholic World Report*, 22 August 2019, https://www.catholicworldreport.com/2019/08/22/falsely-matilda/. Anthony Smith, "A Blight on the Whole Criminal Justice System", *Annals Australia*, September 2019.

should be repeated again and again. For him, this is Australia's Dreyfus Case, as he does not know the Lindy Chamberlain story.

Anthony Smith is equally trenchant—and his thesis parallels that of Weigel. He believes I could not get a fair trial, as there was "no more publicly vilified figure in Australia" than myself. I am inclined to think this is an exaggeration, but I get the drift.

Smith mentions the notorious Carl Beech in the UK and his false accusations against Heath and other public figures[5] as well as the lies of Sarah Parkinson in Canberra against her ex-partner and the problems of Cliff Richard.[6]

He states baldly that John Finnis has performed a "juridical evisceration" of the majority case, which then prompts him to point out that the chief justice wasn't even a practising barrister. He connects these facts with their focus on the "demeanour and persuasiveness of the complainant" as distinguished from "the meticulous analysis by Weinberg".

However, his central point is "the administration of justice is now in absolute disrepute in respect of this case. The precedent is too terrible to contemplate." He then asks rhetorically "Who will be next in line?", while adding, "No one is immune from suffering under this kangaroo process."

The evidence of the prosecution is weak and "bordering on the preposterous". He says "without hesitation" that in the 1980s and early 1990s, "these allegations would have been given short shrift by competent experienced Crown Prosecutors." He would not be aware that the prosecutor's office sent back the case papers to the police three times.

I don't think it unreasonable to connect all the prayers said for me with the providential array of brilliant and courageous writers in Australia and overseas who have written in my defence.

---

[5] In July 2019, Carl Beech was sentenced to eighteen years in prison for fabricating sexual abuse allegations against former UK prime minister Edward Heath and other prominent British politicians. Sarah-Jane Parkinson was convicted and jailed in January 2019 for falsely claiming she had been raped by her former boyfriend.

[6] English singer and actor Cliff Richard was accused of sexual abuse in 2014. The police investigation into the matter was dropped two years later, and Richard was never charged with criminal behaviour.

We shall conclude with an excerpt from Psalm 35.

> *To both man and beast you give protection,*
> *O Lord, how precious is your love.*
> *My God, the sons of men*
> *find refuge in the shelter of your wings. . . .*
>
> *In you is the source of life*
> *and in your light we see light.*

Thursday, 24 October 2019

An unusual day today for a few reasons. It was the warmest day of spring, around 30°C [86°F], with a gentle breeze, so it wasn't unpleasant at all during my nearly two hours in the garden.

For the first time, I spent more than half an hour watering the garden, something I haven't done for more than sixty years. The garden is not entirely to my liking, having many scrawny native plants, tough, with narrow dull green leaves and small flowers, apart from the burst of orange flowers under the central verandah, which the gardener said were grevillea and which he thought were native, perhaps from the northeast of Australia, I guessed. The long leaves are a vivid green and quite succulent.

Three more roses have bloomed to make a total of four with many more on the way, on about ten to twelve bushes. The space is confined, surrounded by a high brick wall and higher brick buildings on two sides, so that it will be seriously hot in summer and the plants need to be tough to survive.

The gardener arrived when I had finished, and I explained that the prison boss had requested me to do the watering. He announced that he, too, would water the garden; perhaps he thought my efforts were a grab for power! But he only watered those parts I could not reach near the prison building. At one stage, he called me down to speak to him, and I wasn't sure what was coming, but he only wanted to show me the only pine in the garden, now two or three metres [seven to ten feet] high, which is a direct descendant of a pine cone brought back from Gallipoli. He also informed me the garden didn't need watering on consecutive days, but I reassured him with the information that I only came on Mondays and Thursdays.

Katrina Lee was my visitor, and she was allowed in early, so that we had about an hour together. She told me Fr Paul Stenhouse was not at all well and would probably soon go into palliative care. He is in pain. I very much regret that I will not be around for him at this time, but will keep him in my prayers.

We discussed my case, the progress of the extracurricular activities on a number of fronts, the disaster of the Victorian appeal, and the prospects in the High Court. Rumour has it that one of the two majority judges in my case will retire next year for medical reasons. I don't know what consequences that might have for his decision, but it would help me understand his reasoning, which is still inexplicable rationally. Katrina was having a meal with [journalist] Andrew Bolt tonight, and I asked her to have a few words with him on his comparing the global warming crusade to a religion. I urged Katrina to explain that there are good and better and inferior religions, just as we have many philosophies, some good and useful, some dangerous and damaging. He should compare the craze to false religion, and he should remember that most of his following are religious people (I think). He has been a formidable defender of mine.

The bulk of my time in the cell until the evening news was spent reading the collected articles from the European papers of 21–22 October on the Vatican financial scandals. Most were in Italian, with one or two in French and Spanish. It is an unusual achievement for me to be reading them a couple of days after publication in an Australian jail, where progress on any front can be slow.

It made me pleased to be out of Rome, as I read the propaganda attempts of the various parties to push their version of events, although I suspect more accurate information is emerging.

It was pleasing to read that in May last year (2018), the Council for the Economy briefed the curial cardinals on the finances, asking them to inform the Holy Father that the deficit had reached a disturbing level, estimated at 63.3 million euros [77 million dollars] for 2019, proving the risk of a default, a dramatic cash crisis, or bankruptcy in the next four years. Revenue is down, costs continue to rise dramatically, assets have lost value, and there are major problems with the pension fund and health costs.

Most of this is not news, but the scale of the losses, mounting each year, the inefficiency of the investments, property losses running into tens of millions of euros [or dollars] in London alone, and the speed of the decline have provoked talk of a crisis more swiftly than I had imagined. It is still a mystery that the Vatican has poured tens of millions of euros into the IDI hospital [Rome's Instituto Dermo-patico dell'Immacolata], which is not a Vatican institution. Galantino[7] claimed this expense as one reason for the first "no profit" from APSA. If their London property losses were recorded accurately, this would have been another important cause.

One or two articles have tentatively defended [Tommaso] Di Ruzza, the director of the AIF [Financial Information Authority, now called the Financial Information and Supervision Authority], which has the responsibility of monitoring the "Vatican" bank, IOR, saying the accusations might be part of a Secretariat of State push to weaken AIF as the powers of both audit agencies have been weakened. This is possible.

The same sad nonsense that I have heard for nearly twenty years is trotted out by APSA, that the properties cannot be valued, so revenue expectations and requirements cannot be made out. No one aspires to value St Peter's or the curial offices or the occasional castle, but the number, nature, and value of rentable properties certainly can and should be estimated.

The London debacle, with at least a €50 million [$61 million] loss, is only one such disaster and a major part of a much wider crisis. I used to say that we don't know how many souls are lost in hell or how many enter heaven, but with money you know you lose or gain, and with contemporary accounting procedures, however imperfect, it is close to impossible to conceal the worst. I fear for the financial future. Chickens come home to roost, and a poor or bankrupt Church can do nothing material to help the poor. We know whether we are prosperous, struggling, or in dire financial straits.

[Domenico] Cardinal Calcagno explained that one of the errors the reformers made was to require the Vatican to conform to business standards. He didn't add that these were standards of honesty and transparency, universally accepted, and that he wanted less for

---

[7] Bishop Nunzio Galantino is the president of the Administration of the Patrimony of the Holy See (APSA).

the Vatican: the fog and muddle that had helped criminals bring the Vatican to its present financial plight. The Vatican is not a business, but its standards of honesty, its hostility to corruption, should at least match what is required by the reviled capitalists. It speaks volumes that His Eminence was unaware of the irony of his claims.

I pray that many good people involved with the Vatican finances will have the heart to continue and be allowed to continue to work for probity and efficiency.

My prayer is that of Psalm 28.

> *The Lord will give strength to his people,*
> *The Lord will bless his people with peace.*

Friday, 25 October 2019

A quiet day, a bit cooler and overcast, without any time in the gymnasium or the garden. I did have my two periods in the newly painted exercise pens, and in the morning I phoned Terry Tobin to inform him of the rumours about a new president of the Court of Appeal. He hadn't heard anything about an illness, but did know of a politician who had recently been offered the position.

Patrick Santamaria called in the afternoon to bring me up to date on my other problem, being confident that the claim for damages should fall over at the November 4th meeting.

We also discussed rumours about the judges, where he was sympathetic to my view that such an illness would explain the bizarre verdict, pointing out that the errors were the talk of all serious lawyers in William St. It was also reported that a day or so ago the said gentleman was seen at the cathedral after the funeral of a fellow judge, standing alone at the entrance, gazing back down the centre aisle.

I cleaned up the backlog of letters and received another collection of news reports from Rome. The London incident continues to provoke a number of substantial articles.

A close friend and relative wrote about the effect my failed appeal had on her circle of devout Catholics. Opinion is still divided but regularly varies with the strength of faith and attitude to the Church: love, hate, or indifference.

Some friends felt physically ill or "gutted", and one rugby enthusiast claimed he didn't sleep for two nights. Others moved in the opposite direction, dropping their fast and starting on the chocolates.

A former school principal phoned to say that God had chosen this cross for me knowing my heart is big enough to cope, and a correspondent added, "Even blind Freddy could see there's a lot of reparation needed today." Two people who are dying are offering up their suffering for me.

She wrote another comment, which echoed the concern of my legal team, that in my case, the notorious allegation of priestly paedophilia, the onus of proof had been reversed, and she also echoed the conclusion of some good lawyers that it was impossible for me to obtain a fair trial by jury because of the poisoning of public opinion. The comment was "It was a dark day for all priests, for they now know that only one allegation is required to put them behind bars." One might quibble about whether this is overstated, but it is important that my innocence on this charge be established in the public mind, for the sake of the Church now and for priests and Church workers in the future.

I feel deeply uneasy and inadequate at being centre stage in this religious struggle, but I am where I am and am coping, through the loving support, the prayers, and the sacrifices of so many wonderful people.

One piece of good news is that Rachel Casey has safely given birth to a son. Both mother and son are well, and she has called the boy Augustine George. I am delighted. *Deo gratias.*

The last word comes from Psalm 145.

> *He is happy who is helped by Jacob's God,*
> *whose hope is in the Lord his God,*
> *who alone made heaven and earth,*
> *the seas and all they contain.*

Saturday, 26 October 2019

One benefit of being overseas in Europe for twelve years is that I know and like Aussie Rules football (which provides the best spectacle), soccer, and rugby union. Tonight after the Allies had finished off Hitler on SBS, I managed to catch most of the second half of the semifinal match in Japan in the rugby union World Cup, when England scored a famous victory over New Zealand, the world champions. It was a fierce match, ferocious tackling, little that was boring like excessive kicking for touch,[8] dominated by man mountains on both sides, especially from the English pack. More than 70,000 were at the game, most of them Japanese, wildly enthusiastic as the exultant English fans sang and sang, a goodly number of them sporting Crusader costumes. I suspect many were would-be Brexiteers.

The Brexit fiasco drags on, with the European Union agreeing to an extension of unspecified length (which will be clarified next week) and [Labour leader Jeremy] Corbyn refusing to support calling an election. Boris told the Labour Caucus to "man up" and do the right thing by the country (by agreeing to an election).

During the afternoon, I returned to another enthusiasm of my school days and watched the Cox Plate from Moonee Valley racecourse, which was won in slashing fashion by the Japanese horse Lys Gracieux. Four foreign horses were in the eleven-horse field, no doubt attracted by the first prize of five million dollars.

The weather was cool, with heavy winds around the state, which did not penetrate into the small enclosed pens where I exercised. In both the morning and afternoon excursions, we had a light shower of rain. I also spent my hour in the enclosed gymnasium, where the buckets are still out in the middle of the basketball court (after a couple of weeks at least) to catch the water (we hope it is water) dripping through the ceiling from the kitchen above.

Saturday is the day of the week when the Church encourages us to remember Our Lady, Jesus' mother. Many of my correspondents mention her fondly. When I went to confession to Prior Benedict last Monday, and as he gave me my penance, he asked whether I knew the Memorare. I replied indignantly that of course I knew it and it as one of my favourite prayers. I might have mentioned already that now when I am asked to pray for some person or some intention,

---

[8] Kicking for touch is a tactic used by a team when it has been awarded a penalty kick. The ball is deliberately kicked out of the playing area, "out of bounds" in American parlance.

I pray a Memorare for that person at the time, as I cannot celebrate Mass for them.

A young Carmelite nun from Des Plaines in the United States, who was professed last year, sent me her commemorative card featuring our painting of Our Lady of the Southern Cross, because it was in Sydney at the 2008 World Youth Day that she received her vocation. Underneath the holy card was written, "We can see Mary as God's smile upon us."

I received my devotion to Our Lady from my mother, from the two schools I attended, where it was an essential and much-loved devotion, and from attending Monsignor Fiscalini's Wednesday night Novena to Our Lady of Perpetual Succour, when St Patrick's Cathedral would be filled with the faithful of every age group. This was in the 1950s and continued for years.

One of the senior Knights of Malta in Australia writes to me regularly, often mentioning Our Lady and more recently highlighting the prayers made to her at the naval battle of Lepanto in 1571, a famous Christian victory over the Muslim Ottoman fleet, and at the even more important victory which lifted the siege on Vienna, more than one hundred years later in 1683, when 140,000 Turkish soldiers were routed by a Polish relief force of 27,000 under King John III Sobieski.[9] The decisive battle was on September 11, when the largest cavalry charge in history, involving 18,000 horsemen overall (according to my correspondent) under Sobieski, sealed the Muslims' fate. This was the reason why the attack on the Twin Towers in New York in 2001 occurred on September 11—a long delayed revenge.

My friend also sent to me a beautiful quotation from Rachel Fulton Brown,[10] who has written on devotion to Christ and the Virgin Mary in the Middle Ages, between 800 and 1200: "She is there in the art and the architecture and the music. She is there in the literature and the liturgy and the liberal arts. She is there in the most elevated expression of human imagination and in the humblest prayers for help. She is there in the politics and in the ideals of marriage, in battle

---

[9] King John III Sobieski (1629–1696) was King of Poland and Grand Duke of Lithuania from 1675 until his death.

[10] Rachel Fulton Brown (b. 1950) is an author and associate professor of medieval history at the University of Chicago.

cries and in pleas for mercy for the oppressed. Medieval Christianity is inconceivable without her."

Dyson Heydon is a distinguished judge, formerly of the High Court, who earlier this year addressed the Knights on the topic of religious freedom. He concluded his address with a stirring peroration from G. K. Chesterton's *Ballad of the White Horse* (1911).

> *And this is the word of Mary*
> *The word of the world's desire*
> *"No more of comfort shall ye get,*
> *Save that the sky grows darker yet*
> *And the sea rises higher."*

WEEK 36

Saints and Sinners

27 October 2019—2 November 2019

Sunday, 27 October 2019

The surprise of the day was to hear of the death of Vivian Waller, the Ballarat lawyer who had worked with J, although I had also heard (I am fairly certain) that J had broken with her. She was a zealous champion of complainants and victims. May she rest in peace.

I had not heard that she was ill and don't know the cause of her death. I didn't think of her as old. Chris Friel had highlighted her contacts with many persons involved in my case, which raised interesting questions, especially about her connection with the mysterious [tweeter Lyndsay] Farlow, who commented regularly. It will be interesting to learn whether any other information becomes available and whether, in this story, too, truth is the daughter of time.

I awoke in time for the televised Mass which was celebrated by Fr Martin Dixon, ordained a few years behind me. He has weathered well and celebrated with devotion and dignity. He described the parable of the Pharisee and the publican as a "non-judgemental Gospel", explaining that not all Pharisees were pharisaical, that we are all a bit like the realist tax collector-publican, disapproved of by both sides. "There but for the grace of God go I", repeating a phrase his father often used.

Joseph Prince spoke on the theme of "Dare to Pray Bold Prayers" in a 2019 production. He was wearing four chunky rings and his high boots, with jeans, a black shirt, and denim top with zips galore and exterior seams. His dress is more flamboyant than it was ten years ago. For Joseph, righteousness comes from Jesus and is not found in ourselves, and he brought on a man dressed as the Jewish High Priest, who represents the Lord. He spoke of the iniquity of holy things; just as the feathers were removed from the sacrifice to be burnt, so our sins are like ashes.

Joel Osteen was his usual indomitable self as he preached on "Don't Settle for Less". When we pray to God for some intention and this is not granted for a long time, we still should continue to pray in hope. Abraham's wife, Sarah, whose age he gave variously as sixty-five, then seventy, and then eighty when she gave birth to her son, Isaac, was an example of someone blessed through perseverance. It also reminded me to persevere in my prayers for an acquittal. He reminded us that we can all find reasons to be offended, that we should be overcomers and not settlers, and therefore we will be in a better position in ten years' time. "Your best years are still in front of you", he rashly promised.

Hymns of Praise gave three excellent examples of Christians doing good in Britain, including a group delivering Gideon New Testaments to a retirement village and to a hotel. I didn't dislike the hymn singing, but it was a bit bouncy for my staid tastes.

I finished reading the collection of articles from 23 October 2019 on the Vatican finance scandals, which did not add much that was new, the counterattack denying any chance of a financial collapse was underway. One colourful article on a site or magazine *Linkiesta* was headed: "Nuzzi Is Not St John and There Probably Will Not Be a Financial Apocalypse"; probably true for the immediate future. This article mentioned Msgr Cesare Burgazzi, who worked in the Vatican Secretariat of State on the finances, who became disillusioned by his discovery of a parallel bank, another IOR, and was then removed from his position through media accusations of sexual misbehavior, which were later shown to be completely baseless. I had not heard of this.

Another report had Joseph Zahra, the Maltese banker, a genuine foe of corruption, publicly wondering in July 2018 why nothing had been done to activate the committee requested by the Council for the Economy in May 2018. It would be nice to know whether such work had commenced, but the silence is ominous.

An article in the newspaper of the Italian bishops, *Avvenire*, tried to provide reassurance by pointing out that deficits were not a novelty in the Vatican and that the losses in 1980 were probably worse in real terms than today's. The attempt was totally counterproductive, because every deficit weakens the capacity of an institution to cope with further losses. Even the bravest spirit would back away from attempting to discover accurately how much money has been lost in the last forty years, concealed from view by primitive bookkeeping and human artifice.

Avvenire did provide some reassurance by pointing out that budgeting procedures for each coming financial year had been introduced by the Secretariat for the Economy and that a set of procedures and regulations to be used in public contracts was being approved. The article didn't mention that we have been in this situation for two years, anticipating their approval.

This is the occasion to pray to the Blessed Virgin Mary, Untier of Knots, with some small changes to the traditional words.

Immaculate Heart, cast your eyes of compassion upon the Vatican, and see the snarl of knots which exists there. You know all the pains and sorrows caused by these tangled knots. Mary, my Mother, I entrust to your loving hands the Holy Father and the Roman Curia. In your hands, there is no knot which cannot be undone.

Most holy Mother, pray for Divine assistance and come to our aid.

Monday, 28 October 2019

We have a new loud and assertive shouter in the unit, who seems to know his way around and was probably a guest here at some earlier stage. He knows at least one of the other prisoners, and a brief, loud dialogue ensued late in the afternoon after lockdown. All has been quiet since, and he doesn't seem mad or violent. The unit's population changes constantly, except for people like myself and Gargasoulas. Victoria has brought in today new regulations which entitle police to ram or shoot rampaging cars which might kill people.

I discovered that Vivian Waller the lawyer has not passed away. Rather, it was her namesake, a sociologist, who died. Neither is she a Ballarat lawyer, as I mistakenly thought, but is based in Melbourne.

It is claimed that she is heavily involved with the Broken Rites organization. The rumours about the judge moving on next year continue. Other rumours have the police commissioner under increasing pressure from the Lawyer X disgrace, while one or two others are watching and waiting to act.

It was a beautiful spring morning for my two hours in the garden, clear and brisk, even a tad cold in the shade. It was like a good spring day in Rome, without that pinch of humidity which often accompanies spring in Sydney. In some ways, a good winter day in Sydney is like spring today down here in Melbourne.

Fourteen or fifteen roses were blooming, including a magnificent large bloom, coloured an unusual reddish-orange. Someone had removed nearly all the wilting orange flowers under the central pavilion. Originally this covered area had been a bird cage (with birds), but the authorities had pity on the birds, and I can well imagine the prisoners not being too keen on seeing the poor birds locked up as we are.

No hose was provided for me to water, and in fact the soil was damp presumably from the rain of the last few days.

David and Judy arrived at midday and were given extra time, about half an hour. The guards were friendly to them.

Not much news. Tim Busch from California had phoned David asking what he had to do to get me out! David brought Windschuttle's latest piece from *Quadrant* and mentioned that someone was alleging *Quadrant* might be in contempt of court for some comment. I haven't seen any of this documentation.

In the evening, SBS ran yet another program on the House of Windsor, the name the Royals adopted during the First World War at the height of anti-German feeling, when bombs bearing their family name of Saxe-Coburg-Gotha started to fall on London! Queen Victoria was designated as the founder of the new House. George V responded to criticism by conceding he was uninspiring, but he would be damned before conceding he was an alien.

The program claimed they were the first to have access to the Queen's private archives in the tower at Windsor. Certainly they revealed that it was George V himself who urged the prime minister, Lloyd George, to rescind the decision to allow Tsar Nicholas of Russia to come into exile in Britain. The King's wily private secretary, well connected throughout the country and aware of anti-Royal and pro-Communist sentiment, persuaded the King to bar his cousin and urged him to break new ground and go out to meet the people. The secretary convinced Lloyd George that the King's greatest security lay in the love and loyalty of the working class.

His letters reveal that the Duke of Windsor (as he became) was a thoroughly unpleasant man, who enjoyed the limelight but hated his royal duties and hated his father. The King himself was prescient, telling Prime Minister Arthur Balfour that his immensely popular son, who had had a ten-year affair with a married woman, Freda Dudley Ward, before his liaison with Wallis Simpson, would destroy everything in the first twelve months of his reign [as Edward VIII]. The Nazis certainly hoped to use him against his younger brother, now George VI. We have documentary evidence of this.

At one stage, the nuncio in Britain told a British member of Parliament that I certainly couldn't be considered a candidate for archbishop of Westminster, because I was a republican. For a host of other reasons, Westminster was never a possibility, and in fact I have always been a supporter of the monarchy in Britain. The system works well. I would be appalled if it was toppled there.

The system also works well in Australia, but we need to stand on our own feet. Modern travel, communications, work mobility, Brexit (if it finally arrives), and a perceived threat from China might all conspire with William and Kate to keep the Royals involved in our system, provided Charles doesn't upset the applecart.

Certainly I pray for Australia first, but I also pray for Queen Elizabeth, as long as she remains Queen of Australia.

Tuesday, 29 October 2019

The big international news was that US special forces had killed Abu Bakr al-Baghdadi, the founder and leader of the Islamic State of Iraq and Syria (ISIS) and its briefly lived caliphate. I hadn't heard of this man, so the significance of his death was somewhat lost on me, but President Trump made a great deal of it, comparing the raid with that which killed Bin Laden, in language which would have been appreciated by his voter base but would once have been described as less than presidential.

Another piece of international news was that Trump had been booed when he attended a recent baseball game. Booing the president is rare in the US, although it apparently once happened to Jimmy Carter. All this provides an interesting contrast with Australia, where prime ministers at big sporting events, especially if they venture onto the oval, are often booed, generally in a good-natured, disrespectful way, rather than maliciously. As Whitlam[1] was once being booed enthusiastically as he walked on to the ground with the head of that football league, he said to his hapless companion, "You must be unpopular!" The Americans are more respectful of high office, e.g., the press corps stands when the president enters for a conference, and devotion to the flag and patriotism are pushed much more there than in, e.g., our schools.

Sr Mary brought me Communion, looking fresh and well after her break. She was able to deny that she had been away on a Pacific cruise with Msgr Portelli. Fake news, she replied. At her suggestion, she will request permission for me to celebrate Mass, and Archbishop Comensoli will concelebrate, if allowed. A wonderful thought, but I am not optimistic.

A half dozen letters arrived today after a quiet day yesterday, and twenty to thirty at the weekend. Recently I received a letter from a German doctor in Königsdorf, which thanked me for my writings in support of "the truly Catholic wing of the Church" and then continued: "In a storm, it does not help the boat with lost orientation to move the lighthouse. Your credibility and prominence made you the target to be brought down. I sincerely hope the last word has not been spoken in your case." So do I.

Another unusual letter came from a Vietnamese-born woman married to an Australian-born husband living in a large Catholic parish in Melbourne's eastern suburbs. She was supportive, quoting different members of her family. One brother, who was described by his mother as "not very strong in the Catholic faith", felt my whole story was "a simple hoax". He told his sister, "In court, he was so stoic, and

---

[1] Edward Gough Whitlam, a member of the Labor Party, was prime minister of Australia from 1972 to 1975.

I felt that should he appeared a little bit softer, even shown some of his emotional eg shedding his tears, than maybe the juries would feel he is more 'average human'." He was very clear that he wanted me to keep fighting, however.

The writer's mother was praying that I would not "lose my faith or commit suicide as it would be the perfect win for the Devil". She concluded, "We need to pray for him." Meanwhile, the writer explained that she and her husband until recently "had got no idea to raise children to become Catholic priests". That has changed. "After what happened to you, both of us realized how much needed to be priests in our society", and they are both wanting to help educate good priests now.

She then turned to the scandal and the hurt the allegations against me have produced. Today I started to read *Getting Back on Mission*, the book produced by Catholics for Renewal for next year's Plenary Council, and I have already found a couple of references that "recent events concerning two senior cardinals have added to the crisis." I am sure this is correct. My correspondent acknowledges such claims; "however, we think it was the contrary." She cites the example of her husband, a lukewarm Catholic. "Since your case was made public ... he was much stronger advocate and concerned spiritually."

Another such example, she continues, comes from her "cousins and cousin-in-law and nieces and nephews too ... I do not know how mysteriously God works on people's minds and soul are but it is so wonderful to experience so. It seems that the more the Dark Tower opening waves of attack, the more people getting so curious they turned to find/explore the facts, and they come out feeling more sympathetic to not only your sufferings in silence but for the Catholic Church as a whole."

I am not sure how many people have been moved in this way, but her story, simply told, is not unique, as I know from other letters. She then adds a theological explanation before quoting, as many correspondents have done, the story of Cardinal Thuan. "Look, on the cross, Jesus Christ pulled everyone up thousands time more than his three years teaching days after days."

This is a hard lesson. If Jesus had not taught, we would not know how to interpret his story, but my correspondent's basic point is true, while still a hard teaching.

I give the last word to my German doctor from Königsberg, who quoted the inscription under a photo of St Teresa of Ávila in his mother's kitchen.

Lord, I do not ask for a lighter burden. I ask you for a stronger spirit.

Amen to that, but I still hope I am acquitted by the High Court.

Wednesday, 30 October 2019

The day was quite warm, around 27°C [81°F] maximum, so that on both my spells in the exercise pen, I took off my green prison top and was comfortable in my shirt. Unfortunately, the gymnasium has been closed since yesterday, probably for repairs, and I have missed two hour-long exercise sessions. I hope and presume they have been fixing the leaks in the ceiling from the kitchen above. I woke about five this morning, what might have been sheer coincidence (such coincidences are God's puns, according to G. K. Chesterton) or the result of less physical exercise or of going to sleep a little earlier.

In speaking with Kartya by phone, I learnt that she had already handed in our document to the High Court registrar, and the prosecution should hand in theirs by Friday. Kartya is keen for us not to miss the scheduled day for documents to go to Canberra. She had been told that we are likely to be informed in December about a hearing on whether we can appeal. I was a bit disappointed, because I had been hoping for this to occur in November.

We don't know the timeline, although Bret believes the court will be sensitive to the plight of a person unjustly imprisoned. However, they make their own pace, and I could well be looking at another six months in jail, or more.

I received from my brother a couple of articles by Friel and Keith Windschuttle's most recent piece, refining his argumentation about the altar servers arriving in the sacristy one minute before the miscreants could have arrived, according to J's story. He was careful not to say the crime was therefore impossible, but I must repeat that not even a credible witness can be in two places at once: in the sacristy being attacked and still in the procession or breaking away from it. Friel continues to roam widely as well as dealing with the trial, exposing what Louise Milligan and Lucie Morris-Marr[2] were doing; how they both might have been used, and how Milligan covered up the discrepancies and difficulties she discovered in J's story. Others might be close to the bones, to most of the truth, but the instigators and the initial accusations are still not clear to me, although the fog might be lifting.

Ed Condon from Catholic News Agency in Rome also had an article alleging APSA violated European regulations by providing a loan of €50 million [$61 million] for a mixed company to purchase IDI hospital in Rome, which is bankrupt with debts of €800 million [$972 million].

The story is that before Pope Francis' pontificate, the Vatican promised this fifty million, claiming it would be paid by Bambino Gesù, the Vatican children's hospital. Naturally this hospital refused, pointing out it could not use Italian government funds for such a purpose. The Secretariat for the Economy had strongly opposed this undertaking, pointing out that nobody else would pay and that we would be handing over a loan to a hospital with no capacity for repayment. My dire predictions were not entirely correct, as the Vatican persuaded the Papal Foundation from the US, calling on all the clerical members to outvote the sceptical lay board members to provide $25 million. This has damaged and might destroy the foundation.

APSA wrote off €30 million [$36 million] of the loan, which explained their unprecedented loss. In 2012, they had promised Moneyval, the European agency to counter money laundering and terrorist financing,[3] that they would not give loans, not act as a bank, and so were exempted from the supervision of the Vatican agency AIF. Moneyval will certainly be interested as these APSA transactions have come to public knowledge.

It will require a miracle for the Vatican not to lose the €20 million [$24 million] remaining of the loan, which it has not written off. With the loss of value for the two London properties (15 percent

---

[2] Lucie Morris-Marr is a British-born investigative journalist and broadcaster based in Melbourne.

[3] Moneyval is the common and official name of the Committee of Experts on the Evaluation of Anti–Money Laundering Measures and the Financing of Terrorism, a permanent monitoring body of the Council of Europe.

depreciation in sterling with Brexit, and at least a 15 percent drop in London property values) and the IDI debacle, we might be looking at losses of 100 million euros [$121.5 million]. At the least, all this, which is not the whole picture, demonstrates massive incompetence.

AIF announced that it had conducted an investigation which had cleared their director, Di Ruzza, and authorised his return to work.

The battle against criminality in the Vatican is probably already won (I hope this is not naïve), but the battle to eliminate incompetence and establish profitability has a long way to go.

So we invoke the leadership of St Michael the Archangel to defend us in all battles, but especially in these financial struggles.

We ask you, O prince of the heavenly host, by the power of God, to thrust into hell Satan and all the evil spirits, who prowl about the world stirring up greed and lies and seeking the ruin of souls. Amen.

Thursday, 31 October 2019

While Sydney was covered in smoke for a second day due to sixty or seventy bushfires and burning off, and some rain was falling in many parts of country Queensland, it was hot in Melbourne for my two hours in the garden, about 30°C [86°F] with a slight breeze.

A few birds were around for some of the time, small, like sparrows, with a black head, white neck, breast, and tail tips, and otherwise brown features. Perhaps they are sparrows!

A few more roses were out, and some small buds were appearing on the low rose bush at the far end of the garden. Unfortunately, the magnificent orange-gold rose, which was near its peak on last Monday, was stripped, only a few of its large petals remaining, flattened and hanging on grimly, with other petals on the ground. As St Mary MacKillop used to say, "We are only travellers here", although we last a damn sight longer than the roses.

No hose was provided for me to hose the garden, so that experiment might be over, the victim of a demarcation dispute, perhaps. I was rebuked for walking around the end of the garden, which had been prohibited on my first outing. The rules often change with the officer. There was no point in complaining or refusing to obey, but

I can see no justification for the rule, as I am visible to surrounding buildings in my allotted area. It might have nothing to do with visibility and be simply another regulation.

Yesterday Boris Johnson shamed the Labour opposition into agreeing to an election in the United Kingdom on December 12th, after weeks of drama and farce, driven basically by the fact that perhaps 70 percent of the House of Commons refused to support the decision of the British people in the referendum to leave the European Union.

Aidan Hartley writes periodically for *The Spectator* from Kenya, where he has a farm in the Highlands. Farm life is wild and exotic, often dangerous, and makes for marvellous reading. He obviously loves Africa. He tells the story of the infamous Idi Amin, president of Uganda, who sent a message to the Queen in 1963 promising to send a cargo boat of bananas to Britain because the ordinary Britons were suffering so much.

Hartley wrote about how all the former British colonies in Africa adopted some version of the Westminster system of government, generally with many ancient trappings, the wigs, the maces, the green benches, as we did in Australia. He then continues, "From where I stand, after a lifetime on the African beat, I see that many of the outrages I covered on this continent in our sad past are becoming the daily norm in British politics today."

Probably most Australians are not aware of, or don't take seriously, the British Labour Party's John McDonnell's proposal to drop the working hours to thirty-two a week or the proposal to seize the assets of 2,500 private schools. Corbyn and his zealots, not the majority of his parliamentary party, are an example of a major party moving away from its traditional voters because it has been taken over by its extremist party members. It is a counterproductive disaffection never likely to be endorsed by a majority vote in the UK.

But on occasion, the majority becomes disaffected, as Trump and Brexit have demonstrated, rejecting the alternative favoured by the "progressive" establishment. For democracy to work, these decisions have to be followed. A majority vote must be effective, and I think that Boris Johnson will be able to achieve a working majority in December so that the House of Commons can and will implement the referendum decision. It would have been unthinkable in Australia for any government not to have implemented the majority's decision in the recent same-sex marriage referendum, even a no vote. I am optimistic, and I don't think anyone will need to offer to send Her Majesty another boat of bananas.

When feelings run deep, it is especially useful to strive to remain calm and wise and to resist the temptations of uncharity, to hate.

St Thomas More's prayer to resist temptation is helpful.

Almighty God, assist me with your gracious help so that to the subtle suggestions of the serpent I never so incline the ears of my heart but that my reason may resist them and master my sensuality and keep me from them.

Friday, 1 November 2019

Today is All Saints' Day, an important date in our beautifully arranged liturgical year. The feast is more important than it ever was in our society, which is dominated by the cult of the young and the beautiful and where society works hard to hide the evidence that we cannot escape suffering and ignore the brute fact that each of us will die. Many people in retirement homes are lonely, not simply because family and friends are (allegedly) busy, disorganized, or lazy, but because selfish people do not want to be reminded of their own mortality, especially when they are without a religious faith.

I remember being surprised, and that was a basic flaw in an adult Christian, by the fact that those most devoted to earthly pleasures, material and sensual, were much less likely to believe in a life after death full of happiness. Unlike the popular versions of Islamic paradise, with its emphasis on the sensual, on beautiful gardens, in heaven, Jesus said, there would be no marriage; but I mistakenly thought that those who sought the good life in the here and now would want the good times to continue.

The Scriptures tell us that the pure in heart will see God and that this happiness, being in his presence, takes us far beyond earthly pleasures, especially when they are pursued selfishly. The truly blind do not see any need to believe.

Today is the feast where we concentrate on heaven, more than on hell, death, and judgement, because we rejoice with those who have made the grade, look to their lives for inspiration, and strengthen our ambition to follow them and be with the one true God. The Letter to the Hebrews reminds us, "You have come to God himself, the supreme Judge, and been placed with the spirits of the saints who have been made perfect" (12:23).

It is Jesus who instituted this New Covenant with his purifying blood. The glorious band of the apostles, the prophets, the white-robed army of martyrs, and all the saints are praising the Holy Trinity, the one true God, in the great cloud, in the wedding feast of the Lamb.

It is the Lamb who has taken the scroll from the One seated on the throne, who broke the seven seals and liberated the ten thousand times ten thousand angels and animals and elders, all of creation who were crying out, "To the One who is sitting on the throne and to the Lamb, be all praise, honour, glory and power, for ever and ever."

The spirit of evil strives to damage the Church from many directions, e.g., Marxism, consumerist materialism, hedonism, ecological pantheism, etc., but all cooperate to flatten the Church, to entice the faithful to be concerned with this world only and to downplay, then ignore, and then eliminate the Transcendent, the Supernatural, the vertical dimension of life. Is salvation more important than ecology or prosperity or class warfare or ... ? It will be interesting to note how many times the German Synod will mention heaven and hell or even mention Jesus himself. In this context, we need to celebrate All Saints' Day, meditate on its message to strengthen our faith, that Jesus wants us to be immersed in the present, the mundane, but insists this will be followed by a supernatural, better than life, tomorrow.

Back to daily life in prison. Yesterday Danny Casey and his wife, Annie, visited for a most pleasant forty-five minutes. Danny had been business manager with me in the Sydney Archdiocese and then worked with me for two years to reform the Vatican finances. We made progress and took heart from the fact that we had strenuously opposed the scandals now coming to light in the international press. It could have been so much better and the Vatican so much richer, and Danny's work was crucial to what we achieved. Like every other significant reformer of the Vatican finances, he was attacked in the media.

The *Herald Sun* was a bit short of news today and ran a story on page 3 that the former Vatican treasurer, now disgraced, was working in the jail garden. They even had a photo where I appeared jovial and benign. The prison authorities were not amused, so that when I had an official visit, I explained that I did the work, only once, because Mr Selisky, in charge of the jail, asked me to do so. As he is on leave, I should not do anything in the garden in the meantime, at least until his return.

Dave Forster, the liaison officer for placements, also called for his usual pleasant meeting. Next week the deputy governor will come, and he might have some information on the future arrangements. I informed them that I am likely to be here for another six months, even if my appeal is successful. It could be less than this.

I conclude with a couple of verses from the hymn of Morning Prayer.

> *The Father's holy ones, the blest*
> *Who drank the chalice of the Lord,*
> *Have learned that bitterness is sweet*
> *And courage keener than the sword....*

> *May all the splendid company,*
> *Whom Christ in glory came to meet,*
> *Help us on our uneven road*
> *Made smoother by their passing feet.*

Saturday, 2 November 2019

One of the hallmarks of Catholicism is our practice of prayers for the dead, that they may be released from their sins. Today is All Souls' Day, when we particularly remember those who have gone before us.

On a number of occasions, I have claimed, only with part of my tongue in my cheek, that Limbo has been pushed off the list, while Purgatory has slipped into Limbo. As faith weakens, or perhaps as we become more self-centred, we don't like the idea of a God who punishes for eternity, or even of a God who purifies through suffering as a preparation for entering into the light and peace of the Creator God.

We understand that you need to be able to drive a car to merit a license, that doctors have to know, that we should be mature and unselfish to be a good spouse and parent. So it is no big jump to concede that we need to be purified so that we are worthy to be in God's presence. That is Purgatory, a cleansing and suffering in the certainty of release into heaven.

It used to be a popular devotion to offer small sacrifices for the release of the souls in Purgatory, as well as praying for them, especially on All Souls' Day. It is one of those rudimentary practices which young Catholics should be brought up to adopt, almost through osmosis, like devotion to Our Lady. We need a revived, perhaps tweaked a bit, Catholic piety, a set of practices and devotions, to be absorbed by young Catholics before the coldness of the oppressive, so-called "permissive society" assails them. Big sinners who repent, those who are specially loved by God, regularly feel the need for atonement, to do penance for their sins. An allied sense, often mistaken and misdirected, is to wonder what we have done wrong to "deserve" this or that misfortune. Our Lord explained that life doesn't work like that, although the wages of sin are real, e.g., regular liars are not trusted, those who live by the sword often die by the sword, drugs and alcohol damage both body and mind. Making amends, doing penance, helps cope with guilt, helps in the struggle to believe in God's forgiveness, in self-forgiveness. More men than women have told me of this, although everyone who believes in heaven wants the scales of justice to be balanced, while acknowledging Jesus provides most of the positive ballast.

Typical Melbourne. Yesterday the temperature was about 30°C [86°F], while today it is raining for the Victorian Derby and quite cool. The gymnasium was reopened, so I performed my round of exercises, eventually, after a few attempts, hitting an unbroken 270 or so shots on my backhand in the table tennis, but I was unable to break 100 on the forehand side. The leaks in the ceiling had been repaired.

I received a copy of eighteen articles from English and Italian language newspapers, of the 26th and 30th October, on the continuing revelations of the Vatican financial scandals. It reads badly, although Jean-Baptiste de Franssu[4] was right to claim that the revelations showed the new regulations were working to reveal these scandals, even when they were unable to prevent the more recent

[4] Jean-Baptiste de Franssu is the president of the Institute for the Works of Religion (IOR), commonly known as the Vatican Bank.

ones. Naturally it is good men like him, insisting that the procedures be followed, who establish the progress. He added that another two factors help ensure proper practices: the need for the Vatican to be approved by international regulatory bodies and the obligation of lay experts on the Vatican boards to maintain their personal reputations for integrity by refusing to countenance corruption.

Three other developments were significant. More details about the Vatican's involvement with the IDI hospital's sordid collapse with 800 million euros [972 million dollars] debt have emerged and about the attempt to extract money from the Papal Foundation to help cover APSA's mistakes.

[Pietro] Cardinal Parolin said the Secretariat of State involvement in the purchase of the Sloane Square property in London was "opaque" and not transparent, to which Cardinal Becciu strongly proclaimed his innocence and his respect for the pennies of the poor and blamed Mincione for disregarding instructions and causing the distress.

It was also encouraging to read that *La Repubblica* had published details of the second disastrous property purchase in 2015 in London, this time by APSA. While (only) 90 million euros [109 million dollars] were invested, 30 percent of this at least would have been lost. No one can claim honestly that APSA wasn't warned against this folly. Apparently it is also mentioned in Nuzzi's book.

Today I will conclude with the short prayer we use after praying each mystery of the rosary.

O, my Jesus, forgive us our sins. Save us from the fires of hell, and lead all souls to heaven, especially those most in need of your mercy.

WEEK 37

Cautious Optimism

3 November 2019—9 November 2019

Sunday, 3 November 2019

During last week, Mr Harris provided me with a white plastic clock radio, whose alarm he set for 5:50 am this morning, so I could get up for *Mass for You at Home*. After setting the machine last night, when the buzzing woke me, my first reaction was to wonder what was happening, but I then realised what it was, rose, turned it off, and dressed for Mass.

For years, I explained that I did not dream, and then some decades ago I learnt that I should have been saying that I didn't remember my dreams. I now dream more than I used to, but I am not an imaginative dreamer, most of the time. However, last night I dreamt that there was a gathering of my long-term friends, where I came upon Claudio Veliz, who asked me to say a prayer! I shall request that Kartya phone Philip Ayres to enquire how Claudio is.[1]

Watched the final of the rugby from Japan between England and South Africa, a brutal encounter of two mixed-race teams, the fruit of empire, where the Springboks stunned the English from the start. The English hooker, a huge man, was knocked unconscious, and the South African pack then crushed the opposition repeatedly. The South Africans deserved their nineteen-point victory in the presence of a capacity crowd of hugely enthusiastic Japanese fans, the heir apparent of the Japanese emperor, the Japanese prime minister, the South African president, and Prince Harry. A prime cast.

[1] Claudio Veliz, an economic historian and sociologist, and Philip Ayres, a literary historian and biographer, are friends of Cardinal Pell.

Initially, my inclination was to support the English team, but I wavered as the social and political benefits at home for a mixed-race South African team victory became more apparent to me. The first black captain, Siya Kolisi, spoke beautifully along these lines, of what could be done by all joining together to work for their 57 million population.

Fr Martin Dixon again celebrated Mass, preaching on the Zacchaeus story, the tax collector who climbed the sycamore tree to see Jesus as he passed. This tree is alleged to exist still, and Martin mentioned that he and his parish pilgrimage had been at the spot, going on to urge us not to condemn outsiders while forgetting the plank in our own eye. At the final blessing, he mentioned the Melbourne Cup on Tuesday and hoped we all would have winners during the week.

Joseph Prince preached on the theme "Believe His Love and Receive All Blessings". He takes extraordinary care to vary his dress with every session. He had a black suit top and dark tie, with white stripes on his biceps and on his suit collar. A few indecipherable words were printed on his shirt collar, no boots, but dull purple sand shoes, with four rings and bracelets and bands on both wrists. His huge congregation doesn't worry, as it continues to come. He reminded us that we sin against God more than we realise; we need poverty of spirit to let God's light in. We are no longer under judgement, because we have professed Jesus and are saved. It is an affirmation of conversion without any need for explicit repentance.

Joel Osteen was again full of folksy wisdom, urging us not to look down on ourselves because we have made a bad mistake. We are not to let people define us, label us because of a lapse. We are redeemed, because we are defined by what Christ says about us. Moses and Peter made big, if quite different, mistakes, and God still chose them to do great things. A desert experience is not necessarily a bad thing, because immediately after Jesus was baptized, he was led by the Spirit, not by the devil, to be tempted in the desert and then to arrive at another place.

I didn't know any of the hymns sung on *Hymns of Praise*, but they were all worth singing. While we also heard of a Birmingham Archdiocese retreat centre designed by Pugin,[2] an American astronaut

---

[2] Augustus Pugin (1812–1852) was a British Roman Catholic architect, designer, and author and a leading figure in the revival of Gothic architecture.

who walked on the moon and then found Jesus, and a deeply Christian "freestyler" who has five world records and does semimiraculous tricks with a soccer ball.

A verse from the morning prayer hymn might take our preachers one step forward.

> *Creator of all things that are,*
> *The measure and the end of all,*
> *Forgiving God, forget our sins,*
> *And hear our prayer before we call.*

Monday, 4 November 2019

The letters which continue to arrive are one of my consolations. I receive five to ten on most days; but on Sunday, I received eighteen, and they were particularly interesting.

One of them from a Footscray[3] woman in her seventies informed me that "God had let us all down" and that while she had lived a Catholic and Christian godly life "for almost seven decades", not so now!!!

I wrote to her yesterday, the same day as I received the letter, something I almost never do. She feels "abandoned by God", has "given it all away", and "no longer" believes.

Then she went on to relate "a strange thing". "Ever since you got in the public eye—say the past two years, every day I say a short fervent prayer for you and that the accuser will fess up." She hopes "God is protecting you from any disrespect and such." Her complaint against God was not provoked by misfortune in her personal life (or at least she never mentioned this), but by the progress of "abortion, euthanasia, SSM and other evils".

I assured her, as best I could, that God never lets us down and that even when we feel we are being treated roughly by God, he has not abandoned us.

I mentioned a couple of things about the complainant, about how he did not want the second trial to go ahead after the hung jury result and that the timeline of the majority of the judges demonstrates that

---

[3] Footscray is a suburb of Melbourne.

the crime is not possible, because the complainant would still have been in the procession and could not have been simultaneously in the sacristy being raped before the servers arrived. Not even the most credible witness can be in two places at once. I claimed to my prayerful supporter that this demonstrated impossibility is evidence of God's providence at work. I truly believe this.

I prayed for this good, just woman and will continue to do so, that she joins the dots together to realise that God is also at work. At different times, each of us can find this difficult to believe. I should have written to her, as I have said on many other occasions, that Our Lord himself had a very tough run, which, at one stage at least, in the garden, he would have been happy to avoid.

Graham Greene, the Catholic convert English novelist, whose style I particularly admire, wrote poignantly of the coexistence in the same persons of faith and sin, faith and weakness, as in the whisky priest in *The Power and the Glory*. My correspondent would be too morally good to be a run-of-the-mill Greene character, but she is evidence of the claim, from the different world of science, that human life is stranger than we can suppose. A great deep, in this case of goodness.

Greene was given an honorary doctorate at Oxford in the same ceremony in which I received my DPhil in the Sheldonian Theatre. He was a larger man than I had anticipated and sat there unmoving and expressionless as though he were taking it all in for his next novel.

I was also encouraged by a letter from a Victorian prisoner, married with children, who had been in and out of jail for thirty years with drug problems, "demons which he is still learning to face". He claims he is not a religious man but believes there was "a person long ago who brought out faith in man, which in turn taught men to help one another and therefore to forgive".

His main purpose in writing to me was to let me know "you have a lot of support from within the ranks of the old-school criminals in jail. What this translates to is 'the general consensus amongst career criminals is that you had been used as an escape goat [sic] by the powers that be, which in this case is the justice system/courts of Victoria.'"

I found this encouraging, because in these matters their judgement was likely to be sound, not just about my own innocence, but about the wider context. Today Fr Joe Murphy was down to see me (more of this tomorrow), and he asked whether I thought the professional reputation of the majority judges would ever recover from their judgement. It should not.

I will let my correspondent provide the final "prayer", or good wishes.

I do hope you fully make it through this ordeal and your faith in man is not lost, but an understanding of the system is gained.

May God bless him.

Tuesday, 5 November 2019

Today is Melbourne Cup day, a public holiday in the state of Victoria for a 3200m [2-mile] handicap horse race, which now attracts the best horses in the world for the $5 million prize money.

It was a perfect day, perhaps 20°C [68°F], for the 81,000 people who attended, and the course was as beautiful as ever, with rose bushes everywhere; 60,000 roses in bloom, according to one commentator. The blooms were out, the result of good timing; as the race has been run for 159 years, there has been time to perfect the preparations.

All around Australia, people stopped to listen to the race, even in Sydney, to my surprise. Many workplaces organize a sweepstake, and groups get together for the afternoon, often with the women dressed up for the occasion. At my boys' college, the whole school stopped to listen to the race. There was no television until 1956.

Horse racing was quintessentially English, loved by the Irish when they became sufficiently prosperous, especially in Australia, where the racing industry is now bigger than in the UK or US. I know of no other nation where most people stop to watch a horse race.

As a youngster, I followed the horse racing and attended meetings in Ballarat at the Dowling Forest track and the Miners' racecourse, now closed. A few of my contemporaries in senior secondary school were already regular punters, a couple of them landing in financial trouble later from their gambling and another, Graeme Sampieri, becoming one of Victoria's biggest rails bookmakers,[4] and a successful one. One

---

[4] A rails bookmaker takes bets along the fence between the different enclosures and the racetrack.

prominent St Pat's College, Ballarat, family, sixty or seventy years ago, was the Bourkes, who owned the Pakenham racetrack.

I lapsed from the sport while I was in the seminary and overseas, only taking an interest sporadically on my return when one of the parishioners had some good horses running, but for some decades I have followed the Melbourne Cup. Generally, I have started to study the form about the time of the Caulfield Cup so I could wager "intelligently" on the big race. I would back a few horses "each way" (for a win and a place), and for many years, especially before the foreign horses came in numbers (I found their overseas form hard to evaluate), I would regularly return a profit.

To my delight, one of the two horses I backed for a win was Vow and Declare, the first Australian horse to win in ten years, and I encouraged my sister to do the same, so she also had a win. It is the only time in the year when I have a wager, although I always love seeing the horses race. I remember my mother and my aunts going to the races, "all dolled up", as we used to say, looking very smart, indeed. Old habits die hard and often return from the dead.

Yesterday, I was visited by Frs Ronnie Maree and Joe Murphy, just ordained priests, and Roberto Keryakos, who will be ordained deacon on Gaudete Sunday in December. All were in the Sydney seminary during my two years there in residence.

It was great that they came down, the second visit of Ronnie and Roberto. Life seems to be going well in the Sydney Archdiocese under Archbishop Anthony, and they didn't have much seminary news as they are no longer there. They were a bit concerned by the results of the Amazon Synod, but were taking it all in their stride. Last night, Tony Randazzo was being installed as the new bishop of Broken Bay, a ceremony they were attending. I think this is an excellent appointment, but I am disappointed that Wagga is still vacant after three years. I was blessed by the two new priests, who will make a fine contribution.

I spent an hour in the gymnasium this morning and immediately hit an unbroken series of more than 100 shots on both my backhand and forehand. A first. I enjoy these gymnasium outings, as they are a change of scene and good physical exercise, which helps me sleep.

My plan to purchase a CD player and five CDs from a special grant application has not sunk, but it has run into heavy weather. A special grant for a purchase over $50 can be made to the jail governor (e.g., for the CD player), but the CD purchases should come from my monthly allowance and can only be made at the rate of one a month; I might have missed the November purchase! I suppose the jail is not designed as a holiday farm.

The horse racing provided a focus and was a pleasant distraction. It is a blessing, part of God's creation, although its financial workings can on occasion be "opaque", although not (as far as we know) as opaque as the Vatican's.

One verse in the hymn for evening prayer calls me to re-centre.

> *Christ be in my heart and mind,*
> *Christ within my soul enshrined,*
> *Christ control my wayward heart;*
> *Christ abide and ne'er depart.*

Wednesday, 6 November 2019

Back to the daily routine after the distraction of the cup yesterday. The day was pleasant in the morning, but overcast and somewhat humid in the afternoon. While many parts of country NSW [New South Wales] have received good rain, up to 100 mm [4 inches], Queensland missed out and will likely have more bushfires.

A couple of *Spectators* arrived and C.J. Sansom's *Tombland*, the last in his series of murder stories set in post-Reformation England, on this occasion featuring the peasant rebellions in 1549. The 860-page text will keep me going for a while. It has received outstanding reviews from all the best sources, and I hope I enjoy it as much as all the others in the series, which I have read.

On last Friday, I informed the medical centre that my ears were blocked. Inhaling warm salty water has helped my sinuses, but done next to nothing for the ears. Today I had a brief visit with the doctor, and he prescribed eardrops, which to my surprise arrived this afternoon. I had to take the drops in the nurse's presence and return the bottle. I was a bit mystified and said that having to return them was a waste of their time. It will be interesting to know the reason for this.

My hour in the gymnasium passed quickly, as I managed to hit more than 100 shots on my backhand and forehand after a few tries. I didn't slip into form immediately as I did yesterday.

Sr Mary brought me Communion and mentioned that a priest might be allowed to celebrate Mass for me at Christmas, but it probably won't be Archbishop Comensoli. This would be marvellous. She brought the usual couple of sermons, and for once I disagreed with Sr Mary McGlone on one small point. I don't believe Zacchaeus climbed the tree wanting to be unnoticed. He wanted to see Jesus, and he might have wanted Jesus to see him. The point I used to make was that Zacchaeus' self-esteem did not prevent him from doing what he believed necessary.

The flow of letters has slowed as I only received four today. One included three more articles, one from the London *Financial Times* and two from Rome on three financial scandals: the Secretariat of State purchase in London for €200 million [$242 million], the APSA purchase of another London property for €90 million [$109 million], and the continuing debacle of the IDI hospital with their €800 million [$970 million] debt, their now laicised and jailed director running around with shoeboxes full of cash, and the unrecoverable €50 million [$61 million] loan from APSA, where the US Papal Foundation was reluctantly involved.

Phil Lawler (30/10/19) wrote about these fiascoes: "I suspect you'll find yourself wondering whether this is fact or fantasy, CNA or *The Onion*, an accurate account or a reporter's nightmare. Is it possible that the Vatican's financial affairs could be so chaotic, so imprudent, so palpably corrupt?"[5] I have sometimes remarked to friends that you could not include some of the antics in a novel because they would be rejected as too far-fetched.

Philip Boyce, the retired bishop of Raphoe in Ireland, wrote me a kind letter. He had been in Rome for the St John Henry Newman celebrations (he had been active promoting the cause), where my "work is appreciated and not forgotten". He added, "May your suffering bring you even closer to our Lord and Saviour. In the end truth will prevail." I believe the truth is emerging, and more people know it.

Another writer from Canberra, whom I don't know, told me he is praying for me and lamented my "loss of freedom, the absence of

[5] Phil Lawler, "Keystone Crooks: The Vatican's Latest Financial Scandal", Catholic Culture, 30 October 2019, https://www.catholicculture.org/commentary/keystone-crooks-vaticans-latest-financial-scandal/.

friends and family, the lack of colour, scent and sound of the trees and birds outside", all the things he is too busy to appreciate. So he thanked me for "making me (him) appreciate the things I have here on the outside". He concluded with good advice: "Keep reading, writing and praying."

Bishop Boyce informed me that when Newman was seventy-eight (my age now) he wrote:

I have ever tried to leave my cause in the hands of God and to be patient—and he has not forgotten me.

I make this my prayer, too, at this time, when I feel more impatient, frustrated by the slow progress of my appeal, than at any other time as the guest of Her Majesty. I don't like the prospect of Christmas in jail; but there are many things worse than this.

Thursday, 7 November 2019

A somewhat unusual day for a variety of reasons. It was cold and spitting rain during my two hours in the garden before my 2:30 pm visit and raining when I went out into the exercise pen at 4 pm.

I mentioned yesterday that the mail had slowed down. It returned with a vengeance today with around twenty letters and three parcels of articles, perhaps a hundred pages of photocopied texts, including Xavier Rynne's reports from the Amazonian Synod and about half a dozen new articles by Christopher Friel on my case. I spent most of the day studying these, although I had seen a couple of them already. In many ways, he is summarising and clarifying his findings, which provide a massive and comprehensive vindication of my position. I need to go back to his article "Investigative Journalism and the Pell Case" to reread a few sections and think through his observations.

I know that the complainant is not telling the truth and that he has no elements of any encounter with me that he can develop and embroider. I also feel that he does not have the imagination or intellect to have put this story together *ex nihilo*, "from nothing". I might be quite wrong here, as he alone and unaided might have used the Billy Doe story from the United States as a foundation for development.

My suspicion is that his recollections could have been shaped and moulded by others in the construction of his story. Another possibility is that he might have been abused by someone else, even near a church or in the cathedral, and adapted that experience. All this involves at least some lower-level conspiracy.

Friel devotes a deal of space to the possibility of a conspiracy and how this might be identified and distinguished from falsehood and nonsense. Perhaps because of a lack of clarity, or perhaps for legal considerations, he doesn't spell out the who, how, and why of his hypothesis or the level of probability he ascribes to it. I had thought this was his position for some time.

What was news from Anne McFarlane, who visited me today, was a couple of questions on which she wanted my knowledge and opinion. I had not heard of either element in the story, but if only one of them were true, it would seem to indicate a significant conspiracy, which might reach back to Rome and my financial work. I have been thinking about her request for leads and suggestions. Robert Richter along with a team of others is continuing his investigative work and remains open to a Roman connection, which represents a radical change in his perspective. I well know from dealing with prosecutors that a possibility is not necessarily a probability, and much more is needed to establish a fact. However, Billy Doe in Philadelphia, Carl Beech in the UK, and the financial scandals in the Vatican are all bizarre, far from normal behaviour. In this world of possibility, truth is once again the daughter, or the child, of time.

Anne also mentioned that her husband, Tim, had met Lord Christopher Patten, the chancellor of the University of Oxford and the last British governor of Hong Kong [1992–1997], whom I had asked to chair a committee to review Vatican communications. (They presented a good report which was largely ignored.) Patten was at the dinner at Newman College to celebrate Newman's canonisation and expressed [to Tim] his best wishes, prayers, and support for my innocence and said he wanted to send me a couple of history books. I sent a message of thanks back to him and requested that he choose them.

Tim has also been involved in a mediation with a flamboyant and notorious underworld figure, who discoursed freely on many topics, including my innocence. Good judgement again. A few lines from Psalm 43 to conclude.

Lord God—
send me your light and your faithful care,
let them lead me;
let them bring me to your holy mountain
to the place where you dwell.

Friday, 8 November 2019

A rather nonproductive day where I had no outing at all, except to the unit common area to speak with the jail's deputy governor.

For the first time in many months, I missed my second exercise in the small pen and lost my opportunity for a phone call. This was probably due to a change of staff. Friday is a quiet day without any visit to the gymnasium or the garden.

Last night, I became quite deaf with my blocked ears, and it was worse for some hours this morning. When the eardrops arrived (twice a day, as I am not allowed to keep them with me), I explained I was becoming as deaf as a post, which was a phrase the foreign-born nurse did not understand. I asked to have my ears syringed, and they muttered some friendly encouragement that it might happen tomorrow.

The deputy governor arrived with three assistants and the unit staff and the two warders, who accompany prisoners on moves; they all stood around and listened to my interview. I was asked my views, and I explained that from the beginning I had requested a bit more company and had lamented that the exercise pen was not the botanical gardens. I expressed my gratitude for time in the gardens and gymnasium and lamented again that the Unit 10 proposals had not progressed. The deputy governor seemed a kindly man, made allowances for my deafness, and explained that I was likely to be here for the duration of my appeal. Then, if the appeal was unsuccessful, the situation would have to be reconsidered. I also mentioned my brief foray into gardening, but the governor said he wasn't going there! The whole meeting was good-humoured, as I explained, when asked about the timeline for my appeal, that the High Court was like this prison inasmuch as both moved at their own pace. He urged me to be careful in replying to prisoners' letters, and I concurred that this was necessary; but I repeated that I tried to reply to each of them. I told him a group of career criminals thought I had been set up, explaining that this demonstrated their good judgement. He didn't comment on the range of my visitors or the 2,500 letters which I had received. Their major concern was my safety, which was made more difficult by my being so well-known.

No new letters arrived today, but I still have a mass of theological articles to read. One unusual short message came from Neuvy in France, with a beautiful coloured photo of the Loire River. The author has written a novel on the history of the first-century Christians in the far west of China, at Urumqi. She belongs to a small expert group which studies the issue. A now deceased Assumptionist priest had been a missionary in the region decades ago, before the library was purged of unwelcome evidence which confirmed his suspicions of an early Christianity. It was also discovered that first-century cliff carvings were not Buddhist as had been thought, but Christian.

The Nestorian Christians after the fifth century had many dioceses in the East, and, I think, in China, but I had never heard of a first-century presence. Whatever of St Thomas' missionary journey to India, it seems that contemporary Christians were active farther north. Another letter from a very strongly Catholic family man, who worked in medical sciences in a jail north of the Murray River and found the work difficult, said that my being in prison helped him continue with his job. God again writes straight with crooked lines.

I have always had a soft spot for James' Epistle, long before I understood the magnificence of Paul's writings and long before I deeply admired them. In some ways James, the brother of the Lord, is the [Raymond] Cardinal Burke of the New Testament.

We should allow James the last word today (Jas 1:2–4).

Consider yourselves fortunate when all kinds of trials come your way, because you know that when your faith succeeds in facing such trials, the result is the ability to endure. Be sure that your endurance carries you all the way, without failing, so that you may be perfect and complete, lacking nothing.

Saturday, 9 November 2019

Today I received a big surprise, something totally unexpected; by me at least. About 10 am the warders informed me that I had a professional visit from my lawyers, and I expected that solicitors Patrick and Nicholas had come to confirm that the fellow suing me had discontinued his efforts. Instead, I was surprised to find Kartya smiling at me and holding a folded one-page letter. She arranged for it to be passed to me through the trapdoor underneath the glass partition which separated us, and I sat down.

The letter was from the High Court, signed on November 6, and had arrived at their office yesterday afternoon. It announced that there would be no oral hearing and that the court in Canberra would announce at 9:30 am on next Wednesday, 13 November, whether my request to appeal had been granted.

I knew this prompt action probably meant that permission would be given, because if they were to refuse in the face of our two splendid submissions, which had been informally commended by judges and senior lawyers as "masterly", they would have given us a hearing.

I also remembered that twice before, I and my team and many outside "experts" had thought I would be freed, and we were bitterly disappointed, especially by the Victorian Court of Appeal. My adult life in the service of the Church and as a sometime participant in public life had taught me that nothing is certain until the deed has certainly been done. This remains true.

The line from my legal team is "cautious optimism", and I have learnt that rarely if ever should we be incautious. Terry Tobin and Michael Casey shared my reading of the development, although Michael, as always, was careful not to encourage me to run ahead of myself.

My mother and father taught me to be grateful and to express my thanks, and my schools reinforced this. For many years I have striven not to be like the nine cured lepers who did not come back to thank Jesus, not because they were ungrateful, but because they were busy doing something else.

I have often preached that we must be grateful to God for his many blessings and to express this. So when I returned to my cell, I prayed in thanks the prayer of the Church and recited the rosary. And God knows I am grateful.

If by some mischance my application to appeal were to be refused on next Wednesday, I would be clear in my mind that the justice system, and not just in Victoria, was broken. But I would be grateful that we knew where we were and were able to front up to the worst and decide to do what we could. I felt a twinge of guilt, too, that I had begun to feel impatient at the prospect of a first decision in December or February and irritated that God was letting things drag on for too long, unmindful of my weakness. In any event, we still have a way to run.

The remainder of this Saturday was also unusual as I watched the last day races of the Melbourne Cup carnival, where I learnt that there were 16,000 rose bushes at Flemington and that the retiring head gardener refused to give too much information on how they organized for the roses to bloom simultaneously and in Cup week.

The gymnasium was closed, and so I missed that hour of exercise.

In the evening, SBS had two good films, the first being an instalment on the Vietnam War that interviewed participants from both sides. The war was a vexed issue for me, as I was strongly in favour of the South Vietnamese and the war when I arrived in Oxford, and Peter Levi, the Jesuit classicist and poet, thoroughly cleaned me up in a discussion on the topic at afternoon tea. I always remained a strong opponent of the Viet Cong, while my concerns were fixed on whether the violence was proportionate to the ends proposed and whether the war could be won. It was a wretched business. I have always remained opposed to the US for overthrowing President [Ngo Dinh] Diem, even if they did not foresee his murder, and I was interested to learn tonight that Lyndon Johnson had been opposed to Diem's removal. Because Communist expansion in Asia did not continue, due in part at least to the Vietnam War, it does not follow that such a threat was imaginary.

The other program was a recent film on Churchill during the six days before the landings on June 6, 1944, D-day, in Normandy, and his opposition to and doubts on this single massive offensive, on the loss of young lives, triggered by his role in the disastrous Gallipoli landings in World War I. He was exhausted and failing in 1944, but his hesitations provide a useful balance to his caricature as a careless warmonger. I am always (still) deeply moved when I hear or read his wartime speeches. Romantic, overblown to some, they remain as powerful for me today as when I first read them as a teenager, although I now realise I would have disagreed with the old lion on many issues. Like Shakespeare's Henry V and Elizabeth before the threat of the Spanish Armada, he turned the English language into a weapon of war, inspired the great mass of his people, and put steel in their souls.

War is always evil, and while I have carefully considered the Christian call to pacifism, I do subscribe to a theory of the just war and feel that violent opposition to Nazi aggression was justified. The bombing of noncombatants, the carpet bombing of civilians through either conventional weapons or the atomic bomb, is another matter and essentially immoral. And I firmly believe that peacemakers are blessed.

As this is Saturday, we close with one of the intercessions from the Office.

Lord God, you strengthened Mary to stand at the foot of the cross and filled her with joy at the resurrection—by her intercession, lighten our sorrow and reinforce our hope.

WEEK 38

More Vatican Finances

10 November 2019—16 November 2019

Sunday, 10 November 2019

A terrible bushfire day in New South Wales and Queensland with one hundred fires burning in the morning. The situation worsened during the day, which in the evening saw seventy fires in New South Wales and fifty in Queensland. Three have died, at least 150 homes destroyed, and more than 100,000 hectares [250,000 acres] burnt. Tuesday is likely to be worse with no significant rain on the way.

When the electricity was turned off on Friday afternoon due to a fire somewhere in the jail, my electric alarm clock went off the rails. I couldn't make any progress in any direction, but Mr Harris set the machine so that it woke me in time for the 6 am *Mass for You at Home*.

Fr Martin Dixon was again the celebrant and preached an excellent sermon on life after death and dying. "Do we live death-denying lives?" he asked, because of our fear of the unknown. He told the story of a young twenty-two-year-old, who was dying in hospital during Holy Week and was agitated and difficult on Holy Thursday. To Martin's surprise, when he returned on Easter Sunday, the young man was calm, explaining, "Today is the day Jesus rose from the dead and the day I will rise." He had travelled through his sickness to a deeper faith.

I must say I found this sermon a bit of a relief from the two messages which followed, good as they were, but never quite arriving at the nub, where we have to repent as well as believe.

Joseph Prince was in black, with no boots and only two rings on his fingers. He had a chain on his right pocket and a monogram on the left back pocket of his jeans. His theme was "Find Hope in God's Covenant with You", speaking of the deep friendship and mutual loyalty of David and Jonathan and of David's loyalty to Jonathan's lame son, Mephibosheth. God will be kind to us, to our children and our children's children. He was shouting a bit more than usual.

Joel Osteen is older, always soberly dressed, never shouts, and his immense congregation is not predominantly Asian, like Joseph's, but of mixed race, if mostly European stock. He is friendly and articulate, slightly oleaginous, but invincibly positive. I don't know how he would preach on why bad things happen to good people! His theme today was "Empty Out the Negative".

When we are disappointed, we have to keep faith alive, live with expectancy. Don't be afraid, just trust in God, as the second divine touch is coming. The Lord himself told us to persevere in prayer, and I found Joel's message comforting in my jail situation. And the news of my appeal announcement had exceeded my expectations.

Elijah had to send his servant seven times before he saw the small cloud bringing the promised drought-breaking rains. Joel told us cousin Elizabeth thought her baby was dead, until he moved in response to Mary's greeting. Unfortunately, we find no evidence in Luke's Gospel to justify Joel's interpretation of a fearful Elizabeth, but we do have to keep our faith alive and live with expectancy.

Songs of Praise followed its usual format with three short accounts of good Christian care, this time with cancer patients, while the hymns were bouncy and folksy. I knew only one of them, "I Heard the Voice of Jesus Say".

The food is always better on Sundays, with roast chicken, and in the evening (or mid-afternoon, to be more accurate) they serve my favourite sweet of tinned fruit in jelly with cream. A pleasant childhood regression.

Generally and especially today, I would not be justified in repeating the grace before meals of an English major during the Second World War, who was living in a college in Delhi, India, and weighed down by the regular fare of hot, greasy curry. "Oh God we don't want to be rude, but must we eat this bloody food?"

This liturgical and literary gem came from Alan Ogden's book *Master of Deception: The Wartime Adventures of Peter Fleming*, a good read. Fleming's job was not to engage in psychological warfare to intimidate, but to try to deceive the Germans and then the Japanese about the Allies' strength and military intentions. India was perilously underdefended, and this was concealed. But generally in Asia, where our forces were short of equipment, a second priority to Europe, the major problem was that no one was clear what the Allied strategy was. Reading between the generally charitable lines, it looks as though Lord Mountbatten, the supreme commander, wasn't too sure himself and was given to changing his mind. I finished Fleming up so I could receive St Thomas More's *The Sadness of Christ*, written when he was in the Tower of London, a gift from Prior Benedict of Norcia.

Four lines from the Book of Wisdom will serve as a conclusion.

> *O God of my fathers and Lord of mercy,*
> *who have made all things by your word . . .*
> *give me the wisdom that sits by your throne*
> *and do not reject me from among your servants.*

Monday, 11 November 2019

Today is Remembrance Day, commemorating the end of the First World War. This was announced over the speakers at 11 am, when I was out in the garden, so I rose to my feet for the minute of remembrance and prayed for the souls of all those who died in that disaster. I wonder how many of these dead have no one who has prayed for them? May they rest in peace.

I have been to Gallipoli to celebrate Anzac Day,[1] visited the Western Front, paid tribute every year to the bravery of those who fought, and defended the celebrations of Remembrance Day and Anzac Day. But there is no denying that World War I destroyed the old order in Europe, removing many of the leadership class and many other good men in all the countries which participated, and preparing the ground

---

[1] Anzac Day commemorates all of the Australians and New Zealanders who served and died in all wars, conflicts, and peacekeeping operations. Originally the national holiday honoured only the members of the Australian and New Zealand Army Corps (ANZAC) who served in the Gallipoli Campaign in World War I.

for Hitler and Mussolini and even the Marxists. I am pleased that Dr Mannix, the archbishop of Melbourne, was one of the leaders against conscription and pleased, too, that he was able to celebrate St Patrick's Day some years later, accompanied by a parade of Victoria Cross winners on white horses.

The war produced the finest poetry, and Wilfred Owen is my favourite. I believe that German arrogance was the driving force, the main cause of the war, but it remains a disaster vividly described by Ezra Pound.

> There died a million,
> And of the best, among them,
> For an old bitch gone in the teeth,
> For a botched civilisation.[2]

I don't have access to a text, but someone claimed that an imperfect citation remains as a compliment. And I am not sure the civilisation was botched everywhere.

David and Georgie visited today, and we spent a pleasant hour plus together. David had been informed by Kartya about the Wednesday announcement and was reassured, although we both agreed not to count our chickens before they were hatched. Apparently Sonny, Georgie's son, is coming along well, a good talker, with a clear will of his own. Given the Burke-Pell genes he has inherited, to say nothing of any other streams of heredity, it is not surprising he is headstrong. Provided he can learn to control it, this is a valuable asset in life.

Just before David and Georgie, Patrick Santamaria and Nicholas O'Bryan, solicitors, arrived with a release form for me to sign. One of the gentlemen, whose case had been thrown out, still alleged I had assaulted him in the pool at St Joseph's Home, in a year when he was no longer there, and was suing me. He eventually claimed he saw me once and then recognized me from television forty years later. I had never swum in the pool, did not know it existed, and both the nuns and a long-term resident gave witness they had never seen me at St Joseph's. Not surprisingly, the gentleman discontinued his case,

---

[2] Ezra Pound (1885–1972), "Hugh Selwyn Mauberly [excerpt]". The original poem has the word "myriad" where the cardinal uses "million".

although he received a significant payment for mistreatment in Ballarat from the Sisters and especially the government system. It is good to have this out of the way.

As I had spent most of the day on Sunday reading Xavier Rynne's reports from the Amazon Synod, remarkable by any standards, I had to draw on my notes and write up yesterday's events this morning, before continuing with these.

While I was out in the yard, I did manage to read a good slab of the tract of the Catholics for Renewal, *Getting Back on Mission*. If they were to carry the day at the Australian Plenary Council next year, which is highly unlikely, they would accelerate the exodus because they believe they can improve the apostolic tradition. When tried, that has never worked.

Tonight on SBS, we had another film on the House of Windsor, on the Duke of Edinburgh. The royals probably get more time from SBS than climate change. Queen Mary featured as the widow of George V, who worked with the Queen Mother to curb the influence of the Duke, whom they distrusted, not least because of his German blood. In her later years, Queen Mary came to the Jesuit church in Farm Street, London, to pray, even summoning the parish priest, asking him to ensure the curate did not come to gape at her. She also occasionally picked up odds and ends from department stores and forgot to pay, something the detective with her would remedy. It was alleged that Princess Margaret had Catholic sympathies, while the Queen remains a Protestant Anglican, although a good friend of both Cardinal Hume and [the late] Cardinal Murphy-O'Connor.

A verse from P Herbert's 1571 hymn:

> *Fountain of Goodness, bless the sick and needy;*
> *Visit the captive, solace the afflicted;*
> *Shelter the stranger, feed your starving children,*
> *Strengthen the dying.*

Tuesday, 12 November 2019

Today was a special day, as Sr Mary had organized for Fr Jerome Santamaria to come with her and celebrate Mass for me, in the usual place in the common area. We had no interruption until Mass was over, thanks to Mr Harris. By a coincidence, I had just been reading a letter from Jerome's father, which was accompanied as always by three or four photocopied articles, and I used the occasion to thank him and pass on my gratitude to his whole tribe, who had been wonderful supporters. Many have written to me.

It was a relief to have the Mass, to have the drought broken, if only for this occasion. For some weeks, when I obtained a text, I read it through as a "dry" Mass, but I found this unsatisfactory; not counterfeit, but not the genuine article which must be reverenced. Neither do I make "spiritual communions", whatever that means, because God is already in my heart spiritually, and I don't have the means to confect the Real Presence.

Neither do I choose to dwell on the fact that I cannot attend or celebrate Mass, but resolutely, each day, I do what I can and should do, which is follow my regular schedule of prayer.

At some times, special times such as Easter, I feel very keenly the inability to celebrate, to worship in the Mass, in the way Jesus prescribed. But Jesus will continue to listen to my small prayers; "poor" prayers would be more accurate than "small".

Catholicism is ritualised and sacramental, the making present of Jesus' redemptive suffering and death. Much more than even the most holy icon, the Mass takes us to the heart of creation and all human history, perhaps especially in this jail setting where a dozen criminals, including myself, are confined twenty-three hours a day—some of them murderers, probably many damaged by drugs, many of them wretched and unhappy, and some very angry. I heard of one murderer, touched by grace, who told the family of the person he murdered not to allow themselves to be consumed by hatred as he had been.

Christ was born in a stable and died on a rubbish dump between two thieves, even if the Last Supper was celebrated with dignity in decent surroundings. I am sure the good God has a special regard for the Eucharist celebrated in jail, just as he blesses all those who work with prisoners, such as Sr Mary.

It seems ungracious to be critical of the TV evangelists, whom I watch every Sunday and from whom I do receive nourishment. But it is a great relief, a return to the richer habits of a lifetime, to immerse myself in the simple Mass ritual and receive Holy Communion. While we had no major eruptions of noise from the prisoners, we were not in St Peter's or accompanied by the choir from St Mary's, Sydney. It was still simple and reverent, the real thing.

Yesterday, while I was taking my afternoon exercise, one of the warders interrupted and gave me a beautifully bound book, containing best wishes, prayers, and greetings from more than ninety-five families, groups, and individuals who participated in the Christus Rex pilgrimage this year from Ballarat to Bendigo. The messages were full of faith, and all were praying for me, so I am sure the good God is listening to them. The book itself was produced by Peter Pauper Press in New York, designed to last, with a solid cover, which at the back and in the front has the reproduction of the sixteenth-century binding for mystical Persian poetry, featuring trees, flowers, and animals. Elegant, even exquisite.

John Macauley, whom I have known for years since he was a seminarian, sent it to me, and Fr Terence Mary Naughtin, OFM Conventual, was the first signature. Other signatories included Fr Mark Withoos, my former secretary and dear friend who insisted there were "no pachamamas" here, and Bernard and Carmel Righetti, who travel down from Smeaton twice a week to stand outside the jail to pray.

In the gym today, on both backhand and forehand, I broke 200 consecutive shots.

Tomorrow morning at 9:30 am, the High Court will announce whether my appeal is allowed.

So I pray [with Psalm 144]:

> *Lord God, reach down from heaven and save me;*
> *draw me out from the mighty waters,*
> *from the hands of alien foes*
> *whose mouths are filled with lies,*
> *whose hands are raised in perjury.*

Wednesday, 13 November 2019

Today was an important day, and, thank God, the High Court did the right thing and gave me leave to appeal.

I slept quite well, although I woke up briefly at 4:45. Naturally, I felt under pressure, but also believed that the evidence was clear-cut, and this gave reassurance. Prayers from thousands could never be wasted, the cause was just; and my eventual exoneration, if it comes, will help the Church in Australia and even more widely. But God's permissive will follows its own patterns, and we still have another big hearing after this. My sleep was better than before the Victorian Court of Appeal verdicts.

When the guards gave me breakfast, I arranged to go out for exercise just after 10 am, rather than at 8:30 am as usual, so I could telephone the lawyers.

At 10 to 10, the guard said I had a professional visit from my lawyers and to prepare myself to go down. As we passed out of Unit 8, one of the women warders who had always been friendly called out, "Good news, George." "Thanks," was my reply, "I didn't know."

Ruth Shann had come down with Kartya, and as soon as I saw their faces, the good news was confirmed. They were delighted. The issue will be heard before all seven judges at some future time, probably in February or March next year.

It remained significant that no hearing was needed, and one retired High Court judge explained that all the judges would have believed there was no need for argumentation at this stage.

In the afternoon, I was able to phone Margaret and David to share our delight. David had been speaking with Andrew Bolt, who said, "Thank God." My message to him, via David, was that his comment was one of the better developments in the whole saga! Terry was also relieved and delighted. Incidentally, David had passed on the good news to Fr Robert McCulloch in Rome.[3]

When I returned to my cell, I felt a sense of relief, an easing of the tension, so I meditated for a half hour on the Te Deum, the traditional prayer of rejoicing and thanksgiving, before I went to the gymnasium for my hour of exercise. On the second or third attempt, I hit over 250 consecutive shots on my backhand but had to try repeatedly before I scored over 100 on the forehand. My weight has dropped again, but very slightly.

On a more mundane level, the medical centre called me so that the doctor could clean out my ears, as I had completed my course of drops. This was happily completed, and my hearing is much

---

[3] Fr Robert McCulloch, an Australian Columban priest, is his Order's procurator in Rome.

improved. My sense of balance played up for a few moments after the procedure, but the doctor explained this was not completely unusual, and after a rest I was able to walk back unaided to Unit 8, Cell 11.

The lawyers had passed on a collection of articles on the financial scandals in the Vatican from the Italian press. Libero Milone, the former auditor of the Vatican, had given an interview four days ago to *Il Messaggero*, where he again expressed his desire to return to work at the Vatican and, more importantly, that his problem with the Vatican should be mediated appropriately or he would take legal action. The most important item was that the former Vatican partner Raffaele Mincione was under investigation by the Procura of Rome for a variety of activities, including the London property purchases.

La Stampa wrote about "all Mincione's flops", listing six or seven and estimating losses of around €23 million [$28 million]. I wonder how much of this went to Mincione only, just as so much Vatican money disappeared in his direction.

La Repubblica had an article on Giuseppe Pignatone, the anti-Mafia campaigner [prosecutor] who has been appointed the new president of the Vatican tribunal, anticipating genuine anti-corruption progress. They commented that in recent times the regime of his predecessor, Giuseppe Dalla Torre, was characterised as being "too slow-moving". In fact, the problem went back for many years, and I had urged Dalla Torre to do his duty and proceed justly and persistently. To little effect. The *sostituto* ensured that most of the sleeping dogs were allowed to lie quietly and undisturbed.

La Repubblica also mentioned a couple of cases which had started, but then seemed to stall. The first of these involved the banker Giampietro Nattino, who had manipulated share prices with help from within the Vatican and had €2.5 million [$3 million] frozen as a precautionary measure. The second case was that of Angelo Caloia, former president of IOR, who some decades ago was involved in the sale of Vatican property worth around €130 million [$157 million] for between €90 and 100 million [$109–121 million]. It remains to be seen how much progress a good man like Pignatone will be allowed to make.

The Vatican's pediatric hospital on the Janiculum Hill, the Bambino Gesù, also scored an honourable mention, listing the shadows still cast by the former director Giuseppe Profiti, who has already come to grief.[4] The president, Mariella Enoc, has worked steadily to clean up the situation and absolutely refused to authorise the €50 million, from the Italian government funds, which Profiti was preparing to use in taking over IDI.

Even efforts to recover some of these Vatican monies were stymied, and *La Repubblica* estimates the Caloia losses at €50 million [$61 million].

The second-century homilist [Clement] was correct.

You fools, compare yourselves to a tree, to a vine, for example. First it sheds its leaves, then it becomes a shoot, then an unripe grape, then in due season it bears ripe fruit.

It is the same with my people. They must first know instability and distress before finding happiness.

Thursday, 14 November 2019

The Prayer of the Church today has the second reading from a second-century homily which begins: "The Lord says: my name is blasphemed among the Gentiles, but woe to him through whom my name is blasphemed! Why is it blasphemed? Because we do not practise what we preach." It is then the pagans claim "our religion is an old wives' tale". If we refuse to do God's will, we fulfil the Scripture prophecy that "my house has become a house of thieves."

The Church of the saints was always an overstatement, as sin has been at work in God's people since Cain's murder of his brother, Abel. Sinners were damaging belief, weakening the body of Christ through scandal even in the second century. Sin is an ancient Catholic tradition, but repentance and conversion are an even stronger hallmark.

Paedophilia has destroyed some religious orders in Australia, damaged terribly dioceses like Ballarat and Newcastle, and obscured our

---

[4] In 2017, a Vatican court found Giuseppe Profiti guilty of abusing his office as president of Bambino Gesù, by using donations to the hospital's foundation to renovate a Vatican-owned apartment used by Cardinal Tarcisio Bertone, former Vatican secretary of state. He was sentenced to one year in jail and fined €5000 [$6039], but the sentence was suspended.

Christian witness. So far, the Vatican financial scandals have not bitten as deeply, especially in Australia, but they are a scandal of incompetence exploited by criminals. I wish every blessing on those in the Vatican who continue to struggle for financial reform.

Australians generally are competent and honest administrators, and the Catholic Church [in Australia] exemplifies this tradition. We must be vigilant, striving to improve our procedures, because the enemies of the Church will exploit any weakness, especially when they can no longer rerun the stories of the worst paedophilia scandals.

When I lamented to the warders that I didn't receive a broom to sweep my cell, one replied that as I had been out and away "all day", this had not been possible.

I had been out most of the afternoon, as Paul Galbally called at 11:50 am to chat about the wonderful development yesterday. He explained that after consulting a senior judge, he was able to state that the option the High Court had given us was the best available. He was delighted, as was Robert Richter, he reported. Apparently Robert had a brief visit to hospital, but all is now well.

The press coverage was extensive, largely predictable, with articles in the *Herald Sun* mentioning the possibility of bail. Paul pointed out that it was useful for us to have so many people unconnected with the case lamenting the decision to allow an appeal. This would demonstrate to the judges the poisoned atmosphere from which the juries were selected.

Anne McFarlane informed me Andrew Bolt on Sky News had put together a very effective audiovisual piece on the ten minutes after Sunday Mass, demonstrating the impossibility of the allegations. This has now spread widely on the Internet.

Paul also mentioned that the High Court computer system crashed because so many people wanted to know the result of my application.

Danny Casey shared the general delight of my friends both in Australia and overseas. He was abreast of most of the information I had gathered from the Italian papers on the Vatican scandals, remarking that he had heard [Cardinal] Becciu had given an interview to a journalist, as he was feeling under pressure, which is not surprising. Danny also suspected that another front might be opening up and that information was coming from multiple sources.

After finishing my chat with Paul, I spent the remaining hour outside in the garden, which was watered in my presence by the officer whose place I had unwittingly usurped. He was in good humour as I explained again that I had ceased because of a demarcation dispute.

Chris Meney and his son-in-law Sam Phillips visited me in a "box" visit, separated by a glass panel, and we had a lovely hour-long chat, double the allotted time. He had obtained family Bibles for me to sign before I presented them to Sonny, my great-nephew, and to Rachel's boy Augustine George. All was well in the family, although Dominic had skidded in Sam's ancient Corolla car and consigned it to history. He wasn't hurt, thanks be to God.

Today a verse from Psalm 43 is appropriate.

> For it is not in my bow that I trusted
> nor yet was I saved by my sword:
> it was you who saved us from our foes,
> it was you who put our foes to shame.

Friday, 15 November 2019

A pleasant nondescript prison day, when the only surprise was a call in the morning from the guards to take me to the medical centre. I presumed it was my thrice-monthly chat with the St Vincent's heart specialist, but it was a video link with a skin specialist to check out the long-term dry sore on the back of my right calf muscle. They confirmed that there was nothing to worry about.

Fr Paul Stenhouse is now sleeping a lot and probably drifting in and out of consciousness in palliative care at the hostel next to St Vincent's. All I can do is pray for him that he dies peacefully and with his pain under control. Terry Tobin informed me that his eyes lit up with delight when he was told that my High Court appeal had been accepted, as he was offering up his sufferings for my cause.

The second part of the afternoon was spent in writing a couple of letters to prisoners, both of whom write regularly. One writes every day and has become a Muslim, giving me about twenty pages on the early life of Muhammad. The story was not new to me, although I had not realised Muhammad was illiterate.

In the evening, I watched a two-hour SBS program on Prince Mohammed bin Salman (MBS), the Crown Prince who has turned Saudi Arabia into a police state, and his dictatorship. He has gone to war with Yemen and Qatar, and the appalling story of the murder of the journalist [Jamal] Khashoggi in the Saudi embassy in Ankara, Turkey, was recounted. The body was dismembered into small parts and flown back to Saudi Arabia. To some extent, the country is being modernized, and the house arrest (and subsequent release for the majority) of many prominent princes and business leaders was ostensibly a drive against corruption. A grim picture worsened by the fact that a fundamentalist revolution would bring worse times.

The bushfires continue north and south of the border, in the north with over a million hectares [2.5 million acres] burnt, some schools and houses destroyed, and three deaths. However, the worst has been avoided by hard work and improved weather conditions.

The letters continue to arrive, a regular consolation, although one or two are weird while still wonderful.

One was anonymous from "some nondescript agnostic Sandgroper[5] living in Queensland", who cheerfully proclaimed his belief that I am "a prized early victim of the burgeoning persecutory age". I have been struck by this vein of pessimism in not a few letters. Apparently, the Desert Fathers had taught that a man should go to a shed (or a cave), and it will teach him everything. He graphically explained that his shed had become a prison and hoped that I "have been able to turn a prison cell into a monk's cell". With my TV, kettle, and chocolates, it is a worldly monk's cell, with a good dose of prayer, as well as health and contentment.

Even in the worst of times, we have had, at least, other reasons to be grateful.

> For as the heavens are high above the earth
> so strong is (God's) love for those who fear him.
> As far as the east is from the west
> so far does he remove our sins. (Psalm 102)

Saturday, 16 November 2019

I have never suffered from Mondayitis, and I am one of a blessed minority of those who thoroughly enjoy their work. A busy priestly

---

[5] A sandgroper is a subterranean insect found in Australia and slang for a person from Western Australia.

life is enjoyable and gives a meaning and satisfaction found in few other occupations, as nearly all "ex-priests" will concede. Similarly, I was never one to be pining for the next weekend.

Prison life is different as I look forward to Saturdays, evidence that one more week is almost completed. We always have a meat pie, or pasty, for lunch, which I now get heated when I return late after my hour in the gymnasium. As I have mentioned, this remains my culinary highpoint of the week, except when the jelly, fruit, and cream are served. As Cardinal Clancy[6] used to remark, "May God forgive our foolish mirth."

My recollection is that recently I heard on the television that the Milky Way has between one and four hundred billion stars. My memory might be faulty, and especially when I was working with money I had to be careful that I was not adding or subtracting two or three zeros. Whatever about the exact number, the Milky Way is immense beyond our imaginings, and only one part of the story of the universe.

This thought was sparked by the report this week that the Anglo-Australian telescope at the Siding Spring Observatory [in New South Wales] had discovered a star, slingshot from the supermassive black hole at the heart of our galaxy five million years ago, which is travelling at six million km [3.7 million miles] an hour, ten times the speed of most stars. At this rate, it will exit the Milky Way in about 100 million years and never return. The black hole responsible for this expulsion, named Sagittarius A, has a mass equivalent to four million suns.

These distances are beyond our imagination, and even when we say the numbers quickly, as we do with the Vatican financial losses, we cannot completely evade their immensity.

It is the God of Abraham, Isaac, and Jacob, whom Jesus called "Father", who created and sustains this unimaginable universe. Equally mysterious is the journey from the macroscopic to the microscopic, to the subatomic world of convertible mass and energy, without venturing into the mysteries of the soul and the brain or without touching the creations of human genius or the beauty of the saints and mystics, poets and artists.

---

[6] Edward Cardinal Clancy (1923–2014) was the archbishop of Sydney from 1983 to 2001.

The one true God is behind all this; no, he is beyond all this, and yet he is interested in each of us and loves each one of us, sending his only Son "to do it rough" with us and suffer and die for us.

As we pray toward the end of each baptism ceremony:

This is our faith. This is the faith of the Church. We are proud to profess it in Christ Jesus. Amen.

WEEK 39

Clash of Mentalities

17 November 2019—23 November 2019

Sunday, 17 November 2019

Today I am going to break with my usual practice for a Sunday journal by not starting with a report on *Mass for You at Home*, the Protestant evangelists, and the UK *Songs of Praise*.

My dear friend Fr Paul Stenhouse is in palliative care, unconscious and dying. He might even have died since I spoke to Terry Tobin an hour or so ago. This afternoon, I opened a letter from the mother of a Sydney priest who had spent a half hour with him at Kensington Monastery on Monday, 4 November. She reported that now "his body is quite wasted, but his mind is sharp." The final issue of *Annals* was being proofread by Fr Michael Fallon, but Paul realised he would not be here for the "wake", the final dinner for *Annals* on 29 November. My correspondent continued, "He is normally calm and rational. He became visibly upset and started to weep when he described one aspect of the lunch. He had insisted that the grandest, most comfortable chair is to be placed at the table and is to remain empty during the meal. That chair is for you, Cardinal Pell. I thought you'd like to know." I am deeply touched by both parts of her account, and I will miss him deeply.

Paul went on to make a beautiful profession of faith and love, and I quote, "He said he is overjoyed at the thought of seeing Our Lord's face." That is the consequence, the reward for a lifetime of faithful priestly service. I felt a twinge of guilt that I had never previously thought of death in those terms; but I do now.

The bushfires continue in northern New South Wales and Queensland, with more than one and a half million hectares [3.7 million acres] burnt. Hundreds of houses are destroyed, but only six dead. The temperatures are very high in most of Western Australia today. All this is only the start of summer. A specialist psychologist who was interviewed explained there were 31,000 arsonists each year in Australia. I was amazed at the figure, many times higher than I imagined, as for me the motivation of arsonists is one of the more mysterious manifestations of evil. Fire is fascinating, of course, an instrument of power for the powerless, the vengeful, and the resentful—and particularly the malign, because it is unpredictable and often uncontrollable.

Msgr Tony Ireland celebrated Mass with dignity and without haste, but it was all over too quickly.

Joseph Prince was soberly dressed in a dark suit and tie, dangerously similar to what he had worn previously. He compensated by wearing three rings rather than two, but his sermon was first class, Christocentric, and drawn from the New Testament. He spoke of repentance, God's lavish love for us; of the lost sheep, the lost coin, the Prodigal Son. We do not find God. He finds us, in all our weakness and sins. Prince pointed out that we judge others by their actions and ourselves by our intentions. This is true too often. His sermon was punctuated by a film excerpt of Jesus' suffering and death on the Cross, dramatised with lightning and a Mel Gibson level of violence.

Joel Osteen was on theme urging us to empty out the negative. As always, he was dressed conservatively in a suit and tie. No open-necked shirt with two buttons undone. God doesn't run out of options, despite the many obstacles we might encounter, because God is not stopped by a closed door which he can pass through, even when we are pessimistic and fearful. I balked when I heard that Moses had led two million in the Exodus from Egypt, but I understood his warning against impatience and his urging that we trust God's timing. Jesus himself told us to keep asking in prayer and faith for what we need, and Joel's theme today spoke to my situation and impatience before the providential High Court decision.

Songs of Praise featured three places of pilgrimage, Mont Saint-Michel, where the statue of Michael the Archangel is still headless, cut off in the French Revolution of 1789; Caldey Abbey off Wales; and Walsingham, the thousand-year-old UK shrine to Our Lady, venerated by both Anglicans and Catholics. At the Anglican shrine, the altar is composed of stones taken from many of the monasteries which Henry VIII destroyed, during the rejection of the papacy, the split with Rome.

We will close with a verse from William Cowper's hymn "Exhortation to Prayer".

> *Restraining prayer, we cease to fight;*
> *Prayer makes the Christian's armour bright;*
> *And Satan trembles when he sees*
> *The weakest saint upon his knees.*

Monday, 18 November 2019

Today is the feast when we remember the dedication in Rome, in the fourth century, when religious freedom was obtained, of the two basilicas dedicated to St Peter and St Paul, on the spot where Peter was buried and on the traditional site of Paul's martyrdom. Today we worship in the second St Peter's, built in the sixteenth century, while St Paul's is a nineteenth-century building, replacing the earlier church destroyed by fire. St Peter's is the best-known symbolic building in the world, at least in a religious sense, better known than the Statue of Liberty or Big Ben or the Great Wall of China, which cannot be seen from distant space, despite the propaganda efforts to convince us otherwise.

However, as Msgr Tony Ireland explained in Sunday's TV Mass, when he spoke on the Temple in Jerusalem, now destroyed, and St Peter's, the most valuable symbol is an individual publicly witnessing to Christ Our Lord, especially when this witness is given under hostile pressure.

It was a perfect early summer day, as the sun was out, very light high clouds, and the air was clear and crisp, without the whiff of humidity which is always present up north, even in Sydney, which stands at the intersection of two weather systems. Someone once claimed to me that this location is an example of the "China syndrome". The birds were about and busy, new roses were blooming as the predecessors quickly wilted, and other native flowers, with small blooms, were also out adding some bright colours.

Not surprisingly, I took off my green prison top as I sat out in the sun for forty minutes. I only had an hour outside, as a fight or fights had broken out among the prisoners. It wasn't directed against the warders, but was between the prisoners. You don't ask how many were involved, or at least I don't, but the prison was "locked down", and other prisoners returned to their cells for about an hour. One of the warders marvelled that the prisoners were fighting when the weather was so good. Windy weather makes primary-school children fractious, so I wonder if any weather conditions worsen behaviour in prison.

Fr Danny Meagher, the rector of Good Shepherd seminary in Sydney, and Della Budwee, the seminary secretary, travelled from Sydney to see me. Both are good friends and strong supporters. Della's mother is still at home with Della and her sister, unwell and aged ninety-four. Her nights are very disturbed, but the sister copes with no nursing help. Danny recounted that the last month in the seminary was difficult, with a variety of problems, but three Sydney men will be ordained deacons before Christmas, and they hope for six new seminarians for Sydney next year and four others. The first years have started their thirty-day retreat, which they all commenced with shaved heads. My seminary house is still vacant, and the new house remains unoccupied, as the Ordinariate bishop is living in Bishop Randazzo's former home.

A couple of articles favourable toward my cause appeared in *The Australian* at the weekend: one by John Ferguson, the crime reporter, and another by Peter Baldwin, a former left-wing NSW [New South Wales] Labor politician, who was famously bashed by right-wing thugs and photographed with a grossly swollen and blackened face. Terry Tobin feels it is the best and most accessible piece yet published, and his left-wing Labor background is also a significant plus. Also reported that on Saturday a Melbourne Fairfax (as they used to be called) paper published an article by David Marr's research assistant, which was basically in favour of my innocence. Danny Meagher expressed his view that public opinion is turning in my direction. For the Church's sake, I hope so.

Some articles have also appeared supporting bail for me and attacking the practice of keeping prisoners in solitary confinement for many months. Apparently an article or two along the same lines had appeared earlier in the *Herald Sun*. A few more months in jail could be offered for the good of the Church, especially the Church in Rome.

I will conclude with a few lines from the sermon of Pope St Leo the Great (fifth century) on Peter and Paul.

We and our forefathers have learnt and know we can trust utterly to their prayers to win God's mercy for ourselves in our labours here on earth. Our sins can bow us to the ground; the fullness of their apostolic merits lifts us up once more.

Tuesday, 19 November 2019

The day began with news communicated by Terry that Fr Paul Stenhouse was hanging on and "sleeping like a baby". He was a workhorse to the end, never complained, and had a tolerance for pain that was remarkable. Few priests in the Catholic story in Australia were able to equal his mastery of languages, his specialist and general knowledge, and his intellectual output. "Christum et ecclesiam vehementer amavit." He loved Christ and the Church deeply and ardently and would have taken a small dose of delight in confounding our expectations. I pray he is not suffering, as he has done penance enough. I was also delighted to learn that Archbishop Fisher had gone to visit him a week or so ago.

To my surprise, Sophie was able to tell us that the High Court had posted, soon after the announcement of my successful leave to appeal, the series of dates when we had to present material to them, the last of these being toward the end of February. Therefore, March is the first realistic opportunity for a hearing. For some reason, I was a bit disappointed, although an earlier date had always been unlikely and a successful application for bail even less likely.

Sr Mary called to bring me Communion and for the customary chat. I asked her to convey again my thanks to Jerome for celebrating Mass for me a week ago. She will complete twenty-five years in service in the jails in December this year and explained, with the agreement of Mr Harris, that the mental state of the prisoners has declined in the last ten years because of the damage done by the new

strong drugs, such as ice; Harris believes many of the prisoners would
be housed more appropriately in a mental institution. We had a noisy
and angry prisoner some days ago, but the unit has been quiet for
some weeks.

Mary brought me the usual sermons by Fr Gleeson, SM, and Sr
Mary McGlone from the US. In the last couple of weeks, Gleeson
has returned to his best while the McGlone homilies are the finest
series I have read for decades. And they are Catholic. She knows
what Christ was "on about". If you are preaching Christ faithfully
week after week, you are constantly niggling your listeners toward
forgiveness, prayer, repentance, purity; toward honesty, service, away
from lies and too much love of money. Too much from the Gospels
can be too much, too discomforting for some TV evangelists, who
take refuge in the Old Testament, which has many interesting stories
where human weakness abounds.

Terry also informed me this morning that Fr Robbie had emailed
the news that René Brülhart, the chairman or president of AIF, the
Vatican agency to supervise the banks and counter money laundering, is resigning or not seeking another term. Some of the press is
interpreting this as a gesture of disapproval. Certainly Moneyval,
the international supervisory agency, was insisting that investigations
proceed, charges be laid and progressed, and it seems little of this
has gone ahead. Day-to-day running of the agency is in the hands
of Tommaso Di Ruzza, who was stood down recently and then was
reinstated, and no one has accused Tommaso of intemperate zeal in
his pursuit of corruption.

On at least some occasions, Brülhart's recommendations were not
accepted. To my mind we have three alternative explanations: (1) René
has the offer of another suitable position; (2) the powers that be are
nervous about his capacity and integrity (this is less likely, given
recent staff changes in the Vatican); or (3) he is unable to direct policy
and is dissatisfied for some reason. This means that another one of the
original Reform Party has moved on, with the ever-present danger
that his replacement will be someone underqualified for the position
and a bit short of courage.

An article by Andrea Gagliarducci reports that my Spanish-
speaking Jesuit successor was in Mozambique at the time the new *sostituto* was nuncio there and that all developments are congruent with

the ambition of the secretary of state to maintain and strengthen the control of the Secretariat of State over all Vatican activity, including finance. This is not healthy, but tolerable if honesty and competence are genuine. Proper audits are essential, preferably internal and external, while the more fundamental problems are to reduce the annual deficit, partly through more efficient investment, and to address the looming shortfall in the Vatican pension fund. The first challenge has not been met, and I don't know whether the pension fund has made significant progress in the last two years, after four years of dissimulation and inactivity financially, although the composition of the new board, which was short of the ideal and a compromise, offered hope for better things.

Lord God, give your Church the help of the apostle Peter, who was a successful fisherman on the Sea of Galilee, and of the apostle Paul, who provided his own income from his work as a tentmaker, so that the Vatican can regularly supply the income necessary for their daily bread in ways that are honest and competent.

Wednesday, 20 November 2019

One of the consolations of my priesthood has been working with Italians, especially in Australia. I have made many good friends and often been impressed by their depth of faith. While it is exaggerating to dismember Italy into three countries—the north long ruled by Austria, the thousand-year-old Papal States in central Italy, and the south—we do have three regions with a frequent absence of sympathy in the north toward the south, who are alleged to be lazy. The story of the southerners in Australia invalidates that accusation, as they have proved to be ferocious workers across the decades. I suspect the southerners were too cunning to work hard when there was no way of getting ahead initially, a situation which changed dramatically with the opportunities for them and their children in Australia.

As the postwar cohort of Italian migrants, mainly southerners, began to grow old in Australia, and even earlier as their relatives aged, priests would regularly be given offerings for a "bad news from Italy" Mass for the deceased.

Today I had good news from Italy. While talking to Danny Casey this morning, he told me that a Jesuit friend of his, a supporter of economic reform, who had invited Danny to the United States to speak on finance and the Church, was enthusiastic about the new appointment to the position of prefect of the Secretariat for the Economy. The new prefect had been the person to whom Danny's friend reported for his financial work, by implication both honest and competent. This was wonderful news and gave me quite a boost. It would be a "game changer" to have a classy player in this position who was allowed to play his game and use his skills. Five to ten years ago, the priority was to stop and eliminate corruption. While this challenge remains, especially with the absence of external auditors, the main challenge now is to stabilise the financial situation, which has worsened more quickly than I anticipated.

In both the morning and the evening, I was unable to contact the Tobins; so I don't know how Fr Paul Stenhouse is faring. I did get through to my sister, who was in hospital in Bendigo for tests on the veins of her legs. Please God we won't have very bad news. The weather was beautiful, although most of Australia is hot, and we now have bushfires in South Australia. I had my customary hour in the gymnasium, meeting all my goals with the basketball, in the ping-pong, and through my improved balance on the treadmill. As always, it is a welcome change of scene.

As I have not been much of a dreamer for most of my life, I have not taken any academic interest in the nature of dreaming, much less in interpreting dreams, although at some stage I learnt about fast and slow eye movements during sleep and types of sleep. My reading has shown that we have no adequate explanation for a goodly number of paranormal events, and I do believe in demonic possession of souls and the possibility of demonic activity. As Christianity declines in Australia, it is almost inevitable that this gap will be filled by the diabolical. But I had never worried much about dreams until I started to receive letters from well-wishers telling of their dreams about me or my case.

The daughter of a school friend wrote to tell me of two dreams. In the first, a Vatican cardinal was given a telegram announcing my innocence, which prompted him to declare there would be no Vatican investigation. This occurred on June 13, and on October 9 she dreamt she was helping me cut and light a Cuban cigar! The dreams gave her hope, and I don't know how she might have known that I do like an occasional mild cigar.

Another dream was quite different, from a woman I had been able to help, who had suffered grievously at the hands of someone whom she had managed to forgive, after a struggle.

She wrote, "Honestly, forgiveness is the pits. Only a fortnight ago I had a blissful dream that X lost his job and his family! I was so depressed to wake up and realise it wasn't true! And I pray for them in real life." All this demonstrates that while Christian forgiveness is hard, it eliminates bitterness and enhances a sense of humour.

Another surprise was that yesterday I received a third letter from my correspondent who insists he is prophesying my future from his dreams. I suspected he might have retired, beaten by the unusual turn of events in my legal history over the last couple of years, which can only be reconciled to his predictions with some difficulty. He confesses that because he is now old, the timing of events in his dreams is difficult.

He is quite adamant that I am innocent and will be released, although he claims he was afraid my Victorian appeal would fail; in fact, he was "sure" but did not want "to take away" my hope. I might be free before my March hearing, he wrote, predicting a couple of developments around Christmas. He is unsure on this, but quite sure my name will be cleared. He wants the legal history of my accuser to be investigated, as something "buried" or hidden could be there. "Something will be found. I have had two clear dreams/visions about that."

The letters are well written, disconcerting mainly in their certainty. He has never mentioned again his bizarre self-understanding of his role and has obviously followed the case. I will continue to record his predictions, with their equivocation and precautionary conditions, and see where we finish up.

For any knowledgeable outsider who believes in my innocence, the more probable conjecture is that there was some type of conspiracy which must involve my accusers' delusions or lies. An *Australian* article mentioned bail by Christmas.

Two thoughts to conclude. We have heard many times from Christopher Friel that "truth is the daughter of time." And I pray the prayer, amended by one word, which I used to recommend to those struggling to believe in God.

God of love, as you exist, please lead us to the truth.

Thursday, 21 November 2019

Once again, I was unable to reach the Tobins (perhaps they are away); so I phoned Chris Meney this afternoon and learnt that Fr Paul Stenhouse died yesterday. May he rest in peace. Chris also confirmed the news that Fr John Flynn, the only Legionary of Christ in Australia, had been found dead in his residence. While he had done fine work for us on XT3, our interactive website instituted at Sydney World Youth Day, he had been off the mission for some years with health problems. I suspect the formation he received with the Legionaries did not help him. While he had done a lot of good work, his last years were sad, although Fr Brendan Purcell kept in regular contact. May he, too, rest in peace, the peace which often escaped him in life.

Chris also passed on the information that the Egmont Group, the worldwide association which shares information in the fight against corruption,[1] of which AIF had become a member under Brülhart's leadership, had announced that they will no longer share information with the Vatican agency. This is a bad blow.

In my conversation with Chris, I had thought that Moneyval, the committee which evaluates anti-money-laundering procedures, was sponsored by Egmont; but this is not so, as Moneyval answers to the Council of Europe. Their spring 2020 visit will be important because in 2017 they indicated that progress was needed in the Vatican procedures against malfeasance. So far, more stalling than progress is apparent, and time is running short.

I don't know how the Egmont announcement relates to René's finishing up, and this was no clearer after I read the articles sent to me on the incident, written by Andrea Gagliarducci and Andrea Mainardi. Mainardi wonders about possible connections between

---

[1] The Egmont Group is a consortium of financial information agencies from 130 countries.

the departure of the auditor Libero Milone, Brülhart, and myself. The departure of Domenico Giani of the Vatican gendarmes and Cardinal Becciu and Msgr Perlasca from the world of finance might be the other side of the coin of the first three departures mentioned.

My Jesuit successor as prefect [of the Secretariat for the Economy] is Fr Juan Antonio Guerrero Alves, a Spaniard from Castile, whose first degree is in economics, who is well experienced in administration in Spain, Mozambique, and Italy, and speaks five languages. I wish him well against whatever remains of the dark forces, because the departure of Brülhart after the banished auditors leaves all reformers uncertain, indeed, uneasy.

In his article, Gagliarducci is correct to understand that contemporary changes will probably mean the Secretariat of State's control is strengthened, and he makes the classical defence of the dark forces in his historical descriptions of the recent financial story in the Vatican.

The Secretariat for the Economy had statutes and was not impeded by not being included in the previous and continuing apostolic constitution *Pastor Bonus*.[2] Its work was impeded by higher authority. The essential struggle was with an old guard, often incompetent, sometimes corrupt, who did not want light shone on their activities and did not want their amateurish, when not corrupt, projects to be curtailed or cancelled.

The theory that was successfully promoted, that it would have been a conflict of interest for the Secretariat to control APSA's investment policies while also running some internal activities not located in the governorate (the Vatican City State), was breathtaking and incapable of realisation in any responsible organization.

It meant the new general manager was to have no control over the investments, which would remain under the control of the same clique whose activities had been described in considerable detail by the investigatory committee COSEA, chaired by Joe Zahra and set up by Pope Francis.[3] More of that story was to become public

---

[2] The apostolic constitution *Pastor Bonus* was promulgated by Pope John Paul II on 28 June 1988 to reform the Roman Curia.

[3] Early in his pontificate, Pope Francis named the Maltese banker Joseph Zahra president of the newly formed Pontifical Commission for Reference on the Organization of the Economic-Administrative Structure of the Holy See (COSEA), which has examined the Vatican financial situation and proposed comprehensive and excellent reforms.

with the passing of the years. Msgr Scarano from APSA was accused of money laundering in spectacular sums and owned an expensive apartment full of valuable art. Hundreds of properties were producing little or no net revenue. Nattino was allegedly manipulating share prices with APSA's cooperation.[4] APSA was giving misleading information on the €50 million [$61 million] for IDI hospital (and incurring this debt for the Vatican). Before my time was out, despite our opposition, the disastrous APSA London property deal would be done, although only €90 million [$109 million] was invested against the €150–€200 million [$181.5–$242 million] London folly of the Secretariat of State.

Gagliarducci reduced the cancellation of the Pricewaterhouse-Coopers audit and the raid on the auditor general's office, the threatening of staff, the charging of Milone (later withdrawn) to a "clash of mentalities" between those defending the sovereignty of the Holy See and those who took a "company-like" position. The real and underlying issue was fear of the truth, of the revelation of the mess that had been concealed. An antipathy to "Anglo" methods, toward those who would "turn the Church into a business", also played well. The fact that many, if not most, Western governments were using standards similar to those we proposed (we had drawn on Singapore's models) cut no ice at all.

Melbourne sweltered under 40°C [104°F] heat today, and it was unpleasant during my two hours in the garden. Peter and Fiona Tellefson called, and we had a pleasant fifty-minute chat. Peter's father, Brian, is coping well six months after his wife, Pam's, death. My sister, Margaret, didn't answer her phone.

A recent response in the Office of Readings speaks to us.

If faith has not supported you on life's journey,
you will not attain the blissful vision of God in your heavenly
*   country.*
Walk the dark ways of faith and you will attain the vision of
God.

---

[4] In 2020, Giampietro Nattino, former president of Banca Finnat Euramerica, was acquitted of accusations of market manipulation and obstruction of supervisory authority.

Friday, 22 November 2019

Marvellous Melbourne. Yesterday we had 40°C [104°F] heat with hot, strong winds. Today was perfect, in the low 20s°C [70s°F], which should have reduced the fire dangers. Yesterday, fifty fires were burning in Victoria alone.

Yesterday, Pakistan was bowled out for 240 runs in the first cricket Test, which is televised. I enjoy watching, but it cuts into my reading and writing time. As I write this late in the afternoon, Australia is 1/285, a magnificent start. Pakistan surprised by selecting a strong sixteen-year-old, one of the fastest bowlers in the world at around 145 km/h [90 miles an hour], Naseem Shah. This is a first, the youngest player selected by any side. I hope he goes from success to success.

Another twenty or so letters arrived today, while I still have some unopened from yesterday.

Also included in the mail was a final copy of *Annals*, Fr Paul's swan song, and it is a beautiful piece of work, one of his best. Once again he included an article in my defence, this time by Tess Livingstone, who told the story of Jean Corish and Lil Sinozic, who were outside the sacristy after Sunday Mass at the time of the alleged "attacks".

James Murray, who wrote in each issue on the media, also described my case as "the most important story on which he has commented: *Pell vs the Queen*". A unique peculiarity for him is the fact that I am a cardinal, and he wonders whether *Wolsey vs the King* destroys this unicity. Whatever the verdict given by the High Court, Murray believes the Vatican, as a sovereign state, should refer the matter to the International Court of Justice in The Hague.

Three days after I made my request for a dressing to be placed on the sore on my back, which had bled, I was called to the medical centre, where the wound was washed, defined as an ulcer which had almost dried, after the initial definition as a "pimple" was abandoned. My ambition was to be sure that it wasn't a skin cancer.

This morning, the young warder asked me to sweep out the first exercise pen, which I did gladly. A couple of days ago, I had volunteered to clean the second pen, which collects debris more quickly and had done so. Despite the newly painted walls in both areas, they are still grotty with chipped and scratched metal doors and panels, but they are significantly improved and without graffiti for the moment.

Although there was no visit, other than to the medical centre, I felt physically better than I had been for some days. Naturally grateful for this, but cannot ascribe any cause. Also feel less disgruntled, once again for no clearly identified reason.

At least one month ago, I finished reading Adrian Pabst's excellent book *Story of Our Country* on the influence of Christian, and more particularly Catholic, social theory on the history of the Australian Labor Party.

No one doubts the importance of Pope Leo XIII's 1891 encyclical *Rerum Novarum* on the new situation in the Western world, brought about through the introduction of democracy and industrialisation, but it is still interesting to see these teachings at work in Australia—not least in Judge Henry B. Higgins' establishment, in the 1907 Harvester case, of a "basic wage" for all workers, sufficient for a husband and wife to live in "frugal comfort" with three children—an influence which was acknowledged by Bob Hawke[5] in the Manning Lecture in 2010. But more of this tomorrow.

I was studying theology in Rome when I read the *Diary of a Country Priest* by the French Catholic author Georges Bernanos. I found it discomforting, not particularly enjoyable, because of my naïveté and youthful optimism. In those heady days in Rome, during and immediately after the Second Vatican Council, I thought the Church would go from strength to strength, a bit like a new Pentecost, by becoming more open, modern, and reasonable.

As a bishop who spent a great deal of time working for reforms, and would do so again (given the chance), I find this quotation from Bernanos, included by Fr Paul in his final *Annals*, explains my discomfort:

The only way to reform the Church is by suffering for her. One reforms the visible Church only by suffering for the invisible Church. . . . The Church doesn't need reformers, she needs saints.

[5] Robert Hawke (1929–2019) was prime minister of Australia and leader of the Labor Party from 1983 to 1991.

Saturday, 23 November 2019

The day was cool again, although bushfires were still burning in the three eastern mainland states. However, the situation was nowhere catastrophic.

Adrian Pabst is a professor at the University of Kent in the UK, well versed in the social philosophers, such as Burke and Mill and Marx, and equally at home in Catholic social theory. He traversed ALP (Australian Labor Party) history with dexterity, avoiding the bushfires, some only apparently dormant.

He noted that the first federal Labor politicians were Protestant and that the Catholics entered later as the sectarian rivalries of English versus Irish, Protestant versus Catholic continued until after the 1950s, although the common suffering in the First World War strengthened a shared Australian patriotism. The percentage of mixed marriages increased steadily, despite the almost obsessional opposition of a few clerics like Archbishop Kelly of Sydney, while the Vatican II endorsement of Catholic participation in ecumenical activities proved a boon and a blessing.

Pabst recounts the "splits" in Labor history over conscription in World War I, financial policy during the Depression, and Communism and Movement[6] influence in the 1950s. He believes the second split over finance was more significant than the conscription quarrel, while also pointing out that Prime Minister Lyons,[7] who left to lead the United Australia Party, presided over a faster economic recovery than Roosevelt's New Deal. We are talking of another world, much poorer, where the majority did not complete secondary education (only a minority went to university), the family farm still existed, the Catholics were regarded like Muslims today, and unemployment nationally was never under 10 percent until the Second World War. From the 1870s, Catholics were united for one hundred years by the struggle for State Aid, government funding for Catholic schools, while the struggle against Communism waxed and waned from the

---

[6] The Movement was a group of largely Catholic political activists, strongly anti-Communist.

[7] Joseph Lyons was prime minister of Australia from 1932 until his death in 1939. He resigned from the Labor Party in 1931 and formed the United Australia Party with members of the Nationalist Party.

Spanish Civil War until after the Vietnam War and, indeed, until the fall of the Berlin Wall.

Ironically, the Liberal leader Bob Menzies broke the barrier against Catholic school funding, while Gough Whitlam, the Labor prime minister, first brought heavy funding, especially to the poorer Catholic schools.[8]

Pabst is a true believer in both Catholic social theory and the Labor tradition, which he defines as one of radical moderation, more Burke than Mill, whose task is to civilise capitalism and democratise politics.

He warns the party against losing touch with its working-class roots; and while recognizing that society has become more liberal socially, he laments the party's drift from the social conservatives. He is not explicit on the elephant in the room, the danger that the ALP will follow the Democratic Party in the US by banning from preselection those who espouse Christian teaching on life (no abortion and euthanasia), sexuality (heteronormative), and marriage, where the preferred model is one man, one woman. The social conservatives no longer constitute the percentage of votes they did even twenty-five years ago, but it will be difficult to govern without them, remembering in particular the ethnic vote. Pabst urges that the ALP must be a home for believers.

Pabst is resolutely opposed to the increasing and extreme concentration of wealth, which he dubs as meritocratic extremism, and warns all parties against the danger of "elites" capturing party organizations, so provoking a popular detachment, a crisis of trust, and even an estrangement from the professional political class. He sees the ALP as a broad church with room for churchgoers.

This book is accessible, useful for the Labor Party, for those in the Liberal Party who are still interested in Catholic votes, and for all those who believe that a (small "l") liberal democracy is the best context for human flourishing. The Australian Catholic University has done us a service in sponsoring this publication.

This was a typical Saturday, with the exception of the Test cricket. A splendid hot pasty for lunch, jellied fruit and cream for sweets

---

[8] Robert Menzies was prime minister of Australia from 1939 to 1941 and from 1949 to 1966. In 1944 he helped to merge the United Australia Party with other anti-Labor parties to found the Liberal Party. Labor Party member Gough Whitlam was prime minister of Australia from 1972 to 1975.

mid-afternoon, and my hour in the gymnasium, where I met all my self-imposed goals.

Today is the feast of St Clement, the third pope after St Peter, whose beautiful epistle nearly made it into the New Testament canon, the list of writings which the Church has recognized, over more than two centuries, as divinely inspired. No angel dictated our Scriptures, and no angel identified the constituents of the "canon". This was one reason why St Augustine accepted the authority of Christ after he had accepted the authority of the Church, because we know Our Lord primarily from the documents written in the early Church communities, which were then formally "canonised" by the Church.

It is also the feast of the great sixth-century Irish missionary and monk St Columban, who founded monasteries in France, but had to move on, when he denounced the morals of the local ruler, to found the Benedictine monastery at Bobbio in northern Italy, which I visited some years ago for today's feast. Columban was also an able writer and is the inspiration of the Columban missionaries well-known in Australia.

In today's Office of Readings, we have these powerful words from St Columban.

Moses wrote in the law, God made man in his own image and likeness.... God, the omnipotent, unseen, unfathomable, ineffable, unsearchable, when making man of clay, ennobled him with the distinction of his image. What comparison has man with God? What is there between earth and spirit? For God is spirit.... A grand distinction for man is the likeness of God, if it be preserved.

WEEK 40

Chickens Coming Home to Roost

24 November 2019—30 November 2019

Sunday, 24 November 2019

Another beautiful day, in the low twenties [low seventies F], with clear heat and clean air, typical of the best weather at the end of spring. The feast of Christ the King, which we celebrated for decades in Ballarat with a procession on the oval at St Patrick's College, was always important for me, so I was eventually surprised to find the feast was only introduced by Pope Pius XI in the 1930s, to counter the pretensions and intrusions of Mussolini.

I gained some understanding of the unease Catholic celebrations such as this and the St Patrick's Day march in Melbourne might have produced in our Protestant and ex-Protestant neighbours when I attended an important Muslim feast at the Gallipoli Mosque in Auburn-Sydney and had to make my way from my parked car through many hundreds of self-confident young adult males. I had no wish to upset them.

The analogy is imperfect, but the Easter Uprising in Ireland in 1916, the Irish Civil War in the 1920s, and particularly the then continuing IRA and Ultra [Ulster] violence in Northern Ireland were clear factors in the Australian public imagination. One difference from today was crystal clear. The Catholic leadership in Australia and the overwhelming majority of Catholics publicly condemned IRA violence, while too many in the Muslim leadership in Australia have been silent on Islamic terrorism, often intimidated into that silence. Progress here remains an imperative.

My alarm again called me successfully for Mass, although I had got to bed after midnight and then read Sansom's *Tombland* until 1 am, resulting in too little sleep and a grogginess in the morning.

Msgr Ireland celebrated the Christ the King Mass, where he had Christ ruling from the Cross and where he demonstrated Christ's kingly mercy by his promise to the good thief of paradise that very day, one of my favourite lines in the Scripture.

During the nine years when I catechized all those 2,000 youngsters whom I confirmed each year, I regularly quoted this line to them and more particularly to those parents who came for the session. For Monsignor, Christ's Kingship is marked by forgiveness, healing, and mercy, and is modelled on King David. I felt he was too tough on David, denouncing him as a scoundrel and unfair trader (all part of the truth), but I don't accept the accusation that he wanted or worked to overthrow his predecessor, except in self-defence.

Joseph Prince preached on the theme "Be Led by His Anointing and Win". He was soberly dressed in a dark shirt, jeans, and jacket with external seams. To compensate for this, he wore four rings, two bracelets, and a pocket chain.

As usual, it was a good Christocentric half hour, where he spoke of the civil war in our body and mind, of sin and how Christ accepts punishment for us. Pride induces us to punish ourselves, while true humility is to accept Jesus' forgiveness from the Cross. Of the five Old Testament offerings, only one, the grain offering, is bloodless, where the anointing oil represents the Holy Spirit.

As though he were answering my query of last week on how Joel Osteen would preach on bad things happening to good people, Joel almost did so. He acknowledged the difficulty of remaining faithful when we cannot see, when nothing appears to be happening, when God is silent. We must always persevere, because what has been promised is on the way; just as we should not weary of well doing, as the due season is coming. God works in secret, just as the eagle's egg hatches, provided the mother sits on it to keep it warm. If the mother were to break the egg to discover what is happening, all would be lost. Joel has stuck with his two million on the Exodus, who are now circling Jericho. With so many, they could have blown the wall down.

Songs of Praise was in Glasgow, for some splendid traditional hymn singing such as "O Worship the King" and "Amazing Grace".

Pakistan rallied in their second innings and nearly made Australia bat again, but was still crushed by an innings and five runs. It is still too early to be confident about our Australian batting lineup.

One of the prayers of intercession for the feast of Christ the King will round out today.

Jesus, heir of all nations, bring all mankind to the kingdom of your Church, entrusted to you by the Father:
—move all men to acknowledge you as the Head in the unity of the Holy Spirit.
Lord, may your kingdom come.

Monday, 25 November 2019

The morning weather was fine for my nearly two hours in the garden, although the sky was clouding over around midday. The birds were noisier than previously, and some of the best roses were well gone. However, others were on their way to replace them. I don't like the tan bark which is used to cover the garden areas and preserve the moisture within. Woodchips remain ugly, even when they are effective.

David visited with his daughters Sarah and Rebecca. All seemed well, as Sarah was about to share in an Australian Research Council grant and Rebecca had finished her year twelve corrections.

Last night, SBS had an excellent two-hour program on Einstein and Hawking, two of the most important physicists of the last century. The program excelled because it explained the notoriously complicated worlds of space-time, black holes, the Big Bang, supernovae, and pulsars in ways that amateur enthusiasts like myself could follow, at least in broad outline. I have little expertise, but I am deeply interested to learn how the Creator God did and continues to "do" remarkable things, whose mysteries we are slowly clarifying. God is a fantastic mathematician with those simple, elegant theorems which explain much about the history and workings of the universe.

A genius like Einstein did not invent these theories; he discovered them, building on previous explanations. Following philosophers of science like Stanley Jaki, OSB, and sociologist historians such as Rodney Stark, I believe it is no coincidence that the Scientific

Revolution, that explosion of knowledge and explanation, occurred in the Judaeo-Christian civilization, where the belief in a benign and rational God encouraged learned men to follow the paths opened by the Greeks and search for the ordered secrets of nature. If thinkers had believed that God was vindictive and cruel, wilful, not rational, but capricious and deceitful, they would have been less disposed to search out the laws of nature, a rational explanation for the patterns of the universe.

It is not hyperbole to claim that Einstein changed our world by discovering the principle of relativity, that mass and energy could be interchanged, that space and time were so intimately connected. Because of him, we now have nuclear power, understand the basic working of the sun and the stars, and have the atomic bomb, where a small amount of matter is converted into an immense amount of destructive energy.

It is of interest that Einstein originally believed in a stable and static universe, which always was, and that it was a Catholic priest, Fr Georges Lemaître, who first proposed the Big Bang theory, the initial explosion which created the entire universe, before which there was nothing. All the galaxies are still moving away from one another at an increasing rate. It was not until 1929 that Einstein accepted this, reluctant at first to draw this conclusion from his calculations. The congruence of the Big Bang theory and the Judaeo-Christian concept of a beginning, even of a stage-by-stage creation, as we see described nonscientifically in the book of Genesis, is obvious and, I suspect, slowed down acceptance of the theory.

While Einstein had been an indifferent performer at high school and at the undergraduate level, Stephen Hawking was a brilliant student at Oxford who went on to spend his academic life at Cambridge. He postulated the existence of black holes, where whole stars are sucked up and consumed once they pass over the "event horizon". Until the show, I wasn't sure whether there was a scientific theory about the end product of the black holes. Did the captured stars finish up in a parallel universe, perhaps in limbo? More recently, Hawking produced the theory of "Hawking radiation", whereby the black holes give out gravitational waves, so that eventually the black hole will evaporate and disappear. While the whole notion of "black holes" is fantastic, like the principle of relativity, Hawking's more recent theory is less implausible, according to the dictates of common sense, a fact which says nothing one way or another about its scientific truth or usefulness.

Einstein was one of those who wrote to President Roosevelt about the danger posed by the Nazis developing an "atomic bomb" and about the necessity to develop one. So the Manhattan Project was launched, which after two years' work exploded the first "test" atomic bomb in Arizona and three weeks later dropped one on Hiroshima. I had not realised the timeline was so tight.

Einstein spent years at Princeton, and his spoken English is very similar to that of Pope Benedict. I have heard many Germans who often speak excellent English, but no one else with quite their lilt and accent.

Einstein probably believed in a Supreme Intelligence, an impersonal God, who, he explained enigmatically, does not play dice. An indifferent musician himself (which is a polite description), he is famously reputed to have said after hearing a beautiful piece of music, "Now I know there is a God."

Despite the fact that Hawking's first wife was a devout Christian, who cared for him faithfully as he suffered with amyotrophic lateral sclerosis, he remained a committed atheist to the end, struggling toward "a theory of everything". I suspect that the "information paradox" which followed from his theories and which perplexed him will ultimately be resolved in ways beyond even his imagining.

These words from Beethoven's "Ode to Joy" from the Ninth Symphony are addressed to the one, true, and good God.

> *All thy works with Joy surround thee, earth and heaven*
> *reflect thy rays,*
> *Stars and angels sing around thee, centre of unbroken*
> *praise.*
> *Field and forest, vale and mountain, flowering meadow,*
> *flashing sea,*
> *Singing bird and flowing fountain call us to rejoice in thee.*

Tuesday, 26 November 2019

Another day, where the highlight was the visit of Sr Mary to give me Communion. She was accompanied by Rosanne, an Australian-born

Chaldean whose parents came here from Iraq in the early 1990s. She told me about the vibrant youth scene among the young Chaldeans and Maronites in Melbourne and gave the welcome news that about one thousand young Melbourne Catholics were going to Perth for the Catholic Youth Festival under the leadership of Archbishop Comensoli. This is good news.

I spent my hour in the gymnasium and did all the usual things. The day was cool, overcast with the occasional shower, which did not occur during my two periods in the exercise pens.

Untypically, I chose to have a spaghetti marinara rather than my usual salad for my mid-afternoon meal, which I put aside until the evening news at 6:30 pm. The spaghetti was warm, an enormous serve, and not too bad, while the warders asked if I also wanted some salad. This is one Aussie custom I don't follow, as I don't eat salad and spaghetti together. I see this as taking a stand on principle rather than as an affectation, like not drinking a cappuccino after 10 am!

I continued my usual practice of replying to all the prisoners who have written to me, penning two letters. Dropped a page also to a Protestant pastor from Werribee who had written a couple of times to encourage me. I noted to him that pastors in all denominations who believe the last word is with Our Lord and the New Testament (rather than modern insights) often feel a solidarity, a mutual sympathy, even though they interpret the Scripture differently on some points. I also mentioned to him the Russian Christian writer Soloviev's powerful essay on the end times, when the faithful remnants from the Christian traditions take their last stand together against the Antichrist. I voiced the hope that Soloviev's vision was grim and too pessimistic.

Spent a couple of hours watching Michael Moore's 2018 film, ostensibly on Trump, whom he compared to Hitler and accused of being more despotic than democratic. Moore's opponents were broader than Trump and included the political establishment of the Democrats as well as the Republicans. He painted Obama in a devastating light, showing him coming to the town of Flint, Michigan, where the town water supply had been polluted with lead through a project sponsored by the Republican governor, publicly siding with the governor, and grievously disappointing his supporters by twice appearing to drink from a glass of water, when he only took a small sip. I don't know the truth behind the allegations, which included the charge that evidence showing the lead poisoning was covered up for eighteen months.

Moore made the good point that when the prosperity, and therefore the numbers, of the middle class are reduced by falling incomes and job loss, democracy is weakened. While religious decline is not as advanced in the US as in Australia, a decline in Christianity expands opportunities for the extremists, while the flight of socially conservative Catholics (pro-life, pro-family) from the Democratic Party on the grounds of moral principle probably weakens the ranks of idealists, "conviction" politicians in the Democrat establishment. Certainly Trump has drawn on Christian discontent and cooperated in their attempts to reform the Supreme Court. I hope Moore is wrong, mistaken in his estimate of Trump's commitment to democracy (certainly Trump is no Hitler in my book). But if Moore was closer to the truth, my prayer would be that the Christian centre in the US would contain and curb any power grab more effectively than the Christian centrist party did in Germany in the thirties. Both Trump and Moore draw their support from different sections of the disaffected, although Trump is more likely to win converts from Moore's followers than vice versa. Moore also showed the student "uprisings" in the US a couple of years ago, when students went on strike for higher wages for their teachers in the public school system, starting in West Virginia. This predates the young people rallies on climate change and even the huge rallies for democracy in Hong Kong, involving people of every generation but led by university students. What is the significance of this?

Social media provides the means to organize such events, but deeper changes are occurring. Who is teaching that children must respect and obey their parents? With blended families and the father increasingly absent, we have other destabilising factors and causes for resentment toward the older generation. When the pagan ideals of youth, health, and pleasure predominate, when the natural law of the complementarity of man and woman and of the generative power of mother and father is no longer normative, profound disequilibrium is the result. We now recognize more clearly the causes of ecological decline and disaster, when we violate nature through deforestation, plastic, and poisonous waste, just as we recognize the damage done by tobacco, alcohol, and harder drugs to our physical health. But we don't apply similar rules to our hearts and minds, to the development of spiritual and psychological well-being through regular love, parental stability, and the Ten Commandments. You cannot maintain a culture by appealing to diversity and banning hate speech, by belittling the Stoics and advocating self-centred wellness.

As an elderly Irish Australian lady from near Ballarat used to opine: "What is in the cat comes out in the kitten."

Young people come from the same stock as their parents, more physically comfortable, but often under more psychological pressure. They don't have the wisdom and experience to make regular substantial gains for society. William Pitt the Younger was prime minister of Britain at the age of twenty-four, but he grew up immersed in the politics of his prime minister father. Few, if any, enjoy similar advantages.

It is a wake-up call to those of us who are older when youngsters denounce our performance. It requires us to look at what we are doing, at the education we are providing, and the social media environment we tolerate for those still at school.

God our Father, we pray that we are the children of the day, not lost in the night, but living in the freedom and hope won by your Cross and Resurrection.

Wednesday, 27 November 2019

Many years ago, I read somewhere, I cannot remember where, that revolutions do not occur when oppression is at its worst, but when there is movement, some improvement, and the oppressed start to have hope. With many others, I believe Pope John Paul II gave hope to his compatriots on his first marvellous journey home as pope, when he told the Poles they were living under a lie.

This is a grand analogy, which does not fit well with my present position in jail, not least because I have no intention of rebelling. What is strange is that I am tempted to impatience precisely at the moment when I am closer to release than at any other time during my nearly nine months in prison. While I did have an expectation of release after the appeal, I realised even then that the result was not guaranteed. Neither is it guaranteed by the High Court, but I do not expect another dismal legal performance like the majority decision.

More than eight months in solitary confinement is a considerable time, and while I would not diagnose myself as suffering from battle fatigue, I regret not being with family and friends for Christmas. Easter brings the central Christian feasts, but it is not a family celebration like Christmas, and it is easier to celebrate a birth than redemptive suffering, even when followed by the Resurrection. And for most of my time in jail, I did not expect to be here at Christmas.

Each day I continue with my routine, without too much trouble, and look forward to my outings in the garden and my three periods a week in the gymnasium, which was closed today, unfortunately. I wonder whether some prisoner blocked the toilet once again, and all are punished by deprivation as a result. This is a surmise.

But I do have to work harder to take each day at a time, keep myself occupied, not least with my prayers, and not give in to self-absorption. My meditation times are riddled with distractions, but my American friend's suggestion of humming the words of favourite hymns is a wonderful aid to meditation and will be particularly useful at Christmas with the carols.

The letters continue to arrive, and among those which were delivered today was one written from Ottawa by a gentleman I had met in Rome. I tend to use the adjective "beautiful" too frequently when I write, but this letter was beautiful, unusual, informative, and encouraging.

My friend wrote on the feast of St Leonard, patron of prisoners, "It was especially important for me to visit Mamertine [Prison] while in Rome and be in the same place where Peter and Paul approached the end of the Good Fight.... The very one in which you are engaged. Don't slack off, for Christ's sake—I pray for you in the mornings and the evenings."

He also claimed that when Our Lord described himself as the Good Shepherd, his listeners would have been "perfectly aware that a stray lamb, once discovered, would have its leg broken to discourage it from wandering again. Lambs heal fast." I had never heard this.

This morning when I phoned Terry Tobin, he informed me the European newspaper articles continue to appear on the Vatican financial scandals. Marc Odendall from France, who was on the board of

AIF, has resigned, following René Brülhart's departure, claiming that only a shell remained of the organization. The Egmont Group had cut off AIF because when the Vatican authorities raided AIF, they removed documents confidential to the group.[1]

More significant was the fact that Claudia Ciocca, who had been doing my job since my return to Australia and was the most committed reformer in the Vatican capable of running the finance organization, has resigned. I had hoped that she would be able to work with my recently appointed successor. I remember just as she was committing to join us, one of the international directors of McKinsey's, where she was working, phoned her to warn against working with a group as disreputable as Vatican finance. What an indictment!

My Ottawa correspondent also spoke of the Vatican finances. During our home meeting "one of your assistants eagerly reported (sotto voce) that another fifty million euros [$61 million] had been found. I thought to myself that I'd had the privilege of meeting you before your assassination. Seems others thought the same, as I read that someone had voiced the same thought, to which you replied: 'No, they will destroy my reputation.' You called it exactly." I do remember making that last comment privately, and as I have written previously, every reformer was attacked in the press and usually blackguarded to the Holy Father.

My friend finished with a flourish. "My mother loved Italian opera and gave us the taste for it—this letter was written to the sound of that perfect voice—Maria Callas—so I can't tell if my eyes are watering for her or for you." I, too, regard Callas as one of the greatest, perhaps even ahead of our Joan Sutherland.

A passage from St Paul writing to the Colossians (1:24) points to the ideal.

I struggle wearily on, helped only by Christ's power driving me irresistibly, and in my own body I do what I can to make up all that has still to be undergone by Christ for the sake of his body, the Church.

---

[1] Marc Odendall, a Swiss-German retired banker, was quoted by Nicole Winfield in "Vatican Financial Watchdog Now a 'Shell' after Police Raid", Associated Press, 19 November 2019, https://apnews.com/article/adece301b0314fdbbf7bee8830fce354.

Thursday, 28 November 2019

For some time, the unit has been quiet, apart from one short-term resident who shouted occasionally and polluted his cell so there was a considerable stench at the other end of the unit. Nothing reached us.

A few noisy ones have made a comeback, and we have just enjoyed a contribution from a serious banger. It is after lockdown, at about 5:45 pm, and some work is being done in the unit. We also have a feminine voice contributing to the dialogue, probably one of the warders.

Another beautiful day in the low 20s°C [70s°F], light high clouds, and cool breezes. Once again, the birds were noisy.

After my pleasant two hours in the garden, a contrast with the hot and windy conditions of my previous garden time. I met with Kieran Walton, Archbishop Fisher's secretary, and Ronan Reilly, who is teaching at a Christian school in Queensland. I knew him as a junior choir boy at St Mary's Cathedral when I came north in 2001. Lively and intelligent, he is a gifted singer and cellist, and is teaching music. He even has a few Catholic primary school choirs singing Gregorian chant. His wife, Beatrice, is expecting their second child in January. Ronan was a lively youth, especially during his university years, brimful of Catholic faith. Sometimes he demonstrated a tad too much zeal. Kieran is a wonderful asset for Archbishop Fisher, a man of sound judgement, who assisted John Howard when he wrote his life of Bob Menzies.[2]

I also received from the lawyers three *Spectators*, another copy of Paul Stenhouse's final *Annals*, and a swathe of European articles on the Vatican finance scandals. While I haven't read them all as yet, the news I had received was accurate, but some details were new and useful for a better understanding.

The reports stressed that René Brülhart from AIF did not have a fixed-term contract, that he had decided to resign on the same day as the Egmont Group excluded AIF, and that his resignation took the Vatican by surprise. All this suggests that the Moneyval review in early 2020 will not go well, that the Vatican might not retain its place

---

[2] John Howard was prime minister of Australia from 1996 to 2007.

on the "white list", with all the unfortunate consequences that would follow from this exclusion. The chickens are coming home to roost.

Cardinal Becciu furiously denounced as "another FALSE article"[3] Ed Condon's accurate account[4] of the London property fiasco and of the accounting procedures which attempted to conceal it, while the American Jesuit Tom Reese, no conservative, recommended that Fr Guerrero decline the Holy Father's invitation to take over the Secretariat for the Economy at this inauspicious time (while conceding the Jesuit fourth vow of obedience to the pope precluded this).[5]

He set out four conditions necessary for success: that Fr Guerrero be given absolute authority to set and enforce financial policy; that he have authority to fire those who would not cooperate; that he have an "unlimited budget" to hire the experts necessary to clear up the Vatican (acknowledging that the Holy Father is a penny pincher); and finally that he have the authority to speak honestly to the press. Reese then wrote, "I doubt that Guerrero will get the authority to do any of these things." So do I.

Most commentators agree that we have a long distance to run on these issues, because the Vatican has probably exhausted the tactic of bunkering down and saying nothing until the storm passes. The Moneyval intervention has not begun, while the annual deficits and the looming pension shortfall cannot be conjured out of existence. The will to be clear and efficient is indispensable, but so too is having the competence and capacity to achieve this.

I was once mildly rebuked by a fellow seminarian when I repeated to him the dominical injunction that we needed to have the wisdom of the serpent as well as the simplicity of the dove (Mt 10:16). "Yeah," he replied, "but in the right proportions."

More than in most periods, the Vatican needs to find the right balance in the world of finance, and in the world of doctrine and discipline after the Amazon Synod.

---

[3] On his Twitter account, 24 November 2019.

[4] Ed Condon, "Vatican Officials: Swiss Bank Suspected of Money Laundering Led to Pell Conflict", *Catholic World Report*, 21 November 2019, https://www.catholicworldreport.com /2019/11/21/vatican-officials-swiss-bank-suspected-of-money-laundering-led-to-pell-conflict/.

[5] Thomas Reese, "Four Powers the Pope Needs to Grant the New Chief of Vatican Finances", Religion News Service, 20 November 2019, https://religionnews.com/2019/11 /20/four-powers-the-pope-needs-to-grant-the-new-chief-of-vatican-finances/.

Friday, 29 November 2019

An abundance of riches; too many things to do. *Spectators* to be read, twenty or thirty letters to be opened, many dozens of pages of articles on the Vatican finances, the first day of the second cricket Test against Pakistan, and another nine articles by Christopher Friel on my case, to which I devoted much of the day.

The weather had cooled down, so that I put on once again my white prison T-shirt, which I had discarded weeks ago. Mr Harris explained that there had been good soaking rain for the gardens.

Further reading of the finance articles clarified some issues for me. Edward Pentin[6] and Ed Condon[7] had done the early work outlining, with basic accuracy, the successive Vatican money scandals, but the Italian papers and, e.g., the *Wall Street Journal* have run articles. So, too, we now have articles from Sandro Magister of *L'Espresso* and John Allen of *Crux*, two of the most senior and important Vatican commentators, although with quite different starting positions. From the beginning, Magister has been a critic of Pope Francis, not vicious or outrageous, but a high-quality writer who is relentless. Allen is from the United States, mildly left of centre, prudent and respectful of the facts, whose attitudes were changed by the [Cardinal] McCarrick affair and the persistent financial scandals.

Coming from a man who chooses his words carefully, Allen's *Crux* article of 19 November is unusually strong and explicit. To the Vatican announcement that Brülhart had completed his term of office and a successor was on the way "to ensure continuity of institutional action", Allen responded: "In other words, nothing to see here, all quiet on the Roman front. Except, of course, that's hogwash."[8]

As president of AIF, Brülhart had no term of office and made it clear he decided to resign. Allen believes it strange that the raids took place when AIF was reviewing IOR and criticising the promoter of justice for not prosecuting money-laundering cases. Like many

---

[6] Edward Pentin is the Rome correspondent for the *National Catholic Register*, where his articles on Vatican finances have appeared.

[7] Edward Condon is a writer and an editor for the Catholic News Agency.

[8] John Allen, "Vatican Finance Guru's Exit Suggests 'Back to the Future' Dynamic on Reform", *Crux*, 19 November 2019, https://cruxnow.com/news-analysis/2019/11/vatican-finance-gurus-exit-suggests-back-to-the-future-dynamic-on-reform/.

others, he suspected an internal Vatican power struggle. It is difficult to avoid the conclusion that anyone who would inspire and execute a raid on AIF, which is linked into a worldwide network fighting corruption and money laundering, is both brazen and inept. AIF has an international status different from that of the dismissed Vatican auditors, and the consequences of continuing to flout Moneyval requirements could be drastic. Just before I began work in Rome, the Vatican had been barred by all the big banks except Deutsche and was only saved by the persistent efforts of an ally on the Deutsche board. Continuing hard work meant the Vatican was included in the "white list" of approved international financial organizations.

This is the grim background to Allen's prediction that "for the Vatican the forecast is less rosy", because it is difficult to avoid the conclusion that "Rome is headed back to the future", where "financial management is lodged with a largely Italian nexus of clerics and lay financiers."

He concludes by acknowledging that Vatican communications cannot be as blunt as his article, but still reminds them, "Just don't try to tell us there's nothing to see here, when the eye test reveals something else indeed."

Magister does not usually write on financial matters, but gives a comprehensive and accurate account of the Secretariat of State London purchase, the involvement of the Papal Foundation, and a short but incomplete resumé of the IDI hospital fiasco.[9] Brülhart's resignation is also reported accurately. I was pleased because Magister acknowledged the "doubtful reliability" of my conviction and my opposition to both the London purchase and the loan for IDI hospital.[10] It is not rocket science to recommend against purchasing at the height of a property "bubble" (and just before a Brexit vote) or to recognize that a bankrupt hospital which is still losing €7 million [$8.5 million] a year cannot repay at the rate of €18 million [$22 million] a year!

---

[9] Sandro Magister, "Money Wars at the Vatican. With the Pope among the Belligerents", *L'Espresso*, 25 November 2019, http://magister.blogautore.espresso.repubblica.it/2019/11/25/money-wars-at-the-vatican-with-the-pope-among-the-belligerents/.

[10] The Dermatopathic Institute of the Immaculate, in Rome, ran up debts of at least €700 million. Fr Franco Decaminada, the representative of his religious congregation at the hospital, was arrested and accused of appropriating €4 million [$4.8 million]. He was imprisoned and laicized.

Magister also recounts the most recent development in the saga of Bishop Gustavo Zanchetta, formerly of the Diocese of Oran in Argentina, who suddenly and mysteriously left his diocese and eventually landed at APSA in the Vatican as assessor. He will return to Argentina on 26 November to answer allegations of misconduct with seminarians. I hope he is innocent and can refute the charges.

I think I will conclude with a thought and a prayer.

Sufficient for the day is the evil thereof (Mt 6:34). May God protect us all.

Saturday, 30 November 2019

An almost cold morning for my early spell outside, but the sun was shining, and it was warmer in the afternoon. The gymnasium was open for my fifty minutes of exercise, where I was up to par with my ping-pong, the basketball, and the treadmill. Another specially warmed meat pie was again the Saturday lunch highlight followed by a lovely apple. Spent the morning writing up yesterday's diary as yesterday was spent reading and then watching the cricket and an interesting program on the Vikings. Apparently York was the headquarters of their kingdom in the middle of the ninth century; the second part of the program spoke of the colonising activities of Erik the Red, who was expelled from Norway around A.D. 1000 and founded settlements on Greenland and then on Newfoundland. In those balmy times, the Church eventually had a couple of dioceses in Greenland, in the Medieval Warming. Neither was that period unprecedented, because the world had experienced a "warm" period one thousand years earlier, around the time of Our Lord. You couldn't blame either of those on carbon dioxide from coal-fired electricity generators, although bovine flatulence might already have been a problem.

I waded through Chris Friel's wonderfully detailed studies on many aspects of my case, especially his thirteen-page analysis of the majority judgement of Ferguson and Maxwell. It is forensic and devastating.

I am becoming more interested in trying to put together the early stages in the evolution of the charges against me. Why were the charges first ascribed to 1997 rather than 1996? When was Sunday Mass introduced as a setting for the crime, as Milligan did not know this? Who helped the complainant? When did the similarities with the Billy Doe incidents in Philadelphia emerge? Was this before or after the story appearing in the *Rolling Stone* magazine? Is there a Roman connection? Who connected with whom, if anyone? All this is previous to the twenty-four changes in his story that the complainant made at committal and trial.

The Holy Father has given an interview once again on his return flight from Japan.[11] The journalists love these encounters (they have told me so), but I and many others dread them.

The Holy Father's financial advisers had briefed him badly, indeed, misinformed him, so that he should have left the topic to others, whatever his ambition to do the right thing and demonstrate his commitment to financial reform.

On three occasions, the Holy Father affirmed his commitment to the presumption of innocence and then went on immediately to speak of crimes or corruption. Once he quoted his promoter of justice as proclaiming "a presumption of corruption in these places".

The publicity for Peter's Pence explains that the money can be spent on papal or curial expenses as well as support for the poor, although many or most donors thought, in the past at least, that the money was for the poor, unlike the diocesan "tax" or contribution. The Holy Father is quite explicit that Peter's Pence can be invested rather than "put in a drawer", but I am not sure this is spelt out publicly in any literature, and the pope himself goes on to say that Peter's Pence should be spent in a year and a half, which is quite incompatible with a property investment (or almost!).

The Holy Father is proud of the fact that the Vatican monitoring system is working well, at least in detecting some crimes rather than preventing them. In a memory lapse, the Holy Father declared that "it's the first time that in the Vatican the pot[12] is discovered from the inside." The Secretariat for the Economy and COSEA discovered many problems worthy of investigation, and the auditor was moved on because of his findings. All the world knew of the

---

[11] For an account of this interview, see Hannah Brockhaus, "On Papal Flight, Pope Francis Talks Vatican Financial Scandal", *Catholic Herald*, 26 November 2019, https://catholicherald .co.uk/on-papal-flight-pope-francis-talks-vatican-financial-scandal/.

[12] This refers to the purchase in London by the Secretariat of State during the property bubble.

Secretariat for the Economy's discovery of €1.4 billion [$1.7 billion] of undeclared assets.

Pope Francis and René Brülhart are now in public disagreement on what was in René's contract, and the pope has rejected the AIF board's clearing of Tommaso Di Ruzza, stating that he is still suspended.

The Egmont Group is described as "private" despite the fact that it is an international instrumentality of many governments, and the appeal is made to Vatican "sovereignty" as legitimising the raid on AIF and rejecting the demands of the Egmont Group. Such an argument was used to cancel the external audit and has been used repeatedly to cover up incompetence and corruption. If there are arguments on the sovereignty issue, they should have been canvassed before entering into international agreements and not only when wrongdoing was alleged or proven. I fear, too, that the Holy Father's confidence in Moneyval is misplaced, especially if he is anticipating an approval rating.

John Allen wrote that the economic reformers were divided between the Anglo-Saxon/Germanic school and the Latin and Mediterranean approach, which, he believes, Pope Francis prefers.[13]

I am tempted to try to send a message to him quoting St Paul, who said that it is not so important whether we are Gentile or Jew. Whether we believe in Christ and are baptised, or not, is the critical issue.

So, too, in Vatican finance, the divide is between those who strive to prevent and eliminate corruption and incompetence and those who are unwilling to do so, for whatever reason.

I conclude with a verse from the Canticle of Sirach (Ecclesiasticus 36):

> *Have compassion on the Holy City,*
> *Jerusalem, the place of your rest.*
> *Let Sion ring with your praises,*
> *let your temple be filled with your glory.*

---

[13] John Allen, "Vatican Finances Pit Anglo-Saxon/Germanic 'Reform' vs. Latin/Mediterranean", *Crux*, 28 November 2019, https://cruxnow.com/news-analysis/2019/11/vatican-finances-pit-anglo-saxon-germanic-reform-vs-latin-mediterranean/.